Cornish Solidarity

STUDIES IN CORNISH LANGUAGE AND CULTURE

Volume 5

STUDIES IN CORNISH LANGUAGE AND CULTURE
Volume 5

Cornish Solidarity

Using Culture to Strengthen Communities

Neil Kennedy

evertype

2016

Published by Evertype, 19A Corso Street, Dundee, DD2 1DR, Scotland. *www.evertype.com*.

A catalogue record for this book is available from the British Library.

ISBN-10 1-78201-196-X
ISBN-13 978-1-78201-196-5

ISSN 2753-1597

Typeset in Baskerville by Michael Everson.

Cover design by Michael Everson, based on a photograph of Carn Brea taken by Fæ, 2011.

Contents

For the Cornish Movement

Unite and unite and let us all unite,
for summer is acome unto day,
and whither we are going we will all unite,
in the merry morning of May.[1]

---

1   Words traditionally sung at Padstow on Mayday.
    www.youtube.com/watch?v=dwSv8YEr78g (May 2012)

Preface

Neil Kennedy has been an active member of the Cornish-language community and a Cornish activist for the past thirty years. In that time, not only has he helped to shape and re-examine contemporary perceptions of Cornish, but has also written a wide range of textbooks, learning resources and dictionaries. He has contributed to recent writing in Cornish, and has spearheaded much work in modern media, music and film, including the ground-breaking ITV Cornish-language programme *Kernopalooza!* (1999). More recently, Kennedy has turned his eye to further academic research into the position of the Cornish, completing his doctorate at the Institute of Cornish Studies at the University of Exeter. The results of his findings on Cornish culture and its effect on strengthening community identity are to be read, for the first time, in this important new book. Armed with his traditional Cornish upbringing, as well as time spent living in another Brythonic language community—that of Brittany—Kennedy has all the right understanding to have completed such a study. His experience in teaching the language, as well as many years spent in minority language development, has meant that he is in a unique position to make an assessment of the condition of the Cornish language and of Cornish communities over the past few decades.

As he outlines in his Introduction to this work, Kennedy's intention here is to both "inform and provoke". These twin objectives are born from his experiences, and from his desire for change and development. In the former, the author certainly informs the reader of the development of Cornish culture in the post-war period, allied to a strong understanding of the New Cornish Studies project of the past few decades. Combined with the latter, he is seeking to review, critique and offer suggestions as to ways forward for Cornish Culture, so that real progress can be achieved.

The title of this work is obviously drawn from the political movement of the late 1990s—rooted in the closure of South Crofty—Cornwall's last, large-scale working tin mine. Cornish Solidarity was a pressure group founded in 1998 by the President of Redruth and District Chamber of Commerce, Greg Woods (who earlier learnt Cornish with Neil). Momentum came from the strength of feeling that arose from that closure, and a general feeling within the territory that Cornwall needed to "fight back" and assert its cultural, linguistic and political identity in an even stronger way than before. In some respects, the pressure group that was Cornish Solidarity was temporary (the group folded in the following years), but moving into the early decades of the twenty-first century, combined with other important markers, the movement pioneered more recent developments, such as the recognition of the Cornish as a "national minority" within the island of Britain, and official funding for the Cornish language.

The closure of South Crofty was a milestone in also prompting the realization that central government and the European Union needed to provide more long-term economic development for Cornwall (though grants and developments agencies) to counter the post-industrial situation the territory found itself in. While Cornish Solidarity's aim was to achieve this kind of support for Cornwall, an ancillary aim was to see Cornwall perceived as a possibility for devolutionary powers. In the period of the Labour government from 1997 to 2010, Cornwall watched with interest as certain parts of the United Kingdom—Wales. Scotland, and Northern Ireland—received more devolved power. Although Cornwall was recognized with the "Council of the Isles" it seemed, however, that the dichotomy between "county" and "country" would not be readily solved. The sense of injustice felt by Cornwall has continued—not least in the Brexit referendum (where Cornwall will seemingly lose economic assistance), and in more recent debate over the so-called "Devonwall" constituency (perceived by activists as another convenient piece of accommodation for Anglo-centric politicians).

Kennedy's starting point for this investigation is his interest in community memory; this anthropological concept then underpins his understanding of Cornwall's position as "an internal colony". Thus, as he identifies early on, much of contemporary Cornish experience is this Cornish community memory juxtaposing and jarring against the accommodated position. What this sets up, of course, is an examination of key indicators of "difference" and how these are used to resist further integration into Anglo-centric culture and indeed, wider globalization. Alongside this, Kennedy proposes that there are different—but often inter-related communities and individuals within Cornwall—who have an impact on this resistance, though often with their own very different cultural and political agendas.

The work begins by tracing the work of those activists seeking a "Cornish Movement" as part of the political drive of the post-war period of the Cornish Movement. The term suggested a new deal for Cornwall, but those pursuing it were seeking it within a fast-changing social and economic climate, connected to in-migration, lifestyle changes and unexpected mass tourism. Kennedy percep-tively notes that his "Cornish Movement" was much wider than the early Cornish Revival, though it still suffered somewhat from the same problems that had dogged the pre-war Revivalist period. However, the "Cornish Movement" was embracing wider political and philosophical changes from British multi-culturalism, European ethnocultural movements, feminism and environmentalism.

Large scale in-migration has been difficult for Cornwall to cope with—particularly in terms of retaining community identity—and so the full effects of this are also examined here. Second homes and holiday lettings are problematical for community cohesion. Kennedy's observations on marginalization are timely in the sense that in November 2016 St Ives Town Council won the right to stop the building of second homes in the town, with a further slew of Cornish town and parish councils wishing to bring in the same restrictions. Such analysis brings the author to then examine insider and outsider perceptions of Cornish experience, and how this affects communities. Crucial here, has been how some public funding bodies and tourist authorities are accused of "wooing tourists", yet as Kennedy suggests, there are a number of writers and activists in twenty-first century Cornwall who are actively redefining and reasserting Cornish identity.

This critique segues neatly into what Kennedy terms a "useable culture". A contested term by its very nature, this concept puts forward the controversial notion that some "cultures" within resistance groups is actually less helpful or not helpful in terms of progressing a culture. In so doing, this involves the author examining the commodification of Cornish culture and the way in which Cornwall is marketed beyond its borders. The argument suggests that only selected items come to be representative and that in fact, these only form flimsy evidence of the wider cultural experience. Capital—that is, what is "gained" from the culture is therefore highly important to debate. When Kennedy considers this, he has to look at places where capital is either mistakenly gained or is falsely represented, often by institutional, media or regional bodies, which want to depict Cornwall in certain and convenient ways.

In this next part of his argument, Kennedy extends Deborah Cameron's term "verbal hygiene" to consider cultural selections and prescriptions. This however, is given further context, when Kennedy looks to examine Hobsbawn's theory of "invented tradition". This concept is associated with most imagined communities across the globe, and those particularly seeking self-determination, but here the author examines how invented traditions have shaped the community's memory. The construct of Celticism itself comes in for deconstruction here. Always a problematical concept, Kennedy re-examines the remit of Cornish Celticity and concludes that although it may be useful, in other ways, it has done a disservice.

In particular here, the author offers a rigorous re-assessment of the culture imagined by the Cornish revivalist Robert Morton Nance. Although aspects of invented tradition are critiqued by Kennedy, elsewhere he puts forward the notion that sometimes invention can be helpful, and offers numerous examples. This leads naturally into a discussion of both Revivalism and what he terms "residual tradition", with Kennedy adeptly noting the collisions and collusions found in the modern admixture of Cornish community memory.

Of particular interest here is the way that Kennedy explored the responses to the building a waste incinerator near to the mid-Cornwall china-clay village of St Dennis. Off the beaten tourist track, here is perhaps the epicentre of cultural debate in Cornwall. St Dennis is seen as a community that is already "wrecked" so the building of such an incinerator will make no difference. Despite mounting a protest, the community there has had to face the fact that such a facility is unlikely be built at Mylor or Carlyon Bay. The geographical focus is connected to the linguistic and cultural link, in the sense that St Dennis may be a bastion of "residual tradition" when compared to elsewhere. In this light of this, the very notion of "Proper Cornishness" and the multi-faceted nature of this concept is given due discussion, with Kennedy demonstrating the term is by no means clear cut.

According to Kennedy, "the Nancean project" needs to be redeemed and continued, but only with certain conditions and objectives newly applied to it. Redemption, suggests the author, is found in what he terms "Cool Cornubia". Here, he offers an antidote to the malaise of the past, with an examination of the way in which "Proper Cornishness" and even Cornish Celticity can be re-branded to make an effect on cultural memory and confidence.

The volume is enhanced by a number of interviews with Cornish residents who offer their own take on the situation, and therefore are representative of the cultural memory. Such work is important, if not now, but for the future – when observers will be able to look over such representations of identity at this key point in Cornwall's history. That Kennedy incorporates this key underlying data into the final research is indicative of what he has achieved in terms of representing "Cornish Solidarity".

The argument achieves its zenith with the chapter titled "Kernow or Kernowland?". Here, Kennedy synthesizes the earlier premises into a convincing examination of the cultural-geographic space that is "Kernow"—examining what this really means. The enquiry shifts here, to become more philosophical—pointing the way, as I have suggested in previous publications in this series—that this must now be the next stage of modes of enquiry within Cornish Studies. Numerous scholars have attested the significance of "Cornish identity" but this means nothing, unless this is underpinned by an understanding of how the Cornish think. Usefully, the author moves to this field offering examining of how pastiche and parody contribute to understanding, and how reality and fantasy intersect. Critically, Kennedy offers a warning too, on how Cornwall—and its cultural twin, *Kernow*—can avoid a second wrong turn. In this, he asserts the confidence of a Cornish standpoint and how this might be achieved. In the remainder of the book, he offers mechanisms for this standpoint: ways which are more sophisticated and connected to Cornish community than perhaps those offered in the past. At his point within the volume, it is possible to see how Cornish communities might progress in the future; an innovative and uplifting vision of this "national minority".

In many respects, we are living in a productive period of research into Cornwall's culture and history. Several recent publications by this publisher and others indicate a high watermark in re-assessing preconceived ideas about cultural history in Cornwall. This work is crucial part of this re-assessment, and will no doubt be read and quoted by many scholars in the future. In this sense, we must congratulate Kennedy on contributing this important work to the academic community concerned with Cornwall. No doubt some observers will find his vigorous reassessment dislocating and unnerving, but herein is its brilliance. Kennedy's research points the way to the future and shows that *Cornish Solidarity* offers a way forward. It also shows energy and a commitment to the success of the Cornish and Cornish distinctiveness well into the middle decades of the twenty-first century—and crucially —beyond that.

Alan M. Kent
Lanbrebois / Probus
December 2016

Foreword

This book is addressed to all who identify affectively with a broad
Cornish Movement of socially engaged, cultural, economic and
political action and it is based on part of my thesis, "Employing
Cornish Cultures for Community Resilience". Between 2009 and
2013 I was lucky enough to be funded by the European Union,
allowing me to undertake research into the potential uses of Cornish
cultures for social cohesion. Under the supervision of the University
of Exeter's threatened Institute of Cornish Studies, I also considered
how Cornishness itself might continue into the future, despite
seemingly overwhelming pressures. Some of what I have to say is
likely to upset some of those I have worked most closely with—but
the intention is to put them at the heart of reflective practices that
build community resilience and continue Robert Morton Nance's
Cornish Project with awareness of the incomparably different
circumstances we find ourselves in.

My inquiry meant that I could come back to Cornwall and see
friends and family, albeit temporarily. Instead of relying on Skype
and email, I could meet other Cornish speakers, eat saffron cake and
feel the full effect of gale-force winds. In 2002 I had moved to
Brittany where, for my sins, I teach English. Although I meant to
stay for a year, I am still there, meaning that I look at Cornwall
yearningly from afar, noting the alarming pace of harmful
development and the erosion of Cornishness at every home visit. In
sharing the frustrations and sorrow of Cornish people and their
friends, at home and around the world, and in acknowledging and
facing up to the situation, this discussion begins to consider some
strategies. It has been informed by the willingness of a very large
number of people to talk about their lives and share their social and

cultural activities. My thanks go to all of them. I should also like to thank Bernard Deacon, Philip Payton and Garry Tregidga, not just for having supervised my Ph.D., but for having largely shaped the New Cornish Studies that allowed it to happen. Some others deserve special mention too. Sharon Lowenna has given steady encouragement and informed discussion, Jenefer Lowe has been ever-ready to talk about Cornish, Kim Cooper and her colleagues from the Cornish Studies Library have been at hand to help, Gus Williams of Camborne School of Mines and Phil Hosken of the Trevithick Society have offered observations and practical support and Jan Lobb, Julie Tamblin and Ed Curry of the Cornish Language Council have maintained a sense of worthwhile purpose.

Introduction

This discussion is meant to inform and provoke consideration by cultural practitioners and policy-makers on the inclusive well-being of Cornwall's population and the affirmative maintenance of Cornishness. It involves questions about cultural use that have to do with feelings and emotions that are slippery and largely unquantifiable. For example, how do you measure the emotional responses to a community narrative or the indirect impact on people's actions when collective memory is stirred by an everyday act, like drinking tea without sugar, eating a saffron bun, using a Cornish shovel or singing "Goin' up Camborne Hill"?[2] Such matters are related here to cultural, social and symbolic capital which furthermore have no fixed values and are similarly hard to measure, let alone equate to a given amount of economic wealth or human well-being. These are subjective phenomena which may be dismissed or ignored, yet they are vital ingredients of community life that must be grappled with if the primary uses of culture are to be appreciated and brought to the fore. The following discussion takes sides, arguing that the cause of the disadvantaged and marginalized should inform policy and cultural practice. It notes, for example, that 19% of children (16,650) in Cornwall live in poverty according to U.K. Government definitions and that inequalities result in local variations between 2% and 58%.[3] Sections of Cornwall's population are rarely heard in public debate, for lack of confidence and morale. These people are less likely to belong to cultural organizations and committees or to respond to questionnaires so the participatory

2   Drinking tea without sugar is attributed to Methodist-led anti-slavery campaigns. The long-handled Cornish shovel recalls mining and working the land and stands for everyday difference. *Camborne Hill* is a song about Richard Trevithick's invention of the steam locomotive.

3   Report: "Deprivation and Child Poverty", Truro: Cornwall Council, 2011.

methods that inform the following chapters were chosen to tap into their experiences.[4]

The heterogeneity of Cornishness means that being Cornish is not the same as sharing the experiences of everybody within the imagined community. I am not an inside participant when it comes to wholly or mainly female activities, for instance and although I have consulted women as witnesses, that is hardly on a level with my easy access to traditionally male domains, including those that I know at first-hand:—landscaping, building and fishing. The principle applies to all parts of society that I do not belong to and that has meant trying hard to seek out their experiences. From an over-simplified perspective though, I am an insider and Cornish speaker. Generations of my family have worked in seafaring, fishing, shipbuilding, farming and mining, a decidedly clichéd background that strengthens their awareness of being Cornish; but as my surname announces, I have some non-Cornish forebears as well. This shapes my interest in espousing an outward-looking vision that envisages exchange, pluralism and recruitment. Objectivity is never possible, whether researchers are insiders or outsiders so, for better or worse, my subjectivity informs my conviction that Cornish cultures and the Cornish language are worthy of being sustained and important for community resilience.

Cornish cultural practitioners, whether amateurs or professionals, represent interconnected communities of practice, bound by networks that ultimately merge with a wider community in the everyday sense. Individual communities of practitioners (Cornish language teachers, musicians and dancers, film-makers, actors and so on) have indistinct boundaries and activities, conceived as expressions of Cornish identity as a whole, diffuse into the cultures of everyday life. Ethno-cultural politics are there even in seemingly banal acts,[5] so researchers, whether "insiders" or "outsiders", can easily slip into ready-made nationalist and ethnic paradigms. The twin dangers in Cornwall are of either ignoring ethnicity—a lack in some non-participant analyses—or of privileging it over other

---

4 Details of the research methods may be found in my thesis "Employing Cornish Cultures for Community Resilience."

5 Cf. Michael Billig (1995), *Banal Nationalism*, London: Sage.

components of identity (gender, class, religion, politics, affective affiliations etc.) to the point of ignoring them and imagining a homogenized, one-dimensional group. The former approach has hitherto been associated with outside academics and government reports while the later has been associated with insiders influenced by the Cornish Movement. Discounting ethnicity has resulted in, "the relative invisibility of Cornwall and the Cornish as a territory and a people in the British national historiography"[6] and since ethnicity is denied—"We do not consider the Cornish to constitute a 'national minority'"[7]—it has been hard to address structural discrimination and disadvantage. Indeed, it was not until 2014— after my inquiry—that the U.K. Government extended legal protection to the Cornish under the Framework Convention for the Protection of National Minorities, despite having undertaken to protect the Cornish language according to the Council of Europe's Charter for Regional or Minority Languages (ECRML) in 2001.

Ignoring ethno-cultural claims has been an obstacle to considering Cornwall separately for administrative purposes and for many years it blocked European regional aid by allowing statistics on poverty to be submerged in those of the more prosperous South-West Region. On the other hand, an overemphasis on ethnicity in Cornish accounts has made it hard to address complexity, heterogeneity and the uncertainties of cultural hybridity and indeterminacy. More belligerent assertions have even been accompanied by objections to studying local differences within Cornwall and to exploring the overlap between Cornishness and Englishness. Both extremes are linked in opposition, each provoking reaction to the other. The casual dismissal of ethnicity by Establishment academics and civil servants gives rise to polemic from Cornish commentators, eager to assert a denied identity and this, in turn, raises worries that their claims must have anti-English motivations. Faced with established views, ridicule and self-righteous moral indignation, Cornish academics and cultural and political leaders are often somewhat

6   Philip Payton, "'A Duchy in every respect un-English': discourses of identity in late-modern Cornwall", in Lancaster *et al.*, (2007), *An Agenda for Regional History*, Newcastle upon Tyne, p. 319.

7   The "U.K. Report on the Council of Europe Framework Convention for the Protection of National Minorities", The Home Office, 1999.

circumspect, choosing not to deal with the pressures upon ethno-cultural identity directly and openly, even when it is crucial to understanding.

The Cornish Movement's paradigms share much with post-colonialism and minority politics elsewhere, homogenizing Englishness as dominant and oppressive and Cornishness as subaltern and victim. It does not matter whether we take Cornwall's historical experience to have been that of an "internal colony"[8] or dismiss the idea as silly because, like it or not, the Cornish Movement operates from such a standpoint and bathes in Celtic nationalisms and British multi-culturalisms. Views of the tribe as homogenous and downtrodden therefore colour and motivate cultural practice so that many work within simple, binary oppositions of "us and them", imagining Cornishness in alterity to Englishness without qualification. Although this favours solidarity, it produces oversimplifications that overlook fractions within an "imagined community"[9] which is thought to have common needs, despite conflicts of interest and internal differences. As in other "minority" campaigns, the emphasis on ethnicity may be so overwhelming that, for example, the specific interests of working-class women or the rural elderly or those of poorly or well-qualified young people are subsumed. Cornish ethnicity has to be at the core of considering useable culture and should inform policy, but it should not be a single-issue obsession. The 2011 census shows that Cornwall's population includes people from all parts of Britain and Ireland and many from further afield so deprivation unavoidably affects some of them, not just the Cornish. English in-migrants furthermore have varied socio-economic and regional backgrounds and individually negotiated relationships with Cornishness. Complexity has informed how and where I have participated, observed and sampled witnesses, including some of these categories:

The economically and educationally disadvantaged,
Qualified and soon-to-be qualified young people,

8   Bernard Deacon, "Is Cornwall an Internal Colony?" in C. Ó Luain (ed.) (1983) *For a Celtic Future*, Dublin: The Celtic League.

9   Benedict Anderson (1991), *Imagined Communities: Reflections on the Origin and Spread of Nationalism*, 2nd edition, London and New York: Verso.

Cultural activists and participants,
Participants in Revivalist music and dance cultures,
Participants in traditional Cornish cultural practices,
Cornish speakers, teachers, activists and learners,
Business people, marketers, managers,
Arts professionals,
Elected councillors,
Academics and researchers,
Policy and decision-makers.

Both the heterogeneity of Cornishness itself and the multi-cultural dimensions of communities are important for considerations of how Cornish cultures may be employed for cohesiveness and resilience.

Chapter 1

The New Cornwall
and the Cornish Movement

The proposition or pro-position adopted here is that distinctive Cornish cultures, including the Cornish language, may be deployed usefully in efforts to create and strengthen sustainable communities and build social and economic resilience, including the strength to adapt and respond to events. The suggestion is motivated by a set of new realities that calls for a rethinking of approaches to cultural tradition and constitutes a seismic change of circumstances. This alters the contextual frame within which culture is performed and understood so thoroughly that any evaluation of its usefulness and value in community development needs to take account. The new circumstances involve material and economic disadvantage, produce social and cultural inequalities and have implications for the primary social and emotional uses of culture. They influence morale which, as an emotional or psychological factor in community life, affects well-being and has potential knock-on effects for the economy. Emotional responses also motivate consciously Cornish cultural and political activities which are here identified as manifestations of a diverse Cornish Movement and related to community resilience.

The greatest changes are demographic. Rapid inward and outward migration has changed the make-up of the population so that, for the first time, a majority of residents does not have a long Cornish family tradition. To put this in a longer, historical context, Cornwall's strong demography in the nineteenth century supported the maintenance and strengthening of a, "Cornish sense of ethnic solidarity and territoriality".[10] Instead of experiencing in-migration of the kind often associated with industrialization, Cornwall had strong internal movements of its mining population and major

10   Philip Payton (2007), "'A Duchy in Every Respect Un-English'", *op. cit.*, p. 323.

emigrations and patterns of overseas working. Relative homogeneity, combined with the dimension of transnationality and global industrial prowess, meant that an already strong Cornish identity was perpetuated with a sense of quasi-nationhood that might not have survived and developed had Cornwall been integrated demographically with other British industrial regions. Yet, whereas nineteenth and early twentieth-century Cornwall had one of the highest proportions of locally-born inhabitants in Britain,[11] data from multiple sources now show that about a third of the population is Cornish, a proportion that varies somewhat according to whether self-definition, birth or parentage is the criterion.[12] It also varies according to locality so that coastal areas have lower proportions and former industrial districts with lower house prices have higher proportions. There are, however, no areas with an overwhelmingly Cornish population. For clarity in this discussion, "indigenous" is applied to people who consider themselves Cornish and have a degree of family continuity in Cornwall, however tenuous, and "native" refers literally to those born in Cornwall or Plymouth (since the maternity hospital that serves East Cornwall is in Plymouth) regardless of identifications and background. These problematic definitions, central to questions of identity and cohesion, invite comparison with other parts of Europe such as The Basque Country and Corsica that have experienced large-scale in-migration but which retain ethno-cultural identities.

These demographic changes are a side-effect of tourism, "on a seemingly cataclysmic scale".[13] Five million tourists visit Cornwall

11 *Ibid.*; Census data: 1891, 1901, 1911.
12 In Cornwall Council's "Quality of Life Survey" (2007), 25.9% of respondents self-identified as Cornish; Kerryn Husk (2012) gives 25%; In the CAPITA EMS Pulse School Census for the Dept. of Education, 41% of pupils self-identified; Other sources: Carrick District Council, "Private Sector House Condition Survey", (1996); Peter Wills (1999), "Information from the Parish Housing Surveys and Household Survey Reports of Cornwall Rural Community Council", CoSERG; Ron Perry *et al.* (1986), 44% were "indigenous"; Discussions: Cornwall Council website (20th October 2011); Ian Saltern, "Cornish National Minorities Report 2", (2011); Joanie Willett (2008), "Why is Cornwall so Poor? Narrative, Perception and Identity", Ph.D. thesis, University of Exeter.
13 Alan Kent, (2000), *The Literature of Cornwall, Continuity, Identity, Difference 1000-*

each year and the industry represents around eleven percent of the economy.[14] As well as having both positive and negative economic impacts, tourism changes representations and perceptions of Cornwall and the Cornish with consequences for consideration in this discussion. At the same time, traditional industries (metal mining, China-clay extraction, quarrying, farming, fishing, engineering, ship repair) that formed the basis of occupational cultures and identities have all but gone, producing a set of experiences that is shared with much of industrial, maritime and agricultural Britain. This involves the loss of the material and symbolic foundations of community and produces multiple crises of identity (including those of gender roles, linked to work) and morale. Cornwall has simultaneously experienced similar social trends to the rest of North-Western Europe, including transformations in social structures and patterns of consumption, as well as local experiences of globalization.

Since the mid 1960s, there has been a trend away from administration and decision-making in Cornwall towards institutions based either on the "South-West Region" or "Devon and Cornwall" (part of a wave of centralization in the United Kingdom.). This applies to everything from public utilities and the police to the civil service, government offices and quangos—including bodies responsible for regional development and arts funding.[15] As institutions have expanded, creating thousands of middle-class jobs and decision-making roles, Cornwall has lost out to centres in Bristol, Exeter, Plymouth and Swindon, so much so that when it was afforded Objective One status by the European Union, it became the only such region where the funds were administered externally. Indeed, central government has continued to transfer public jobs out of Cornwall even while European Union aid is received for job creation. All of this means that regional aid "funds jobs in Bristol" and that many important decisions are "not taken in Cornwall by

2000, Bristol: Redcliffe Press, p.12.

14 ONS figure for 2011.

15 An early example was Devon and Cornwall Constabulary, 1967; See CoSERG Report: "South West Regional Strategy 2006-2026 'Wrong Region, wrong assumptions, wrong strategy'" www.cornwallcoserg.org.uk/ (Accessed 19 May 2011.)

people who understand what is needed".[16] Critics see this form of centralization as leading, not just to job losses, but to bad governance and cultural impoverishment[17] as it depletes Cornwall of an articulate, home-grown body of people with local knowledge, loyalty and motivation—the "organic intellectuals" who might contribute to all domains.[18] The Mebyon Kernow councillor, Dick Cole, describes Cornwall as, "always tucked away in some unelected, unaccountable South-West body that wouldn't know Talskiddy from Tolvaddon."[19] and the prominent independent councillor, Bert Biscoe remarks that, "'Regional arrangements', such as 'west country', be they cultural, administrative, economic or political, are designed to solve other people's problems, but not Cornwall's."[20]

For many Cornish people, not just declared nationalists, inclusion in larger administrative areas is furthermore anathema because it ignores Cornwall's identity claims and historical integrity. This was evident is discussions of the proposal in 2010-11 to create a Cornwall and Scilly Local Enterprise Partnership to replace the South-West Regional Development Agency. It has also been the theme of campaigns against new electoral boundaries that include parts of Cornwall and Devon in the same parliamentary constituencies for the first time. At the "Keep Cornwall Whole" rally (10th October 2010), hosted by Saltash Town Council, speakers, including members of parliament, mayors and community figures, linked the issue to the *de facto* creation of an administrative "Devonwall" (the derogatory term used by critics) and a raft of economic and cultural issues that "need Cornish solutions" and "a Cornish voice". Symbolic references were made to Athelstan's confirmation of the Tamar boundary in 936 A.D., just nine years after he had, "cleansed

16 Complaints from councillors, cf John Angarrack (2008), *Scat t'Larrups. Resist and Survive*, Padstow: Independent Academic Press, p. 82.

17 Cf. Joanie Willet (2008), "Why is Cornwall so Poor? Narrative, Perception and Identity", *op. cit.*

18 Antonio Gramsci's term; See B. Deacon, "And Shall Trelawny Die? The Cornish Identity." (1993) in P.J. Payton (ed.) (1993), *Cornwall Since the War: The Contemporary History of a European Region*, Redruth: Dyllansow Truran and Institute of Cornish Studies, p.215.

19 Dick Cole, recorded B.B.C. Radio Cornwall (12 December 2008).

20 Bert Biscoe, letter to *An Baner Kernewek*, no. 73, August 1993.

the city [Exeter] of its defilement by wiping out that filthy [Cornish] race".[21]

These demographic, economic, administrative and institutional circumstances have weakened traditional culture but heightened a defensive awareness of identity and produced a tangible sense of marginalization and embattlement that seeps unavoidably into the conversations and banal acts of everyday life and social media discussions. In keeping with this widespread, popular discourse Bert Biscoe writes:

> The reluctance of central institutions to acknowledge the distinctiveness of Cornwall and her people…is probably the greatest single contribution to the present social and economic malaise of Britain's poorest region…[22]

Little analysis of the continuities and discontinuities that the new circumstances produce has been undertaken and still less consideration given to how new residents engage with Cornishness or could do so in the future but these are important areas to grapple with if Cornwall is to have a sustainably inclusive society. What is clear though, is that there has been a sea change, justifying the name "New Cornwall" which one or two analysts have appropriated from earlier uses.[23]

An Movyans Kernowek: The Cornish Movement

The name "New Cornwall" here describes a multifaceted situation of which assertions of difference are a major component. These expressions are motivated by the recent transformations and may be seen as a "response to the everyday deluge of Anglicisation",[24] but

---

21 William of Malmesbury, *Gesta Regum Anglorum*, 1125, cited in Susan Pearce (1978), *The Kingdom of Dumnonia*, Padstow: Lodenek Press.

22 Bert Biscoe in S.Parker (ed.)(1998), p. 150; cf. Bernard Deacon (2000), *The Cornish and the Council of Europe Framework Convention for the Protection of National Minorities*.

23 E.g. Bernard Deacon (2007), *Cornwall: A Concise History*, Cardiff: University of Wales Press; Applied by R.M. Nance to an imagined future (1925, 1949), inspiring the magazine *New Cornwall*, launched by Richard Gendall (1952), eds. Helena Charles, then Ann and Richard Jenkin.

24 Bernard Deacon with Sharron Schwartz and David Holman (2004), *The Cornish*

they also build upon Pan-Celtic discourses that emerged in the nineteenth century and upon much older narratives of a non-English origin. Commentators present them as having maintained Cornish identity and ensured that, "Cornwall and its people, despite the fears of observers in the 1970s, became more 'Celtic' as the millennium reached its end."[25] An array of forms, referred to with religious echoes, as the "Cornish Revival" (An Dasserghyans Kernowek),[26] or simply the "Revival", imagines the re-invigoration of a flagging culture and the resurrection of real and supposed past elements in projects of cultural retrieval similar to those of post-colonial situations. This "Revivalism" is one of several aspects of a much larger "Cornish Movement" (An Movyans Kernowek), a misleadingly unitary title for what has become a plural, heterogeneous and highly fragmented constellation of cultural and political activities, united by an overarching Cornish sentiment.[27] Multiple, inter-connected "Cornish scenes" concern themselves with differing cultural, social and political activities.[28]

In this discussion a terminological distinction is made between "The Revival", which includes language revitalization, cultural retrieval and reconstruction, and the wider "Cornish Movement" which also embraces manifestations of group awareness and feelings that put less emphasis on reviving past cultures (language, music and customs) and more upon socio-economic issues and maintaining present practices. Revivalism represents a large part of the Cornish Movement, in other words, but not all adherents are motivated by cultural revival or involved in it. Unlike "Revival", which suggests a narrower focus on Celticism and connotes a quasi-spiritual quest, the more secular-sounding "Movement" encapsulates a broader range of responses to new and changing circumstances, including symbolic, political uses of culture for socio-economic ends. Despite

Family: The roots of our future, Fowey: Cornwall Editions.

25 Ibid.

26 Charles Thomas, "An Dasserghyans Kernewek", at the Celtic Congress, 16-20 April, 1963.

27 "Cornish Movement" was perhaps coined by F. Cargeeg c.1930 as "an Mevyans Kernewek"; For discussion see, Caroline Vink "'Be Forever Cornish!' Some Observations on the Ethnoregional Movement in Contemporary Cornwall", in P.J. Payton (ed.), Cornish Studies, no. 1, (1993), pp. 109-119 (112).

28 Inspiring the magazine Cornish Scene, Sarah Foot (ed.) in the 1980s-90s.

their plurality, it is useful to think of these phenomena as a single movement because collectively they constitute a current that favours a sense of difference, having the sense of a collective voyage, even if the precise course is disputed and uncharted. In using the label "movement"—as in applications from the arts—there is a suggestion of innovation, creativity and radicalism, all of which have long co-existed with preservationist, conservative and atavistic motivations for interest in Cornishness. The impossibilities of delimitation compare to other uses of "movement" where people combine in actions that produce affective identifications beyond organized membership—as in the Labour Movement, the Feminist Movement, the Environmental Movement and so on, all of which are plural, nebulous and diffuse while being thought of as entities.

The Cornish Movement has been categorized as an "ethno-regional movement",[29] as an "ethnic revitalization movement"[30] and as "ethnonationalism",[31] underlining similarities with counterparts such as the Breton *Emsav*,[32] where cultural identity and cultural production influence commerce, public policy and politics. The historian Charles Thomas has called it, "a Cornish national-consciousness movement", noting that:

[I]t may well be another century before most native Cornish cease to think, subconsciously and automatically, in terms of 'Cornwall' and 'England', an Us-and-Them syndrome...[33]

The post-war Movement has been motivated by economic inequalities, in-migration and anti-metropolitanism and includes forms of political and cultural nationalism that have been partly

29 Caroline Vink, *op. cit.* (note 151); Michael Hechter and Margaret Levi, "The comparative analysis of ethnoregional movements", in Ethnic and Racial Studies, vol. 2, no. 3, July 1979.

30 Jane Smith Korey (1992), As we belong to be: The ethnic movement in Cornwall, England, Ph.D. Thesis, Brandeis University.

31 Amy Hale (2001) "Representing the Cornish: Contesting heritage interpretation in Cornwall", in *Tourist Studies*, vol. 1 (2), pp. 185-196, (2001), London: Sage, p. 185-196.

32 See Jean Olivero (2010), *op. cit.*; Ronan Le Coadic (1998), *L'Identité bretonne*, Deuxième édition, Rennes: Terre de Brume - Presses Universitaires de Rennes.

33 Charles Thomas (1986), *Celtic Britain*, London: Thames and Hudson.

framed by Welsh and Scottish models.[34] Its origins are often traced uniquely to the Celto-Cornish Revival that emerged from antiquarianism in the late nineteenth century but in reality the movement has multiple origins, not only in Celticism but in the development of Cornish Associations (overseas and in London) and Cornish institutions during the nineteenth century, and in distinctive political and religious experiences that coupled Methodism with radicalism. None of the proposed labels adequately describes a phenomenon that spans the left-right political spectrum, manifests itself in social movements and economic initiatives, increasingly incorporates environmentalism and multiculturalism and inspires the arts and popular culture. While sharing a sense of Cornwall and attributing symbolic roles to the Cornish language, the Movement's manifold manifestations are sites where ideas about what it is to be Cornish and what kind of place Cornwall should be are argued over. They are places where "ascribed and elective identities"[35] meet untidily so that it is unrealistic to distinguish between clear insider and outsider versions. As representations, differing performances of identity both inform (help) and misinform (hinder) efforts to develop cultural strategies, such as those of Cornwall Council, and are at the heart of discussions about "regional distinctiveness", branding and cultural tourism.[36]

The effects of the Cornish Movement extend far beyond overtly Revivalist or nationalist circles, influencing the main political parties and the character of civil society.[37] For example, in 2012 all of Cornwall's members of Parliament were learning Cornish and several had a track record of pursuing devolved government.[38] In

---

34 See Bernard Deacon, Dick Cole and Garry Tregidga (2003), Mebyon Kernow and Cornish Nationalim, Cardiff: Welsh Academic Press, pp. 18-22. See B. Deacon *et al.* (2003) *op. cit.*

35 Stuart Hall's terms (1973), cf. S. Hall and Paul du Gay (eds.) (1996), Questions of Cultural Identity, London: Sage.

36 E.g. Cornwall Council's "White Paper for Culture", Truro: Cornwall Council, (October 2012) and earlier "green paper".

37 Philip Payton (1996), *Cornwall*, Fowey: Alexander Associates, p. 290; B. Deacon *et al.* (2003), *op. cit.* (note 158).

38 See "Dydh da—M.P.s to learn Cornish", www.thisiscornwall.co.uk/Dydh-da-ndash-MPs-learn-Cornish/story-17546252-detail/story.html (Accessed 12 December 2012.); Communications from Andrew George, M.P.

recent years, the Movement's discourses have underpinned bids for Objective One assistance, the Combined Universities Campus and recognition for the Cornish Language from the Council of Europe and the United Kingdom government.[39] Indeed these bids are inter-connected since individuals and groups from the Movement took the initiatives, simultaneously arguing that Cornwall should be disentangled statistically from South-West England for economic reasons and making cultural and historical arguments for recognition as one of Europe's historic regions. The symbolic existence of the Cornish language proved decisive, while the existence of the Cornish Movement demonstrated that the identity existed in the present. The Movement's influences pervade much of everyday life and have had a major impact on "Cornwall since the war"[40] yet there has been little critical assessment of its socio-economic impact or potential. Many concerned with promoting multiple interpretations of Cornish culture see it as straightforwardly positive without giving further thought to which versions of Cornwall are foregrounded and which intra-group stories are relayed. This is—or should be—controversial because it has inevitable consequences for Cornwall's image and could influence decision-making. It affects how "people in Cornwall" (an expression used in public discourse to discretely include Cornish and non-Cornish residents) feel about themselves and their communities, with consequences for material areas such as employment and in non-material areas such as self-esteem.

In-migration

Since the late 1960s, an abrupt tipping point, the imagery of tourism and alternative lifestyles has fuelled counter-urbanization and speculative housing, attracting thousands of new residents, mainly from urban England who, contrary to common assumptions, are mainly of working age and more likely to be so than the indigenous Cornish.[41] Chronic poverty and unemployment have simultaneously

39 Testimony from councillors; Discussion in J. Willet, *Why is Cornwall so Poor? Narrative, Perception and Identity*, (2010), *op. cit.*

40 Philip Payton (ed.) (1993), *Cornwall Since the War, op. cit.*

41 See Malcolm Williams and Eric Harrison (1995), "Movers and Stayers: A comparison of migratory and non-migratory groups in Cornwall, 1981-91", in P.J. Payton (ed.), *Cornish Studies*, no. 3, (1995), pp 176-193; Bernard Deacon,

led many people to leave yet the population rose from around 342, 300 in 1961 to 532, 300 in 2011, an average rise in the order of ten percent per decade, making Cornwall's population fifty-eight percent higher than in the mid twentieth century.[42] At the same time, the indigenous Cornish population is estimated to have fallen from around 260, 000 to below 180, 000.[43] To put this in perspective, Cornwall's growth rate since 1961 has been more than three times that of England, more than four times that of Wales and approximately seventy-three times that of Scotland. This growth is on an exceptional scale in Britain where only six or seven counties (all closely connected to London) have similar rates[44] and its causes and consequences have attracted interest from social scientists.[45] It is also unusual because it has not been fuelled by labour shortages but has, "always outstripped the creation of jobs, thus embedding chronic unemployment and driving wage levels down",[46] so while Cornwall has had impressive periods of job-creation, these have not been the motor for population growth nor enough to satisfy growing demand. It is only since around 2005 that Cornwall's relative employment and income figures have improved, coincidentally corresponding to a slowing down of in-migration.[47] Population growth is set to continue though, because far from opposing it or extrapolating from a recent slowing down, Cornwall Council's Core Strategy caters for, and encourages, rates of development and migration greater than those of the last decade and far exceeds local

Andrew George and Ron Perry, (1987), *Cornwall at the Crossroads*, CoSERG: Redruth.

42   From the 2011 Census. The last decade shows a 6.7% rise.

43   Estimates in Jane Howells, "Preliminary report on the Cornwall Council Core Strategy preferred approach equality impact assessment", Cornwall: Bewnans Kernow, (23rd February, 2012).

44   Bernard Deacon, "Population change in Cornwall 1951-2001", eric.ex.ac.uk/ exeter/bitstream/10036/199s6/1/PopulationchangeinCornwall1951- 2001.pdf, (Accessed 10 November 2010.)

45   E.g. Ronald Perry, Ken Dean and Bryan Brown (eds.) (1986), *Counterurbanisation: case studies of urban to rural movement*, Geo Books, Norwich; Mary Buck, Lyn Bryant and Malcolm Williams (1993), "Housing and Households in Cornwall: A pilot study of Cornish families", Plymouth: University of Plymouth.

46   Bernard Deacon (2007), *Cornwall: A Concise History, op. cit.*, p. 213.

47   NOMIS Labour Force Statistics; Information from Cornwall Community Intelligence Team.

needs estimated by CoSERG and the campaigning group, "It's our Cornwall", to be 12,500 houses based on analysis of internal trends and the housing waiting list.[48] Indeed it is argued that only five percent of the proposed housing is for local need and that, in the words of the former M.P., Andrew George, "Our housing stock has more than doubled but our housing problems have got worse", while "Allowing Cornwall to carry on being a developers' paradise will do nothing to help the deep seated housing problems of locals."[49] Cornwall's internal demographics point to zero growth or a slight decline but the proposals mean that the population will be around 637,400 by 2031.[50] That is if opposition fails and economic trends continue.

Another effect of tourism and speculative development is the growth in the number of second homes which is believed to have a strong effect on house prices and community life. The Office of National Statistics reports that 10,169 people in England or Wales own a second home in Cornwall, higher numbers than any county. There are estimated to be more than 14,000 such homes, with concentrations in coastal villages such as Padstow (29,3%) and St Minver Lowlands (42,9%).[51] In nearby Polzeath and Trebetherick the Council Tax list shows that more than half of houses are either second homes or empty.[52] Widespread concerns are summed up by a news report describing Mousehole as having been, "left empty by [the] scourge of second homes", quoting a man in his seventies, Leon Pezzack, who talked of "a disintegration of our society".[53] It is a side-effect of tourism that is not lost on Malcolm Bell of Visit Cornwall who talks of needing to, "mitigate the negatives and build on the

---

48 See www.cornwallcoserg.org.uk/ and www.thisiscornwall.co.uk/Campaigners-say-Cornwall-growth/story-16623925-detail/story.html, (Accessed 1 August 2012)

49 Andrew George M.P., www.thisiscornwall.co.uk/Nimbys-blame-affordable-housing-shortage/story-11486176-detail/story.html

50 Estimates cited by Jane Howells (2012), *op. cit.*

51 Andrew Wallis, Cornwall Councillor, has provided a breakdown by parish, www.cllrandrewwallis.co.uk/the-full-list-of-second-homes-by-parish-in-cornwall/ (Accessed 15 January 2013.)

52 ourcornwall.org/?cat=21 (Accessed 15 January 2013.)

53 Leon Pezzack cited by Simon Parker, www.thisiscornwall.co.uk (17th November 2012.)

positives" and "dovetail" tourism with, "improving the quality of life for Cornish people" and using planning to tackle the, "unacceptable burden on the local community" whereby "local people can't afford housing".[54] The issue came to a head in 2010-11 when it was revealed that an unknown number of owners had voted in marginal seats and had probably changed the outcomes of elections, notably in the case of George Eustice, Conservative M.P. for Camborne and Reduth who had won by a margin of 66 votes (20 April 2010). In what might signal the beginning of a determined fightback, Cornwall Council stepped in with "a strict interpretation of the law" to reduce this phenomenon and, in November 2012, proposed using new powers to end council tax discounts. Then, in May 2016, following eighty-three percent support in a referendum, the Council adopted a Neighbourhood Development Plan for St Ives and Carbis Bay that makes full-time occupation of housing by local people a condition for planning permission.

The demographic and housing situation is the proverbial elephant in the room of discussions about "regional distinctiveness". Quite simply, Cornwall is distinctive because the indigenous Cornish make it so, yet if recent trends continue they will be no more than twenty to thirty percent of the population by 2031. Ethnicity and in-migration are difficult matters to talk about, though. They touch sensibilities about racism and, in any case, Cornish ethno-cultural claims tend to be met, not just with indignation and lack of sympathy, but with ridicule and dismissal of the idea that a distinct ethnicity exists. Furthermore, the in-migrants and second-home owners in question are predominantly white, English and middle-class, just like most institutional decision-makers, meaning that the latter may feel targeted. For many Cornish people, the issue is emotionally-charged and produces both polemic and quiet, gloom-laden fatalism. Against this background it is understandable that when making the case for the Cornish language and cultural activities, participants are inclined to avoid reference to these circumstances; yet, as previously noted, practices and artefacts that are labelled Cornish only make sense if embedded in indigenous culture and society:

54 Malcolm Bell in A film by John Howe and Richard Stevens, Digital Media students at UCF, 2010. www.youtube.com/watch?v=KPIGqCJWXpk

If the Cornish people are not there underpinning it [Cornish identity], then all the talk about 'Cornish culture' or 'the Cornish heritage' will be just idle talk. We will have an empty culture with a disjointed identity. Cornwall will be populated by ghosts of its past—it will no longer be Cornwall in any real sense of the word but merely another spot on the map.[55]

Despite reticence about raising the issue in institutional settings, demographic trends pre-occupy cultural practitioners and community activists. Some are all too aware that the commodification of cultural distinctiveness may continue apace without actions to ensure the material conditions needed for the continued presence of the Cornish themselves and the transmission of their living cultures. The organization, Bewnans Kernow, is a partnership of sixty-five bodies concerned with a broad span of indigenous culture which has responded to proposals for further population growth with a report that expresses alarm and claims that, "In-migration to Cornwall has had a strong adverse influence on the ability of the indigenous Cornish people to maintain a sustained population."[56] The report touches upon the uses of culture, stating that, "Cornish culture and Cornish distinctiveness powerfully strengthen community cohesion and are key drivers in Cornwall",[57] and suggesting that these "drivers" will be compromised if the Cornish are further marginalized:

Marginalisation will affect the political, social, cultural and economic spheres, and will increasingly limit the ability of a diminishing indigenous population to influence these spheres.[58]

Marginalization and a Last-of-the-Mohecans psychosis
These demographic transformations and projections have intensified fears that Cornwall's distinctiveness will be eroded and even that, "the whole essence of Cornishness could be lost within a

55 CoSERG (1987) *Cornwall at the Crossroads.*
56 Jane Howells (2012), *op. cit.* p. 16.
57 *Ibid.*
58 *Ibid.*

generation".[59] Because of narratives of a Cornish national and ethnic identity, this disquiet goes beyond concerns about the countryside, rural deprivation or even localism, having much in common with rural Wales. In both cases worries about housing, employment and the physical and cultural landscape are joined by anxieties around the maintenance of culture as a way of life and the survival of the group as a Celtic nation. In Cornwall, this gives rise to a widespread feeling that the "imagined community"[60] and identity are in imminent danger and although this produces militancy and resistance, it also leads to pessimistic acceptance and an "end of Cornwall rhetoric":[61]

> What and how people feel is one of the most important things about culture and identity, and many of the Cornish [...] feel a sense of being "wiped out". This is reflected in the reality of a diminishing ratio of Cornish people to other people in Cornwall.[62]

To varying degrees, many members of the community see the erosion of their way of life, culture and community as inevitable and irreversible, reflecting feelings of powerlessness and the impression that developments are irresistible and beyond democratic control. Repeatedly, conversations return without prompting to these themes, expressing "disabling feelings of despair, defeatist acceptance and grief",[63] and forms of resignation that undermine well-being.

---

59 Loveday Trevenen Jenkin (2011) www.bbc.co.uk/news/uk-england-cornwall-12995737; cf. Charles Thomas, *The Importance of being Cornish in Cornwall*, Institute of Cornish Studies, Redruth, 1973; CoSERG (1988), *op. cit.*; B. Deacon (2012), "The Unimportance of being Cornish in Cornwall", Address to the Institute of Cornish Studies, CUC Campus, Tremough, 24th November 2012.

60 Benedict Anderson (1991), *op. cit.*; See Alan Kent (2000), *op. cit.*, p.12, for discussion of "perceived... extinction".

61 Bernard Deacon (2007), *op. cit.* p. 215; cf. Daphne du Maurier (1967), *Vanishing Cornwall: The spirit and history of Cornwall*, Harmondworth: Penguin.

62 Jane Howells, *op. cit.*

63 Neil Kennedy (1995), "Racial equality in Cornwall", in Commission for Racial Equality, "Challenging Racism in the South-West: report of a one day seminar for Cornwall", Truro, pp. 18-211.

This favours a lack of confidence, dynamism and creativity that can be misperceived as apathy and encourages the kinds of self-deprecation and rejection of personal background that commonly accompany assimilation into prevalent cultures. A need, identified by some cultural practitioners, is to actively move beyond manifestations of a self-fulfilling "cult of loss".[64] Prominent themes of loss and defeat, increasingly joined by narratives of historic victimhood, are suspected of producing cultures and identities that are closed, moribund and nostalgic or of leading to a "Last of the Mohicans"[65] psychosis of the kind expressed by the writer Roy Phillips:

> This book is dedicated to the likes of [list of names]. They represent the last of the Cornish, who are following their beautiful language into oblivion.[66]

There are claims that sections of Cornish society are marginalized politically, economically and culturally. Jane Howells refers to a process of "disenfranchisement" and warns that as the Cornish become a smaller proportion of the population, "this is likely to have a knock on effect on the ability to access resources and opportunities."[67] With regard to planning, she notes that, "consultation of representative Cornish organisations has not only been inadequate but non-existent." This means that the impact of policy upon the indigenous community and its cultures has been ignored, flouting Cornwall Council's recognition that "The Framework Convention for the Protection of National Minorities" applies to the Cornish and the commitment within it that, "All parties shall refrain from measures which alter the proportions of the population in areas inhabited by persons belonging to national minorities."[68]

Howell's comments are characteristic of a new set of Cornish discourses, drawn from British multi-culturalism and minority

---

64 Alan Kent (2000), *The Literature of Cornwall, Continuity, Identity, Difference 1000-2000*, p. 283.

65 The Mohicans are still with us in Oklahoma and Wisconsin.

66 N. Roy Phillips (1987), *The Saffron Eaters*, Devon Books.

67 Jane Howells, *op. cit.*

68 Jane Howells, *op. cit.*

politics, which has largely superseded the "Cornwall for the Cornish" rhetoric of the 1960s and 70s. Thus, the tendency is towards using the terms "ethnic group", "minority" and "indigenous" and speaking about "rights" and "equality", often with reference to legislation and charters.[69] Accompanying arguments began to filter into official channels in the early 1990s and featured in conferences and reports of the former Commission for Racial Equality:

[T]here is a substantial number of indigenous Cornish people who feel themselves disadvantaged, compared with 'incomers', in relation to class, income, housing, employment and various other aspects of daily living.[70]

These discourses have strengthened and are articulated with growing confidence and demands for, "special care and responsibility for maintaining the homeland of this ethnic group in a sustainable fashion."[71]

An aspect of Cornwall's demographic circumstances is what Bernard Deacon has called, "an ethnic division of labour" and "a superimposition of cultural divisions on class divisions", noting that it results, in part, from wider geographical labour markets for middle-class jobs and higher rates of middle-class migration.[72] Large numbers of outside candidates apply for jobs, encouraged by the message that Cornwall is, "a place where people are delighted to settle"[73] and Cornish candidates are said to suffer indirect

---

69 See Bernard Deacon, "The Cornish and the Council of Europe Framework Convention for the Protection of National Minorities", Redruth (1999); John Angarrack (1999), *Breaking the Chains: Propaganda, censorship, deception and the manipulation of public opinion in Cornwall*, Camborne: Cornish Stannary Publications.

70 An anonymous council officer cited in, Eric Jay, "Keep them in Birmingham: Challenging Racism in South-West England", (1992), Bristol: Commission for Racial Equality; Neil Kennedy (1995), *op. cit.*

71 Jane Howells, *op. cit.*, p. 15.

72 Bernard Deacon (2007), *op. cit.* p. 215; See B. Deacon in Cornwall, *The Cultural Construction of Place*, Chapter 1, Patten Press & Institute of Cornish Studies, Penzance: University of Exeter.

73 See www.investincornwall.com/living-in-cornwall/ (Accessed 16 November 2012.)

discrimination because of assumptions that they must be un-dynamic and un-ambitious if they stay in Cornwall. Deacon's analysis agrees with work by the geographer, Ron Perry, who undertook the first detailed studies of counter-urbanization in the 1980s, noting that it produced a socio-economic demarcation between the Cornish, who then constituted much of the working-class, and in-migrants who made up most of the middle-classes:

> [T]he picture that emerges from our study is of a Cornwall swamped by a flood of middle-class, middle-aged, middle-browed city dwellers who effectively imposed their standards upon local society.[74]

Growing public concern, from the 1970s onwards, centred on the impact this had on access to housing. It was apparent that the Cornish were being financially confined to less attractive areas. CoSERG described them as having been, "shunted onto windswept council house reservations on the outskirts of our coastal villages", where they had, "seen their communities disintegrate in front of their own eyes within just one generation."[75] David Penhaligon, M.P., popularly identified as a Cornish champion, stated that, "If you want to find the Cornish go to the council estates."[76] and the issue of marginalization led the mild-mannered Conservative, David Mudd, M.P., to warn of unrest on the lines of riots in Toxteth and Brixton.[77] In dramatic, Biblical tones, Paul Laity, Q.C. claimed that the Cornish were, "hewers of wood and carriers of water", increasingly confined to jobs that serviced the better-off.[78] To address the absence of detailed information and overcoming resistance to monitoring the Cornish as a category, Cornwall Rural Community Council, housing departments and academics undertook studies which sought data but by the 1980s the linkage between Cornishness and low socio-economic status had, in any case, been established in public

74   Ronald Perry, Ken Dean and Bryan Brown (1986), *Counterurbanization: International Case Studies of Socio-Economic Change in Rural Areas*, Norwich.
75   B. Deacon, A. George and R. Perry (1988), *Cornwall at the Crossroads, op. cit.*
76   David Penhaligon M.P., 21/6/1978 in Parliament (Hansard).
77   Comments in *The West Briton*.
78   Paul Laity Q.C. at the Cowethas Flamank conference, Perranporth - 1992.

discourse, even finding its way into jokes, such as, "What do you call a Cornishman in a three-bedroom house?—A burglar."[79] Cornish nationalists could ratchet up the rhetoric and portray council housing and low-standard private estates as, "the Cornish equivalent of American ghettos or South African shanty towns, places where low paid locals are shut away out of sight."[80] Prevalent representations masked the problems so that outside perceptions contradicted the reality:

> For outsiders, Cornwall is peace and tranquillity, a haven to which one might retire from the mad rush of modern life; for insiders Cornwall is often poverty and poor housing and a struggle to make ends meet in a low-wage economy.[81]

Of course, deprivation and poverty do not really respect ethnic categories and the worst-off Cornish have material needs in common with disadvantaged in-migrants that they do not share with better-off natives. This said, there are, nevertheless, correlations between poor socio-economic circumstances and Cornishness that are part of the context for considering whether Cornish cultures might be useful for resilience and cohesiveness. Given the scale of change, recent decades may have produced greater cultural and generational fault-lines than those of language shift, from Cornish to English, in the seventeenth and eighteenth centuries[82] or industrial decline and mass emigration in the late nineteenth and early twentieth centuries.[83] While the former produced a linguistic rift and loss of associated cultural items and the later undermined economic purpose and esteem, the recent changes may have interrupted the inter-generational transmission of identity, culture and knowledge more deeply, producing a rupture at the level of family and

79 Allegedly printed in *Cornwall College Rag Mag.*, c. 1985.

80 John Angarrack (1999), *op. cit.*

81 Philip Payton (1996), *op. cit.*

82 See Nicholas Williams (2006), *Cornish Today*, (Third edition), Westport: Evertype; Brian Murdoch (1993), *Cornish Literature*, Cambridge; Philip Payton (1992), *op. cit.* p.92.

83 See Philip Payton (2005), *The Cornish Overseas: The Epic Story of the 'Great Migration'*, Fowey: Cornwall Editions Ltd.

community. This is because the scale and speed of migration means that most people—notably the young—are not as immersed in the banal, everyday narratives of community identity as previous generations. The fact that a far lower proportion of people have Cornish families means that Cornishness (as distinctions, as daily narratives, as dispositions and attitudes etc.) is not a ubiquitous feature of life and is often absent in the work place, public spaces and social settings.

In-migration and centralization combine against the maintenance and expansion of a native middle-class, producing breaks in transmission and cultural (re)creation on a scale that does not happen in communities with confident, empowered elites and intelligentsias. There is a resulting failure to develop definably Cornish institutions and networks to replace the work-based and mainly Methodist, religious institutions that formerly served as spaces and channels of cultural transmission. In Althusser's analysis, institutions form part of an "Ideological State Apparatus"[84] by which cultural mœurs and norms are transmitted but, as seen across Europe, institutions may also be regional, local and counter-hegemonic, serving to create and disseminate geographically and culturally specific knowledge and discourses. In Cornwall, these are not adequately communicated institutionally because there are few spaces in the media and education that are defined by Cornish people. In this context the Cornish Movement is the main means by which identity narratives are passed on outside the family and might be regarded as a counter-hegemonic, regional apparatus in waiting.

Taking Stock

In the 1980s and 90s, political opposition to the above trends stagnated, as campaigners began to see their efforts as futile[85] but multiple critiques emerged nevertheless and fused environmentalism, Cornish nationalism and socio-economic demands in an oppositional groundswell. With their concern for the disadvantaged in housing and jobs, these critiques largely avoided nimbyism but

84 Louis Althusser (1971), "On Ideology and Ideological State Apparatuses", in *Lenin and Philosophy and Other Essays*, New York: Monthly Review Press.

85 Information from witnesses; See Philip Payton (1992), pp. 200-201; Bernard Deacon (2007) *op. cit.*

attracted accusations of parochialism that still beset opponents of unsustainable development. In terms that call to mind some sustainability agendas, the independent Cornish Social and Economic Research Group (CoSERG) argued in 1987 that Cornwall was "at the crossroads" and faced its "greatest ever challenge".[86] Communities needed "a breathing space"[87] to allow job creation and infrastructure to catch up with population growth, to protect the environment and avoid cultural and socio-economic destabilization. Without this the problems of local people would worsen and Cornish identity would weaken to the detriment of community cohesion. Uncontrolled, market forces and bad governance were allegedly threatening the very existence of a distinct Cornwall and a change in direction was urgently needed, one that would prioritize "local housing needs" and build on "regional strengths" such as Cornwall's prime maritime position,[88] local knowledge and identity, much as is being successfully achieved by strong native elites in Brittany.[89] A pause in the "speculative house-building spree" would let in-migrants "put down roots". The polemic and the arguments had some influence on oppositional discourses but were unheeded by outside decision-makers and, as the Core Strategy demonstrates, they have had no lasting effect on Cornwall Council planners. From the critics' perspective, Cornwall has been frog-marched beyond CoSERG's crossroads and taken down an unsustainable dead-end. Since Cornwall did not get the breathing space they thought indispensable, have their gloom-laden predictions come true? Some obviously have but the purpose here is to take stock of the situation, acknowledge it and seek constructive ways forward that identify opportunities in its various continuities and discontinuities.

One of the most important aspects of the new circumstances is that they produce oppositional responses and the promulgation of local knowledge as those concerned with maintaining Cornishness claim spaces within existing institutions and create alternative scenes. I

---

86 B. Deacon, A. George and R. Perry, (1987), *Cornwall at the Crossroads*, Redruth: CoSERG.

87 *Ibid.* (p.47, p.157).

88 Peter Wills, (1992), *Water, Water Everywhere*, Camborne: CoSERG.

89 Cf. Jean Olivro (2010), *Project Bretagne*, Rennes: Editions Apogée.

have observed this in many settings:—within the networks of a handful of Council officers, amongst academics and students across higher and further education institutions, amongst the organizers of community events and in the use of the internet to disseminate information where mainstream media are lacking. These are, of course, examples of network building based on identity-led social capital, but they are also marginal. A primary school teacher at the Krowji in Redruth (2011) described this way of networking as, "lurking in the cracks" and "getting together with like-minded people", comments that reveal the felt absence of institutions and awareness of trying to make-do. Widespread concern for the erosion of communities and tradition has not yet translated itself into sufficient research into socio-cultural discontinuities, despite academic attention to economic and demographic change and to individual areas of culture. It might nevertheless be concluded that Cornwall is poised at the beginning of a post-Cornish moment where disappearing cultural components have not been replaced with anything lasting or embedded, yet some analysts draw attention to a vigorous performance of Cornishness that recalls the "stubborn refusal of Cornish identity to go away" and its conscious maintenance as "a passion to exist".[90] In these accounts, the new circumstances have driven a "re-definition and re-assertion" of identity,[91] paradoxically strengthening awareness while undermining the material and observable realities of difference.

Some insiders represent current challenges as the latest in a long history of endurance and struggle, in a discourse that owes much to eighteenth-century narratives of an ancient history of resistance to Saxon invaders[92] and later accounts of wearing economic hardship in mining. Corresponding cultural activities produce, "the knowledge that Cornwall and the Cornish people are still very much

90 B. Deacon (2007), *op. cit.* p. 216; A.M. Kent (2000), *op. cit.* pp. 11-12; Comments by Alison Davey at the CAVA conference, October 2011; Rob Burton, "A Passion to Exist: Cultural Hegemony and the Roots of Cornish Identity", in P.J. Payton (ed.), *Cornish Studies*, no.5, (1997), pp. 151-163.

91 Bernard Deacon and Philip Payton, "Re-inventing Cornwall: Culture Change on the European Periphery", in *Cornish Studies*, no. 1, pp. 62-79 (63).

92 E.g. William Borlase (1769), *Antiquities Historical and Monumental of the County of Cornwall*, Bowyer and Nichols, London, p. 40; Fortescue Hitchins and Samuel Drew (1824), *The History of Cornwall*, Helston: William Penaluna, p. 725.

alive and kicking even after 500 years of very mixed fortunes."[93] In challenging the alleged extinction of Cornish ethnicity in the eighteenth century, Bernard Deacon has observed that, "the way that people think about themselves and their identity does not just rest upon the 'facts' of history but on the way that history is remembered."[94] Identity narratives that are founded on the past may, furthermore, produce histories which have meaning even if they do not correspond to present, material realities. Thus, forty years ago, Charles Thomas observed that, "the knowledge of the existence of a separate language, as distinct from a full knowledge of that language itself, is probably sufficient ... to foster a sense of otherness".[95] His view seems to have been borne out by a growth in symbolic references that is out of all proportion to the small number of Cornish speakers. Similarly, today's Cornish identities are partly maintained by what might be called remembered difference. The tangible, observable things that make the Cornish recognizable are far fewer but the idea of difference is nevertheless supported by faith in its existence and by collective memory and post-memory that are discursively produced and transmitted. Thus, while the distinctions of a Cornish way of life have lessened, this does not stop in-group histories from asserting difference. On the contrary, identity narratives are intensified and newly generated precisely because Cornishness is under threat and this furnishes material for both enabling and disabling "useable histories"[96] and useable culture. In brief, identity does not require difference to be a quantifiable and tangible reality or to take the form of obvious visible or linguistic distinctions.

The extent to which ethno-cultural awareness has not only survived but translated itself into a more explicit, national identity was brought into sharp focus by a survey conducted by *The Guardian*

93 Loveday Jenkin & Peggy Morris in Simon Parker (ed.) (1998), *Cornwall Marches On!*, Keskerdh Kernow 500: Keskerdh Kernow Ltd.: Truro, p.3.

94 Bernard Deacon *et al.* (2003), *op. cit.* p. 6.

95 Charles Thomas, *The Importance of being Cornish, in Cornwall*, Institute of Cornish Studies, Redruth, (1973), p.10. Thomas died in 2016.

96 Cf. Michael Keating, "A regional history of modern Europe. Territorial management and the state" in Bill Lancaster *et al.* (2007), *op. cit.* pp. 149-164.

in 2011.[97] Respondents were asked to state whether they considered themselves British, English, Irish, Northern Irish, Scottish or Other. When plotted on a map, the results show a sharp demarcation which, as *The Guardian* put it, "closely follows the line of the Tamar River".[98] To the west of this line most respondents identified themselves as "Other". The result agrees with research by Joanie Willett that found that forty-one percent of people questioned felt either "Cornish and not English" or "more Cornish than English", a proportion that incidently suggests some in-migrants, or their children, choose these identifications.[99]

The New Cornish

Those in-migrants who have "put down roots" are sometimes called the "New Cornish" and some use this, or similar tags, to describe what Stuart Hall called "elective identities".[100] This ambiguous naming, which may be read either as a distinction *from*, or an identification *with*, the "Old Cornish", reveals differing encounters with perceived difference and negotiated relationships with it. The 2011 census did not include a tick-box to indicate Cornish ethnicity, despite a campaign since the 1980s, but a specific code was none-theless allocated for analysis of "write-in" responses.[101] Cornwall Council and the census officers delighted activists by intervening with a publicity campaign to explain how people could register Cornish identity and be recorded.[102] They suggested that, "the

---

97 *The Guardian* 12 October 2011, m.guardian.co.uk/uk/2011/oct/12/uk-citizens-reject-british-survey?cat=uk&type=article (Accessed 21 November 2012.)

98 *Ibid.*

99 Joanie Willett, "Cornish identity: vague notion or social fact?" in Philip Payton (ed.), *Cornish Studies*, no. 16, (2008), pp.183-205.

100 Stuart Hall (1973), *op. cit.*

101 Requested by Dan Rogerson M.P., for example.

102 Widely covered in *The Western Morning News* and the news site, This is Cornwall. The Census Office and Cornwall Council published information on how to register Cornish ethnicity: cornish-census2011.org/. See also: www.cornwall.gov.uk/default.aspx?page=26948; www.telegraph.co.uk/news/uknews/8395003/Census-2011-council-urges-residents-to-proclaim-Cornish-nationality.html; news.bbc.co.uk/2/hi/uk_news/politics/8389745.stm (All accessed in November 2012)

Cornish National Identity question is inclusive of all of Cornwall's residents" as well as "Cornish people living in major cities such as London, Plymouth and Bristol". In the event more than 73,218 people in Cornwall chose to actively write Cornish on their forms.[103] Some established in-migrants expressed their desire to do so and were encouraged by "born and bred" natives (at the Bewnans Kernow conference, 12 February 2011, for example and via social media). In an encounter at Mabe, a woman who had moved there more than thirty years previously had tears in her eyes when friends told her, "Of course you can put Cornish."[104] This phenomenon of "going native" and identifying with place and community seems perfectly normal and hardly worthy of comment, except that it does not always happen. There are many cases around the world of higher status outsiders maintaining distinction from natives. Cornwall has points in common with "attractive" rural areas of England (The Cotswolds, The Lake District etc.) that have experienced gentrification[105] whereby the "superior" cultures of affluent in-migrants replaces those of locals who sometimes adjust culturally by, for example, changing the way they speak. In other words, hegemony is at work, but what is clear from identifications in Cornwall is that there are negotiable processes whereby individual in-comers elect or reject all or part of the local culture and natives variously reject or adopt the cultures of in-migrants. In 1988, CoSERG observed that:

> it is not too difficult these days to find those who, despite being brought up or born in Cornwall, and even having traces of a Cornish accent, will fiercely deny they are Cornish, because their parents hail from Hemel Hempstead or some such place.[106]

---

103 ONS Census report KS202EW released, 11 December 2012.

104 Conversations at the Mabe-Primelin Twinning Association, Mabe Community Hall, April, 2010.

105 Cf. Gary Bridge, "Bourdieu, rational action and the time-space of gentrification", www.jstor.org/stable/3650668 (Accessed 8 February 2011.)

106 B. Deacon, A. George and R. Perry, (1988), *op. cit.* p.156.

Observing the extent to which Cornish people were taking on the attributes of in-migrants in the 1990s, Ron Perry and his colleagues concluded that, "integration and assimilation" was "a one way process of urbanisation rather than ruralisation",[107] and it is indeed easy enough to find people who sound like they come from South-East England, even though they have always lived in Cornwall and have Cornish parents. Yet CoSERG noted that there were also people who adopted a Cornish identity and were thought of as Cornish by natives.[108] In accordance, Mary McArthur predicts that "it is possible that the incomers of today will become (or produce) the Cornish of tomorrow",[109] and in her work on housing and family structures, Mary Buck suggests "a fairly high level of assimilation".[110] Data provided by the CAPITA Schools Census have also attracted interest. Since 2005 pupils have been able to select the category "Cornish" in the question on ethnicity and in 2005, 27% of pupils opted for this. The surprise, though, is that the proportion grew steadily to 41% (28, 584 pupils) in 2011, an increase of about 5,000 pupils since 2009.[111] This may reflect confidence in making this choice, as it becomes normal and less likely to attract ridicule, but the high proportion also suggests that an important number of the children of in-migrants consider themselves Cornish and that in turn hints at their parents communicating affective identifications. In comments that suggest connections between identity and social capital, Paul Masters of Cornwall Council's Chief Executive Office, connects the pupils' responses to commitment to community, suggesting that it offers the hope that, "people will be more interested in looking after the place for future generations and volunteering within their communities."[112] The former Cornish Language

---

107 Ron Perry *et al.* (1995), "Movers and Stayers 1971-91", Department of Sociology, University of Plymouth.

108 B. Deacon, A. George and R. Perry, (1988), *op. cit.*

109 Mary McArthur, "The Cornish: A Case Study in Ethnicity", unpublished M.Sc. dissertation, University of Bristol, 1988, p.97.

110 Mary Buck *et al.*, *Housing and Households in Cornwall: A Pilot Study of Cornish Families*, University of Plymouth, (1991), p.51.

111 The Cornwall Pupil Level Annual Schools Census (PLASC), See www.thisiscornwall.co.uk/Children-Cornish-pride-latest-school-census/story-14334357-detail/story.html, (Accessed 26 April 12.)

112 *Ibid.*

Officer, Jenefer Lowe, suggests that the findings show awareness of Cornwall's "distinctiveness", including the language, and levels of personal identification which, "can only be good for Cornwall and Cornish culture".[113]

Wooing in-migrants has been a theme since the 1970s when some Cornish nationalists, including the campaigner, teacher and publisher, Len Truran, were arguing that they could integrate in-migrants and "make them Cornish".[114] In Corsica and the Basque Country[115] many in-migrants and their descendents are strong champions of the Corsican and Basque languages and identities, giving credibility to the view that culture can contribute to integration and lead to assimilation. In analysing responses to questionnaires from Cornwall, Joanie Willett discusses the theoretical view that, "newcomers to a community can assimilate into the new identity through a process of learning".[116] She contrasts this to views that, "family may be critical for identity transmission" and prescriptive and essentialist views of identity that exclude the idea of recruitment. Some cultural practitioners cite participation in Revivalist culture to claim that there has been a change in the way in which Cornishness is valued by in-migrants so that, as a young musician put it, "not so many people rubbish it". Encouraging though this sounds, the picture might be more complicated than suggested by appreciation of compartmentalized activities or by the uptake of Cornish house-names, flags and other signifiers. These mean different things to different people, so while there is certainly serious participation and symbolic display by in-migrants who sincerely identify with Cornishness, there are also superficial visual and recreational uses that may have more to do with exhibiting counter-urban lifestyles to peers. This has been remarked by Cornish Oafs, an online comic act launched by two Cornish learners, Liam

---

113 Communications from Jenefer Lowe, Cornish Language Development Officer.

114 Information from Ted Chapman, former treasurer of Mebyon Kernow (d. 2010).

115 For discussion of Basque identities see, Lieven de Winter, Margarita Gómez-Reno and Peter Lynch (eds.) (2006), *Autonomist Parties in Europe: ethnic politics and the revival of the territorial cleavage*, Barcelona: Institut de Ciències Polítiques i Socials.

116 Joanie Willett, "Cornish Identity: Vague Notion or Social Fact?", (2008), *op. cit.* p. 185.

Thomas and Luke Stevens in 2012. In one of their online clips a fictional artist says, "Well, I got fed up with the rat-race and moved down to Cornwall, aka Kernow. I've got the car sticker and everything."[117]

Identification by many in-migrants with something Cornish is shown by their involvement in cultural events, campaigns and community initiatives but not enough is known about the phenomenon to draw the conclusion that it means valuing Cornishness as a whole. In brief, it is possible to take up an isolated activity without embracing an entire culture. People may feel part of a community or identify with it without adopting its way of life and culture. Cornish culture is heterogeneous and we do not really know which strands appeal to which New Cornish participants and how they imagine and value them. Consequently, we cannot be sure whether the assimilation, tentatively identified by Mary Buck, involves general cultural acquisition—such as taking on new attitudes or local accents—or whether it is limited to social and structural adaptations, such as making friends. It is apparent that some in-migrants feel common cause and identification with the indigenous Cornish while others do not and may feel a degree of antipathy towards them. It also seems clear that cultural activities provide contexts for social relationships that draw people into the community. For instance, a journalist who has learnt to speak Cornish expressed the sentiment of many, saying in Cornish, "I'm not Cornish but most of my friends are and everything I do now is Cornish, so I feel like I am."[118] In a discussion with seven people from Falmouth who had worked in shops or the docks and were nearing retirement, the topics included regret for changes in the town and the conversation was laced with local expressions and insider references even though three of them had moved to Cornwall as young adults. This common enough experience suggests that, in working-class contexts at least, people may come to identify strongly with Cornishness and incorporate this into their personal identities, even taking on outward distinctions such as accent, body language and shared references. The affirmative proposition is therefore to

117 See www.facebook.com/CornishOafs (Accessed 17 November 2012).
118 Comments in Cornish by Matthew Clarke of Kernow-Pods, and Radyo an Gernewegva.

embrace the potential for progressive and inclusive community building suggested by the naming "New Cornish" and examine what is happening so as to inform intervention.

"Those who were born here and those who were drawn here"

Some years ago, a well-known Revivalist, Howard Curnow, wrote that, "The Cornish Movement" was:

> in a position to adopt a programme of mature, responsible action... [that] would embrace cultural achievements, political recognition, our economic future, and, most importantly, a popular acceptance ... of what it is to be Cornish AND/OR to be living in Cornwall.[119]

Questioning a new generation of activists about what that could mean reveals promisingly inclusive views and actions that recognize the need for alliances of common interest between the indigenous Cornish and incomers. They refer to issues as diverse as the economy, housing, the environment, devolved government and public services, linking them to a sense of community. They also appear united in distinguishing between, "those who are with us and those who are against us",[120] making it clear that the former are welcome in all areas of community life and recognizing that in-migrants are far from being a homogenous group and that neither are the Cornish. In signalling their wish to include the New Cornish, the musicians, Skillywidden, use the phrase, "those who were born here and those who were drawn here". Comments like this show awareness of the risks of Anglophobia, presented as a moral dilemma in Marcus Tanner's pessimistically entitled, *The Last of the Celts*:

> How far can they [rural 'Celtic' communities] go, and how far will they be allowed to go, towards resisting the flow of English immigrants, second-home owners and pensioners without slipping into outright racism?[121]

119 Howard Curnow, in *An Baner Kernewek*, No. 69, August 1992.
120 Comments at the CAVA conference, Perran Porth, October 2010.
121 Marcus Tanner (2006 [2004]), *The Last of the Celts*, New Haven: Yale University

This is a key issue and it is hard to provide an easy answer. Ethno-cultural identity is part of what many wish to sustain and the "distinctiveness" that it produces has been identified as an asset, so how can Cornishness be carried forward and upheld so as to spread harmony and cohesiveness rather than discord and division? The short answer is that it cannot because of conflicts of interests but in taking sides the Cornish Movement can continue to construct projects that avoid conflating conflicts with ethnic division. Cornwall's newly composed communities share some common interests and a physical space, so some of the answers surely lie in exploring place-centred culture and using it to cement new bonds. We should understand, however, that geographically located culture is not the same thing as ethnic culture. As may be seen in Australia, North America and large cosmopolitan cities, the development of common values and loyalties may involve civic identities which celebrate place but have little or no reference to a common ethno-cultural identity. Awareness of this takes the discussion into further areas of controversy and raises more questions about what place Cornish ethnicity and linked cultures can have when the indigenous Cornish are a still-shrinking minority of the population. What workable strategies can be imagined for its survival and where do the New Cornish fit in? In keeping with the attention to diversity in this discussion, the leaders of the *Kernocopia* community arts project suggest that, "[O]ur communities are fragmented along multiple lines—'incomers' and 'locals', 'Cornish' and 'furriners', 'hooded wannabee-gangstas' and 'old fogeys'..."[122] but they nevertheless believe that, "art and cultural intervention *do* have the ability to change" and that:

> Through uncovering Cornwall's diverse and distinct stories, and bringing them to life through creative, participatory and immersive experiences, Kernocopia intends to make a tangible contribution to the health and well-being of our communities.[123]

Press.

122 *Kernocopia*, project proposal for 2013-14.

123 *Ibid.*

Various sections of the population need to work together so a unifying identification is in everybody's interest. Some analysts have speculated about the emergence of a civic Cornishness that includes the New Cornish and they have observed the pragmatic embrace and encouragement of this by strands within the Movement.[124] From the Cornish Language Office to Mebyon Kernow, there have been clear statements, not only of inclusiveness, but of a civic idea of community that goes beyond ethnicity. Civic identity is not a straightforward matter, though. It can be understood as usurping or replacing ethnicity, thus reducing a deeply tribal sense of Cornishness and complex cultural acquisitions to something relatively superficial that people can opt into or out of with the ease of changing address. As a result, something of a false opposition has emerged between ethnic and civic identities in identity politics. The prominent campaigner and polemicist, John Angarrack, has been vociferous in dismissing the "civic nationalism" of Mebyon Kernow and reasserts the relevance of an ethnic nationalism that he nevertheless constructs as open and welcoming to the New Cornish.[125] Listening to his argument though, it very much sounds as though Angarrack is talking at cross purposes to advocates of civic identity. The latter have not abandoned ethnic Cornishness and Angarrack has not suggested exclusivity so their differences appear more semantic than real. They have all apparently realized, tacitly at least, that there is a demographic reality that makes exclusivity untenable. The indigenous Cornish can no longer make public policy decisions or even elect representatives without the support of friends and appeals to common interest with people who have moved to Cornwall.

The opposition between civic and ethnic nationalism depends upon theoretical and ideological assumptions that are rooted in dualistic thought of the kind criticised by post-structuralists as supporting hierarchies but excluding ambiguity and indeterminacy. As a dichotomy, it therefore compares to other binary simplifications in discussions of Cornishness (Insider/Outsider; Cornish/English; Celt/Saxon...) and to problematic constructions of "Celtishness" in

124 See Cole, Deacon and Tregidga (2003) *op. cit.*; See also, J. Willet, *op. cit.*, p.200.
125 E.g. John Angarrack (2008), pp. 82-86.

opposition to Engishness. The proposition, therefore, is to move beyond an "either or" (*an eyl pò y gila*) discussion to adopt an aspiration that combines ethnic and civic identities (*an eyl hag y gila*). Although "the myth of the civic nation"[126] can be a smoke-screen for ethnic identities, many are multi-ethnic and multicultural, while ethnic identities themselves can be internally plural and indeterminately bounded. In fact, plurality is often the whole point of developing civic identity in the first place, because it allows different sections of a population to develop common purpose and to respect and like each other, thus functioning as a single society that gets things done. Ethnic and cultural heterogeneity may even be one of the unifying myths around which civic identity is constructed, so that it is celebrated with affection.

Cornish cultures can be an interface which favours recruitment into indigenous society so that they define Cornwall instead of becoming more sidelined. A civic identity that makes symbolic reference to indigenous Cornishness may produce benefits, leading to Cornish cultures acquiring symbolic value and esteem so that motivation and affective support for socio-cultural projects and language revitalization increases. A related idea, explored later, is the possibility of using existing Cornish practices to enhance the social capital of the whole of society, the suggestion being that this might favour civic identifications with valorizing benefits for ethnocultural identity.

---

126 Bernard Yack, in R. Beiner (ed.) (1999), pp. 103-118.

Chapter 2

An Introduction
to Useable Culture

This discussion embraces the idea that a definably Cornish cultural tradition may be employed inclusively and constructively to strengthen communities that have been socially weakened by economic and demographic changes. An opening premise is that the ever-changing relations between communities and their cultures are crucial to how they work socially and therefore to how they function economically. The subjective view is also taken that local cultures and languages have worth as part of the collective stock of human experience and knowledge. Indeed, maintaining them features in the aims of government and international sustainability agendas and they are part of what diverse critics and activists around the world wish to retain under the homogenizing conditions of globalization and consumer capitalism.[127] It is proposed that Cornish cultures, like others, include local knowledge and resources that may be employed in addressing and setting objectives in such diverse areas as economic initiative, education, housing, land management and environmental planning.[128] Serendipitously, a piece of unusual graffiti on the site of the planned Cornish History Centre reads, "Never underestimate the power of local knowledge." (2012) and in economic and community strategies for Cornwall both the "knowledge-based economy" and "regional distinctiveness" are seen as underlying "sustainable economic development".[129] Even so, few

127 Cf. Sustainability agendas of the E.U., Council of Europe, U.K. Government, Cornwall Council, U.N., Welsh Assembly, Scottish Executive.
128 Cf. Jean Olivero (2010) on planning in Brittany.
129 E.g. Cornwall Council's "Sustainable Community Strategy" and "New Agenda" for planning. Comments by Cllr. Carolyn Rule on the Tremough Innovation Centre, 12 January 2011.

attempts have yet been made to genuinely link these elements or coherently explore what they could mean.

Arguments based on cultural difference and the symbolic presence of the Cornish language helped campaigners to justify Cornwall and Scilly's becoming a European economic region, distinguished from the larger and generally more affluent "South-West Region". The "existence of Cornish as an emblem of regional distinctiveness" is credited with having been, "an important factor in Cornwall being awarded Objective 1 status."[130] More generally, cultural difference has provided identity-based motivations for multiple economic, social and political projects and campaigns and has supported insistence on maintaining Cornwall's administrative integrity since attempts to create a Greater Plymouth or "Tamarside" authority and alter its boundaries in the 1940s and 1960s.[131]

The mobilization of identity for campaigns as diverse as regional status and opposition to hospital closures flags up non-commercial and social and symbolic uses of culture and points to a need for discussion of the less apparent ways in which geographically rooted cultures are valuable. Local cultures may strengthen slippery, abstract ingredients for community resilience, such as solidarity, motivation, aspiration and morale. An intention is therefore to take the step from historical description of cultures and discussions of identity (vital foundational themes in the "New Cornish Studies")[132] towards considering how particular assemblages may contribute to long-term community resilience. This search for usefulness, whether futile or achievable, involves focusing on the collective status of the Cornish community and of disadvantaged fractions within it. The potentially euphemistic term "regional distinctiveness" is disam-biguated as meaning Cornishness and the discussion explores what that means and could mean in the future. Despite assertions of Cornishness, Cornwall Council's regional distinctiveness agenda has

---

130 www.magakernow.org.uk, (Accessed 24 June 2011.)

131 J. Paton Watson and Patrick Abercrombie (1943), "A Plan for Plymouth", Plymouth: Underhill (Plymouth) Ltd.; The Redcliffe-Maud Report (Cmnd. 4040), The Royal Commission on Local Government in England 1966-69; See Philip Payton (1992), *The Making of Modern Cornwall*, pp. 211-115.

132 See Philip Payton (ed.), *Cornish Studies*, 2nd series, vols. 1-20, University of Exeter Press.

so far compartmentalized the issue, failing to develop joined-up policies that link culture and identity to social and economic issues.

The following discussion pursues the objective of social cohesive-ness with attention to the roles culture plays in the relationships that are the basis of functioning communities. The intention is to make the linkages between culture and the emotional and social under-pinnings of regeneration explicit and reflect upon the general hypothesis that distinct Cornish cultures provide vital ingredients for well-being. It is claimed that culture can strengthen feelings associated with belonging to a community and even engender a will to strive, invest and contribute to it beyond self-interest. This, it is suggested, is an economic and social asset that sometimes leads to unselfish motivations, desires and vocations that, by being based on sentiment and non-economic aspirations, defy what some might think of as rational economic actions. Culture may be used for many things, involving conflicts of interest in which there are winners and losers but an indispensable part of regeneration is improving the conditions of the worst-off. This means taking partial views on the ends to which culture should be put rather than just finding uses for it irrespective of whether the disadvantaged benefit.

Primary uses, human need and well-being

Inherent in this approach is the idea that culture has uses, a view that may raise the objection that it transcends functional considerations but this reaction relies upon the idea that use implies something material or economic. While culture may indeed have commercial or straightforwardly practical applications, its engage-ment of the senses and the emotions may be considered to involve other kinds of use in areas of psychological, emotional, spiritual and aesthetic need. These may be thought of as primary uses so that, in Marx's terms, cultural practices may be said to have "use-values". Culture, in the comprehensive sense, common to anthropology and cultural studies, is furthermore the basis of relationships and therefore society. Some non-material uses, outside the logic of economic exchange, address human needs which include having relationships with others and belonging to a community. In theoretical accounts derived from Abraham Maslow's hierarchy of need, these involve interpersonal requirements and relate to friendship, love and related feelings.[133] They concern "belongingness" or the psychological need to be part of a group.[134] In hierarchical presentations, these are commonly ranked just above physiological need and physical security and safety and are said to support a further level of psychological need in the area of esteem, which includes confidence, self-esteem and respect of and by others. The point is that culture is involved in meeting—and sometimes not meeting—these needs and therefore connects to what Maslow, and much of present-day psychology, calls "self-actualization", whereby individuals realize their potential once their needs have been fulfilled. Maslow argues that because most people's needs are not fully met, they operate on lower levels. Their psychological potential is not optimized, limiting their personal expectations, desires and ambitions as well as their ability to function socially—and therefore economically.

Our sense of leading worthwhile, fulfilling lives, our physical and mental health and our state of mind, may not be neatly correlated to measurements of wealth but may have much to do with culture. Cultural "distinctions",[135] as the arbitrary and subjective basis of identities and belonging play a role in determining social standing through the workings of hegemony. They may thus be involved in undesirable and disabling psychological effects such as an inferiority complex, depression, stress and a personal sense of incapacity. All of these are sometimes discussed in relation to Cornishness, even if this has yet to generate much published work,[136] and they are recurring themes in work on disadvantage and marginalization

133 Abraham Maslow, "A Theory of Human Motivation", in *Psychological Review*, 50, (1943), pp. 370-396.; cf. Maslow (1954), *Motivation and Personality*, New York: Harper and Row Publishers.

134 See N. Kunc (2011), *The Need to Belong: Rediscovering Maslow's Hierarchy of Needs*; S.T. Fiske (2009), *Social beings: A Core Motives Approach to Social Psychology*; R.F. Baumeister and M.R. Leary, (1995), "The Need to Belong: Desire for Interpersonal Attachments as a Fundamental Human Motivation", *Psychological Bulletin*, 117, 497-529.

135 Pierre Bourdieu (1979), *La Distinction, Critique sociale du jugement*, Le Sens Commun (coll.), Paris: Minuit.

136 An exception is, Allan Ivey and Philip Payton, "Towards a Cornish Identity Theory", in *Cornish Studies*, no. 2, (1994), pp. 151-163.

where the term "deprivation" often encompasses, not just relative material poverty, but also social exclusion and social problems. In public discussions the obviously subjective and relative terms of reference, "well-being" and "quality of life" are also common and are used variously.[137] Here they are taken to have something to do with the fulfilment of psychological as well as material needs and stand as catch-all designations for non-deprivation. The idea that psychological needs have implications for well-being and health is established, often from diverse situations where a lack of esteem is linked to pathological effects such as domestic violence, alcoholism, suicide and self-harm. The low status of some cultures has been recognized as contributing to such affects and cultural valorization and enrichment have sometimes been the basis of projects to address them.[138] In fact, language revitalization has been presented as helping to reduce social pathologies and enable communities, notably in North America and Australia where indigenous languages have underpinned wider, validating projects.[139] Producing psychological benefits may therefore be one of the main ways in which culture and language might contribute. There is no inference that Cornish society is particularly marked by social pathologies but what is suggested is that sections of it suffer from reduced morale as a result of low status and marginalization linked to economic, social and economic circumstances. This does not lend itself to statistical measurement and receives little attention. The role of culture's primary uses in morale is also ignored in economic projects and strategies that are, by-and-large, undertaken and imposed from outside the community by professionals who have no direct

137 Louis Tay and Ed Diener (2011), "Needs and Subjective Well-Being around the World", *Journal of Personality and Social Psychology*, vol. 101 (2), pp. 354–365; G. Hofstede (1984), "The Cultural Relativity of the Quality of Life Concept", *Academy of Management Review*, vol. 9 (3), pp. 389–398.

138 Cf. Jean Olivero (2010), pp. 153-155, re. suicide and cultural status in Brittany; T. Blakely and K. Dew (2004), re. Maoris; For suicide in Cornwall see, S.A. Hill *et al.*, "Changing patterns of suicide in a poor, rural county over the 20th century: A comparison with national trends." In *Social Psychiatry and Psychiatric Epidemiology*, vol. 40 (8) (2005), pp. 601-604.; cf. "Health and Wellbeing - Focus on healthy adults", Cornwall Council, Community Intelligence Team, 2009.

139 E.g. Ojibwe, www.tpt.org/?a=productions&id=3, (Accessed 29 November 2012) and communication from Anthon Treuer, Bemidji State University.

emotional engagement as insiders and who usually lack similar experiences and feelings produced by economic disadvantage and cultural marginalization.

Culture always serves a purpose then, whether we are aware of it or not and the uses to which it is put may be beneficial or detrimental. Using it beneficially to address morale can be related to what Diane Reay calls "emotional capital",[140] encapsulating a sense of individual and collective worth which need not correspond to economic standing or material measures. Considering primary use and related intervention leads to an idea of *usable culture* which connects with the notion of "useable history",[141] and which reminds us that cultures, like histories and correspondingly "imagined identities",[142] have often been the basis of political and social projects, for better or worse. Here the interest is in progressive community regeneration as engaged practice, and the notion of usable culture for this purpose, underpins the following chapters. Asking how culture might be used to these ends replies to the frequently-asked, rhetorical questions (from the assumptions of modernism) posed to the supporters of "regional and minority" cultures and languages, of the type, "What use is it?". It also goes beyond the contrary polemic of minority politics which inhibits reflection on whether there is a useful point to these cultures abd asserts their intrinsic value defensively and without question.

Narratives and representation

The Cornish cultural project leader and performer, Will Coleman, connects community narratives to all areas of life, suggesting that, "Stories have been at the heart of all cultures and can heal, inspire, delight, enrage but, can ultimately change our view of ourselves, other people and the world around us."[143] Indeed, culture and

---

140 See Diane Reay (2004), "Gendering Bourdieu's concept of capitals?: Emotional Capital, Women and Social Class", in L. Adkins and B. Skeggs (eds.). *Feminism after Bourdieu*, London: Blackwell.

141 See Michael Keating (2001), "Rethinking the Region. Culture, Institutions and Economic Development in Catalonia and Galicia". *European Urban and Regional Studies*, vol. 8 (3), pp. 217-234.

142 Benedict Anderson, *op. cit.*

143 Will Coleman, *The Western Morning News*, 26 June 2007.

identity may be thought of as being constructed through stories and their performance. Here, this is taken to include the practices of daily life where even banal acts convey ideas discursively. Culture, history and heritage are inextricably connected and come together as the stuff of narratives and representations. What is more, this is a multidirectional set of relationships in which cultures, histories and heritage are in turn shaped by narratives which may be generated within the community or received from outside. Culturally mediated stories may be used (beneficially) or misused (harmfully) in constructing representations and imaginings, thus relaying narratives that connect to the primary uses introduced. These stories include those of continuity and tradition that underpin all ethno-cultural communities, as well as those which valorize or de-valorize the group and inform or undermine agency. Through the performance of culture, insiders represent themselves to each other, recreating and disseminating ideas they have of themselves but their narratives are not immune from outside versions and do not always produce stories that are enabling, beneficial or rooted in valedictory histories. Both insider and outsider narratives (as crude, often inseparable categories) can be disabling, negatively stereotypical or harmful in other ways. It is unusual to engage in representation consciously, wisely and with sophistication so the tendency is for prevalent discourses to be reproduced in matter-of-fact ways. In Cornwall, the intensity of tourism-inspired representation makes it especially hard for insiders to develop and maintain useful narratives that can compete, even amongst sceptical insiders. When it comes to representing Cornwall, commercially, administratively, politically and artistically, dissenting insider voices are drowned by the sheer volume of contradictory messages that furthermore gain credibility and legitimacy from their closeness to the centre and received wisdoms. Strong discourses (i.e. those which have a legitimate genealogy and often a degree of financial backing) favour one-size-fits-all agendas for regeneration which contain problematic assumptions about Cornwall that ignore local knowledge and therefore fail to address needs and aspirations. In response, the following discussion considers maintaining useful narratives and intervening in representation. Cultural leaders and innovators already intervene to project and relay images that they prefer but supporting well-being implies further thought about which narratives could be useful and which cultural selections might support them. The intention is not to offer an over-arching prescription as the right way to do things but rather to consider how useful narratives are compromised and what to do about it.

Commodifying Cornish difference

An added reason for attending to the primary uses of Cornish culture is a developing emphasis on selling it that binds it to tourism. Quite simply, items may be packaged profitably and used in branding and marketing, and people may work in cultural industries. Throughout Europe, cultural heritage underpins diverse programmes and marketing strategies where regional distinctiveness, as an asset, associates culture and the economy. Consumers are willing to pay for difference, authenticity and local flavour, which, in the case of produce, is increasingly guaranteed by labels of approved origin. This is another manifestation of expanding commodification, not just of culture *per se* but of connected place, identity and life generally. In some discussions, the Cornish language and cultures are seen, first and foremost, as saleable and marketable and this is one of the ways—often the only way—in which performers, cultural entrepreneurs and local government officers suggest that they might be useful. The conversion of cultural difference into economic value has been established since the early twentieth-century marketing of the "Cornish Riviera" but now it is more explicitly and intensely used in targeting niche markets and the demand for cultural tourism. High on the shopping list of saleable items are the consumable spectacles, cultural practices and symbols which were, until recently, associated unambiguously with Cornish nationalism and shunned by public bodies. An everyday example is *Baner Peran*, the Flag of St Piran, revived from sparse historical references and recast by Helena Charles and Richard Gendall (early members of Mebyon Kernow) after the Second World War as a symbol of nationhood and the desire for political autonomy.

Baner Peran, gwydn ha du, otta va a-uhon.
Brâssa othem byscath veu. Deun warbarth, Kernowyon.[144]
('The flag of St Piran, white and black, there it is above us.
Never was there greater need. Come together, Cornish-
men.')

In the intervening years it has gradually been adopted as a
ubiquitous, all-purpose symbol by Cornish people in general, almost
inevitably appearing at public events and often on public buildings.
In a significant gesture during the Queen's Diamond Jubilee pageant
of 2012, it was flown with the flags of the other constituent nations
of Britain on the royal barge, Gloriana. As recently as the 1980s,
though, the flag was controversial and threatening enough to be
banned from many public places, including town halls, schools and
harbours.[145] Indeed there are anecdotes from the 1970s of education
officials warning teachers not to fly it and of the police removing it
from a town hall. Now, despite continuing oppositional uses, it is
part of the mundane iconography of branding and regional
promotion, safe enough to appear on supermarket shelves. Selected
imagery from consciously Cornish cultures is incorporated into an
increasingly commodified, leisure-orientated Cornwall with apparent ease, perhaps because much of it is folkloric and picturesque,
sharing some of its genealogy with the imagery of tourism. It may
thus be read in ways that correspond to the three Rs in prevalent
portrayals of Cornwall: *romantic, rural,* and *remote.*

A recent trend is the reinterpretation and incorporation of
nationalist-inspired items, alongside elements that have long been
used by tourism (pasties and piskies, cream teas, legends etc.), to
provide visual supports for the phenomenon that Bernard Deacon
calls, "Lifestyle Cornwall".[146] This is a version that is branded as
"upmarket" and "exclusive" by tourism promoters, estate agents,

144 "Baner Peran", a song by R.R.M. Gendall. Unpublished learning resource
    [n.d.]. Original orthography: Baner Peran, gwidn ha diu, yta va a iuhan. /
    Brossa othom beska ve. Dean warbar Kernowion.
145 E.g. The Town Hall and Prince of Wales Pier, Falmouth c. 1979.
    Communications from Ted Chapman (d. 2010).
146 Bernard Deacon (2007), *A Concise History of Cornwall,* Cardiff: University of
    Wales Press, p.227.

property speculators and more controversially, by the institutions of regional regeneration. It further develops prevailing images of safe difference and leisure and foregrounds recreation—obscuring modernity, work, social challenges and deprivation as well as contradicting the possibility of native dynamism. Lifestyle Cornwall, as a brand or image, is thus at the heart of conflicts of interest between economic sectors and between sections of the population. Tourism, heritage industries and attendant development pressures have come together to multiply representations that offer a fashionable set of Cornish experiences. Like earlier touristic imagery, that of Lifestyle Cornwall stands accused of carrying assumptions about Cornish people that influence decision-makers unfavourably so that "Cornwall is poor because policy is based on what some people expect it to be rather than what the overall experience of life in Cornwall is."[147] Bernard Deacon describes it as, "feeding in on Cornwall's image as being a slightly green, a bit of a mini California".[148] It is an assemblage that involves "iconic" landscapes and sites, "high end facilities", quality restaurants and "excellent local produce"[149] and it is now central to institutional notions of what Cornwall's brand should be. Even Newquay, associated in recent decades with Ibiza-style clubbing, binge drinking and crime, is rebranded as "The British California" in advertising that associates surfing and designer beachwear with a healthy, stress-free lifestyle, complete with harbour-side meals.[150]

A new wisdom is that cultural distinctiveness may be used in branding Cornwall as an all-year-round recreational destination with corresponding "quality products". The argument is that things that "make Cornwall different" have economic value, a point understood, even by those with only the vaguest idea of what Cornwall's cultural difference might consist off. Even some of those who are suspicious of commodifying culture see it, with resignation,

---

147 Joanie Willet (2010), *op. cit.*, p.5.

148 Bernard Deacon, interviewed by Cornish National Cinema, youtube.com/watch?v=LbMaI0XaqNE (Accessed 5 January 2012).

149 E.g. Uses by Visit Cornwall; cf. www.cornishcottageholidays.com (Accessed 24 November 2012).

150 Newquay's "official" promotion film, launched in July 2011:

www.youtube.com/watch?v=2ZnaxtR9ki8

as inevitable and think local people might as well be the merchandisers and economic beneficiaries. A concern for job creation and income echoes the deliberations of an earlier generation who, faced with hardships at the end of the nineteenth century, resigned themselves to tourism as a means to address emigration and poverty, despite having misgivings and regrets: "[O]ne is bound, if he cares for his countrymen, to consider any cure thoughtfully suggested."[151] The language of the market-place, even in critical approaches, raises questions about what the objectives and assumptions of some initiatives are. What, for instance, is meant and understood in such claims as, "the culture of Cornwall is a collaborative brand"[152] or the suggestion that Cornish culture is "good for business"[153] and what might different kinds of commodification mean for various sections of society, including those who do not stand to gain financially?

While market discourses view culture as a commodity, others view it as too precious to be dealt with commercially, belonging to a domain that is outside that logic. Commercialization produces opponents whose concerns are evidence that people value (and wish to control) culture in non-economic ways. Conflicting ideas spill over into discussions of sustainability and development in more complicated ways than as simple oppositions though. One reason is that those concerned with maintaining culture and heritage have to deal with financial constraints that pressure them to generate income for projects and justify them within a commercial rationale. Activists have likewise collaborated with tourism, often despite themselves, and have sought to package culture, including the Cornish language, despite their non-profit motives. This is part of a global phenomenon, where people seek to make money from their cultures, either to earn a livelihood or to fund the cultures themselves. In Cornwall the readiness of some to go down this route may also be linked to a (childlike) desire for the "recognition" of difference from the (parental) "centre" and a wish to bring Cornish identity to the

---

151 Sir Arthur Quiller-Couch, *The Cornish Magazine*, vol.1, (1895), p. 236.

152 C. Tims and S. Wright, DEMOS Report (2006), *op. cit.* note 34.

153 E.g. Matthew Clarke, "Cornish Culture in Business",

www.businesscornwall.co.uk/blogs/guest-blog-cornish-culture-in-business-123, (Accessed 13 April 2012.)

attention of others for political aims. A dilemma is that the benefits that campaigners wish for may be accompanied by (mis)representation, misappropriation and economic forces that compromise material, psychological and social need. Notably, they may confirm inferiority through portrayals of picturesque otherness and encourage migration trends that increase demand for jobs and raise house prices. These are amongst the most pressing issues to address in Cornwall where tourism has been the motor for demographic and social changes that produce marginalization and make it hard to address employment and housing needs. Cornwall is often cited as an extreme case of an attractive area with house prices that are unaffordable to people with typical local incomes, and holiday-home ownership has even produced a recent decline in the resident population of some coastal areas.[154] Financial exclusion from the housing market and strong competition for jobs in some sectors may be linked directly to selling distinctiveness so any discussion of culture becomes nonsensical without reference to them.

If the outcomes of existing ways of selling cultural and geographical differences are expensive housing for everybody and unaffordable housing for many, then it would seem wise to think about whether more of the same might add to this and other problems. In short, selling culture or using it to sell other things may profit some while producing collateral damage for others, but regeneration should not simply mean generating income without thought for who gains, who loses and what happens next. In most institutional discussions these risks are not dealt with and they may also be ignored by Cornish activists when seeking enhanced status for cultural practitioners. They may be so thrilled by the immediate opportunities for promotion and publicity and so preoccupied by displays of identity that they disregard anything that inconveniently complicates a seemingly straightforward proposition to combine profit with cultural development. Shallow approaches may also allowing regeneration institutions to justify themselves statistically by demonstrating an expansion of business. In simple terms though, it is often possible for people from outside a community, or its disadvantaged sections, to expand the cultural sector and commodify aspects of heritage

154 "Cornwall 2011, Demographic Evidence Base", Cornwall Council.

without consulting, employing or otherwise benefiting insiders—so a commercial uptake of Cornish culture could happen without addressing disadvantage or strengthening resilience. We have only to consider the 1980s and 90s, when a relatively low proportion of tourism-related businesses were in Cornish ownership,[155] while the industry itself depended upon differences that were produced by the Cornish.

These issues concern efforts to "promote" the Cornish language and the neo-traditional music scene where emergent projects, linked to branding, tourism and commodifying cultural production are on the agenda. Viewing culture as saleable also raises issues of ownership because, although cultural products (artifacts, performances and so on) may be marketed and sold, by their generators or others, cultures are perceived as belonging to groups. Their intangible components, such as memory, story, myth and symbol, are sometimes supported by the very practices and objects available for commerce. Sometimes commercialization means that some elements are no longer viewed as the exclusive property of the communities that produced them and may therefore become less useful for marking and communicating identity and belonging; yet in other instances, the fact that they have worth for outsiders may lead insiders to take pride in them and therefore in themselves. Practically speaking then, commodification is neither all-good nor all-bad and a challenge, if it to be pursued as policy, is to find ways of using symbolic elements without losing ownership or reproducing stereotypes that harm the wider economy and self-image.

Cultural items or a whole culture?

There might be two approaches to assessing the usefulness of cultures, an itemized or piecemeal approach, whereby component practices or elements are considered in their own right and a holistic one, where all of the constituents are evaluated together as one, multidimensional construction. Using the first approach, we could take individual elements and consider how they are valued by different sections of the community. We could take the music and

---

155 Gareth Shaw and Allan Williams, "Tourism and employment: reflections on a pilot study of Looe, Cornwall", (Department of Geography, University of Exeter) in *Area*, vol. 20 (1), (1988), pp. 23-24.

dance forms that are labelled Cornish and inquire into participation and perceptions, for example, or we could ask how much worth is attached to the Cornish language by a diverse public. Indeed these are the obvious cases that would be identified by researchers who are guided by Cornish nationalist and Revivalist and paradigms. For those concerned with commerce, the selection of individual artefacts, customs and practices as marketable items suggests itself as an obvious route, but such a compartmentalized approach has short-comings. It risks forgetting that cultures are whole, polymorphous, constructions where elements are embedded in contexts that are social, economic, historical and geographical with dimensions of gender, ethnicity, generation and class. Within these situations, items have specific meanings, resonances and something of an "aura", akin to the notion Walter Benjamin applied to works of art.[156] The seemingly woolly concept of aura allows us to recognize that practices and artefacts, as items with relationships, can produce tacit and emotional responses and have primary uses for human need, already serving a purpose before economic exchange is considered. Semiologically speaking, they are polysemous signs which may be attributed different meanings by different people or, for that matter, by the same people according to time and situation. Broadly though, customary meanings are partially anchored within socially-mediated meaning systems. Individuals relate to customary maps of meaning that are constantly drawn and redrawn within the group and informed from outside. Once removed from this context, elements are ascribed new meanings so that their use and value may have little bearing on how the whole culture is perceived.[157] A piecemeal approach does not therefore allows us to get at the worth attached to whole cultural identities.

Just as socio-cultural spheres have been seen as having relative autonomy (partly through discourse and hegemony) from economic and material circumstances, so cultural components may be independent of one another and of social structure. It is possible to

156 Walter Benjamin, "The Work of Art in the Age of Mechanical Reproduction", trans. Harry Zohn, in Benjamin, Illuminations, London: Jonathan Cape, 1970, pp. 219-53.

157 Cf. Bernard Deacon and Philip Payton, "Re-inventing Cornwall: Culture Change on the European Periphery", in *Cornish Studies*, no. 1, pp. 62-79 (63).

take elements, some objects, customs or items of cuisine for instance, and attribute worth to them while holding contradictory views that devalue the whole culture. Identities are "elected and ascribed"[158] with reference to whole categories, not isolated elements, so while outsiders may pick out bits they fancy, they need not endorse the cultural group. Elements may be imbued with Otherness and appeal to the senses and the imagination but the very features that attract may simultaneously be held inferior to the person's own culture. The meanings given will not be those understood in their original context so we cannot extrapolate from the worth attributed to one item, or a range of items and assume more about that attached to a whole cultural group. People may eat chicken tikka masala and listen to rap while holding essentialist, reductive, or openly racist, views of the ethnic groups and cultures they are drawn from, and by the same token, it would be simplistic to assume that somebody—even an insider—who likes pasties or neo-traditional music has wholly positive views of the Cornish. Mixed processes of leisure-motivated appropriation and commodification sometimes lift items from embedded contexts and divorce them from traditional meanings and social and emotional uses. They may be valued in new situations while broader constructions of Cornishness are not. A few examples will illustrate this. At Bolster Day in St Agnes (a carnival and theatre event based on the legend of a giant) a couple of middle-aged musicians who had learnt a repertoire of Cornish dance tunes and who enthused about Celtic festivals, told me that the "locals" were boring and that "We don't have that much to do with them." The impression was of somewhat Bohemian incomers drawing upon local elements to create their own scene, much as American sub-cultures have appropriated Native American material. On another occasion, participants in a race between former Fal oyster boats, teased the only man with a Cornish accent, going into Long John Silver-style imitations and making indecent quips about incest, the inference being that locals were inbred yokels. Although the distinctive boats were appreciated, the event was uncomfortable for those who shared

---

158 Stuart Hall's terms, cf. Hall (1980 [1973]), "Encoding/decoding", in Centre for Contemporary Cultural Studies (ed.): *Culture, Media, Language: Working Papers in Cultural Studies*, 1972-79, London: Hutchinson, pp. 128-38, cf. Stuart Hall and Paul du Gay (eds.) (1996), *Questions of Cultural Identity*, London: Sage.

their origins. If we accept cultural ownership, this involves misappropriation and sometimes empties elements of customary meaning so that they become unavailable as symbolic resources for the Cornish. For example, the knit-frock, a distinctive fisherman's jumper, enjoyed renewed interest in the 1980s, thanks to a well-researched book,[159] but it was later taken up as middle-class leisure wear and commercialized so effectively that derivatives may now be bought in London and Paris. It is now unlikely to be read as a local symbol but might instead suggest that the wearer is, as some locals put it, a "yachty" because it fits the nautically-themed, leisure-wear image promoted by *Armor Lux* in Brittany and *Sea Salt* in Cornwall. Pasty shops have sprung up in places like Bath, Gloucester and Wells, and in London's Oxford Street and Tottenham Court Road, where they may be associated with holidays but hardly with mining and Cornish food-ways. To summarize, the success of cultural items is not automatically beneficial for a community's standing and well-being so we need to think about the Cornish and their culture as a whole assemblage. This also requires us to consider how a multidimensional set of cultures within Cornishness is constituted and perceived as a single identity.

Critically considering commodification and primary uses together allows a search for public policies and strategies where the desirability and impact of economic uses on culture's roles in relationships, feelings, and even psychological health, are taken into account. Generating profit is then seen as a possible means to support communities, not an end in itself. One way forward may be to avoid polarized, for-or-against arguments of the kind that formerly characterized debates on tourism. The broad purpose is therefore to discuss culture's potential usefulness as a contributor to meeting a range of needs and to specifically consider it as affecting the ability to build sustainable futures and enjoy levels of solidarity and harmony that are conducive to the capacity to adapt and exercise agency. This neither shuns commodification nor embraces it as an unassailable logic but highlights emotional and social uses to ensure they are not ignored when commercial uses are considered.

---

159 Mary Wright (1979, 2008), *Cornish Guernseys and Knit-frocks*, Polperro: Polperro Heritage Press.

Chapter 3

Cornish Culture and Capital

To consider wider social and emotional uses of culture we may turn to a multidisciplinary framework based on plural notions of capital from sociology, cultural studies and economics. The closely intertwined terms *human, cultural, social* and *symbolic capital* (amongst others) are variously understood and applied but all essentially imagine other forms of economy in parallel to that of money and goods. Some of these extensions are closely linked to economic capital, commercial exchange and the accounts of finance that we all recognize from everyday understandings of "capital", but others are only indirectly related and have more to do with the workings of society in general. Choosing capital as a focus at all, even as an analogy, implies staying within the logic of exchange and binding cultural life to economics in one way or another but the suggestion here is that it might also be taken as a byword for communities' stock of useful cultural practices and connected social behaviours.

This chapter has two starting points. The first is "social capital", using work by James Coleman,[160] who explores it in relation to human capital and economics, and Robert D. Putnam who centres closely on social solidarity and well-being.[161] The second is the work of Pierre Bourdieu whose interest in social and economic inequalities and their connections has produced an elaborate analysis that emphasizes polymorphous forms of capital—including social capital—and moves away from simplistic, pyramidal ways of

---

160 James Coleman (1988),), "Social Capital in the Creation of Human Capital", in *The American Journal of Sociology*, vol. 94, Supplement: "Organizations and Institutions: Sociological and Economic Approaches to the Analysis of Social Structure", pp. S95-S120.

161 Robert D. Putnam (1995), Robert D. Putnam, "Tuning in, tuning out: the strange disappearance of social capital in America", *Political Science and Politics*, no. 28, (1995), pp. 664-83; Robert D. Putnam (2000), *Bowling Alone: The Collapse and Revival of American Community*, New York: Simon and Shuster.

imagining social hierarchies.[162] Taken together, Bourdieu, Coleman and Putnam provide approaches, firstly to studying social networks and relationships and secondly to considering the relative status and value attached to individuals, groups and cultures. Their ideas may be expanded to consider psychological/emotional need through esteem and belongingness so the purpose is to present an overview to inform considerations of culture's connections with well-being. Coleman's direct links between economic and social capital furthermore point to culture's non-commercial uses being economically enabling.

All of these theoretical frameworks, based on capital of one kind or another, have a Marxist genealogy, even if that is not immediately obvious, so it is useful to consider one or two of Marx's basic notions and how they might relate to the proposition that culture has primary uses and assumptions in favour of commodification. Firstly though, it is worth remembering that some terms used have widespread, common-sense meanings that relate to taken-for-granted truths. This explains some of the difficulty encountered when striving to take discussion beyond the understandings and "truths" that underpin institutional attitudes and which are nearly all rooted in achieving further commodification. One of Marx's most important concepts, when it comes to reflecting upon useful culture, is that of "use-value"—the worth that something has when used to meet a human need.[163] Marx extends his understanding of human need beyond the material, allowing connections with emotional and psychological need: "The nature of these needs, whether they arise, for example, from the stomach, or the imagination, makes no difference."[164] Use-value may, in other words, relate to all areas of need,[165] not just the obvious physiological and security needs which might be easier to relate to the profits of commodification. Note that "use-value" is not the same as "value" or "exchange-value"[166] but

---

162 See Stéphane Chevallier and Christine Chauvre (2010), *Dictionnaire Bourdieu*, Paris: Ellipses, p.20.

163 Cf. Karl Marx (1990 [1867]), *Capital, Volume 1: A Critique of Political Economy*, trans. Ben Fowkes, London: Penguin, p. 126.

164 Karl Marx, *op. cit.*, p.125.

165 Cf. Abraham Maslow's "Hierarchy of Needs" (1954), *op. cit.*

166 Cf. Yu Wujin, "Thing, Value, Time, and Freedom: A Consideration of Some

is instead the inherent property or content of "a thing which through its qualities satisfies human needs of whatever kind".[167] This need not have anything to do with trade. For a locally-inspired illustration, somebody may catch mackerel and grow potatoes, both of which have use-value as food to be eaten at home rather than sold. Just as things that are made and produced have use-values that need not be converted into exchange values, so cultural practices may have primary uses in meeting non-material needs. In fact, it would not really be stretching Marx's definition to regard these primary uses straightforwardly as use-values. Such intangible uses have to do with the relationships and feelings that underpin identity, community and society.

Things becomes commodities when produced for market exchange so that they have "exchange-value" and may be traded or sold. It is this process of "commodification" that is involved when culture and heritage are turned into commercial products (perfor-mances, spectacles, artefacts, representations, paid visits, experiences etc.) and exchanged for money. We may consider primary uses of cultural elements independently of commercial potential, though. Singing a repertoire of songs amongst friends may correspond to emotional uses for example, irrespective of the potential for commer-cial performance and exchange-value. Capitalist societies convert much of their production into commodities as a taken-for-granted aspect of life and the suggestion that more aspects of culture should be commodified is an extension of the corresponding logic and expectations that have strengthened under conditions of global, liberal capitalism.[168] Commercialization has intensified and reached further into our lives, as has the acceptance that this should happen. Proposals to commodify culture and heritage and to use symbols of regional, national, local and ethnic identities to produce "added value"[169] are aspects of this trend. Once commodification happens, cultural elements become consumable and acquire exchange-value.

key Concepts in Marx's Philosophical System", trans. Jie Tang in *Frontiers of Philosophy in China*, vol.1 (1), (Jan., 2006), pp. 114-123, Springer, p. 117.

167 Karl Marx, *op. cit.* p.125.

168 See Arjun Appadurhi (1986) (1986), *The Social Life of Things. Commodities in Cultural Perspective*, Chicago: University of Chicago Press.

169 E.g. www.objectiveone.com/client/cases/InvClusterPDFs/Plough2Plate.pdf

Commercial production—including non-material aspects such as services and performances—still involves primary uses, though, and while some aspects of culture can easily be turned to economic profit, others are less amenable to this because they are less tangible or aesthetically marketable. One-dimensional discussions that reduce cultural elements to saleable resources concentrate exclusively on profit without regard for other roles, arousing the suspicion that commercialization sometimes compromises or alters their primary uses and undermines well-being by lifting them from social context.[170] This is not to say that commodification has to involve a complete or permanent abandonment of other uses. On the contrary, it has been recognized that commercial uses sometimes enhance primary uses and there may be a two-way process whereby elements are de-commodified and retained in everyday life, or commercialized and de-commercialized in specific contexts. Arjun Appadurhi describes how they may move back and forth between a "commodity state" and simple use at different moments, meaning that they do not have one-way trajectories or fixed meanings.[171] Thus, aspects of culture need not be stripped of their primary uses when commercialized and commercially disseminated elements may be incorporated into people's lives, enhancing identities and fulfilling other uses. This happens with elements from tourism, such as Cornish ice-cream and surfing, which have been woven into everyday life as sources of identification and pleasure.

An influential extension to the concept of capital is "human capital" which emphasizes the skills and knowledge available to business and industry. Regeneration discourses often consider how to enhance the capacities of people so as to provide economic potential, extending this to qualitative considerations such as attitudes and characteristics (conscientiousness, ambition, reliability, versatility etc.), rather than just measurable or qualification-based components. Attention to knowledge as a resource in the "knowledge economy" or "new economy" is but a recent manifestation, reflecting economic changes. While attention to work capacities is part of

170 Wujin Yu (2006), *op. cit.*, p.116. (Marx's dialectical materialism is only concerned with the material in so far as it plays a part in human relations and activities.)

171 Arjun Appadurhi, *op. cit.*

the common-sense "real world" where production and job creation is the currently-available route to material comfort, it does not, on its own, take account of the breadth of human needs. It may even invert priorities so that the economy becomes the goal rather than the means to well-being. Variations of "the economy needs skilled workers" somehow render human needs secondary to the impersonal requirements of financial capital and, however sound the economic reasoning, the means seem to become the end. It may even be implied that the people available are not suited to the economy's needs and that better ones are needed, perhaps from somewhere else. This privileges capital's need for labour, rather than people's dependence on paid work as a means to meet their needs.

This has particular resonance in Cornwall because of a special set of institutional attitudes that has characterized discourses around the economy since at least the 1970s.[172] These are rooted in portrayals that stem from tourism and Cornwall's history as a supposedly *remote* setting for romantic fictions and—in clear contradiction—an *accessible* leisure area. Despite Cornwall's long industrial experience and international connections, these portray it as being far from modernity and industry and create expectations that the people as rustic, backward and insular—connecting with escapist ideas that many are fond of. Thus, the realities of human capital may be less influential in shaping what is believed than exposure to fictional representation. Consequently, economic strategies since the 1980s have made frequent references to "dynamic in-migrants" but have rarely featured dynamic and qualified people from Cornwall itself.[173] In the 1980s and 90s this prejudicial emphasis was compounded by informing would-be investors that wages were low and casting Cornish workers as "honest, reliable and productive" and not given to "absenteeism" and "industrial unrest"[174]—an overall image of honest country folk who were dependent workers but not decision-makers, innovators, entrepreneurs, managers, scientists and intellectuals. Things have improved with initiatives such as the graduate programme, "Unlocking Cornish Potential" but these

172 For criticisms see, J. Willet (2009), *op. cit.*

173 Cf. B. Deacon, A. George and R. Perry (1987), *Cornwall at the Crossroads, op. cit.*, pp. 29-30 and pp. 67-8.

174 *Ibid.* Cornwall County Council leaflet (1986) cited on p.29.

enduring discourses resurface in approaches which assume the desirability of attracting able people from outside, rather than meeting local needs or building upon existing strengths. This informs attempts to attract businesses with unsubstantiated claims about the nature of in-migration as a source of human capital:

> Over the past few years Cornwall has seen significant inward migration, particularly of young, innovative and highly skilled people.[175]

It is hard to view some promotional work as addressing local needs and their discursive formations illustrate links between representations of the Cornish, their collective status and their access to jobs and housing. This recalls criticism of broadly functionalist applications which put gender or racial inequalities down to human capital without considering other influences and it is a reminder that socioeconomic deprivation involves past as well as present factors.

Human capital is often understood as being limited to obvious work-based skills and qualifications but relationships and behaviours are involved as well. We may extend it to non-economic domains where the components of knowledge, skills, feelings and behaviours help build relationships, initiatives and networks. That takes us to social capital and the part played by culture in its generation. Amongst Putnam's definitions of social capital are the following:

> features of social life—networks, norms, trust—that enable people to act together more effectively to pursue shared objectives.[176]

> connections among individuals—social networks and the norms of reciprocity and trustworthiness that arise from them.[177]

---

175 www.investincornwall.com/living-in-cornwall/ (Accessed 20 April 2012)

176 Robert D. Putnam (1995), "Tuning in, tuning out: the strange disappearance of social capital in America", *Political Science and Politics*, 28, pp. 664-83.

177 Robert D. Putnam (2000), *Bowling Alone: The Collapse and Revival of American Community*, Simon and Shuster, New York, p. 19.

The constitutive norms of social capital are acted out within culture and are linked to such components as beliefs and attitudes, imagination and both tacit and explicit knowledge. Putnam's view is that social capital is useful, not only for individuals but for society as a whole. It may establish norms such as honesty, trust, helpfulness and friendliness that rely upon mutual obligation and our need to be respected and accepted members of society and to be credible in our roles. This means that social capital is closely interconnected with culture's primary uses and well-being, also having something to do with economic capacity.

There are various slants on this. Coleman largely sticks with the emphasis on rational actors that dominates economics, proposing that, "social capital constitutes a particular kind of resource available to an actor"[178] which contributes to human capital. This involves social structures and facilitates actions by "persons or corporate actors" that it makes ends possible.[179] Putnam develops complementary ideas, suggesting that societies with lots of social capital produce "generalized reciprocity"[180] whereby useful behaviours become socially-produced norms. Rather than working as conscious, investment and return, this involves the promise of exchange in that people expect others to do things for them and it only works because individuals do not have to "balance exchanges instantly".[181] Social capital thus spreads to increase well-being. Coleman's account involves obligation in the form of virtual "credit slips", calling to mind the saying, "One good turn deserves another". He attributes the "norm that one should forgo self-interest and act in the interests of the collectivity" to the family context or special, local circumstances, such as building "young nations" or "nascent social movements"[182] and even suggests that, "Voluntary organizations are brought into being to aid some purpose of those who initiate them."[183] This could apply to the Cornish Movement and indigenous Cornish society as a whole, but Coleman's dismissal of

---

178 James Coleman (1988), *op. cit.* p.98.
179 *Ibid.*
180 Robert D. Putnam (2000), *op. cit.* p. 21.
181 *Ibid.* (2000), p. 21.
182 James Coleman (1988), *op. cit.*, pp. 104-105.
183 *Ibid.*, p.108.

unselfish motives for helping others is questionable. He writes from a hard-headed emphasis on self-interest he calls "methodological individualism".[184] Social capital exists in relationships and, although it may be presented as "a resource for persons",[185] organizations may be "corporate actors", providing a principal that we can extended further to cohesive groups. Different kinds of community are distinguished, those where, "people are always doing things for each other" and those where, "individuals are more self-sufficient and depend on each other less".[186] Essentially Coleman is talking about neighbourliness even if his language of social commerce turns this into a question of exchange. Culture becomes useful in this rationale when it contributes to the structure within which social capital works and belongingness (a human need) may be essential to that. Actions are said to be made possible by intra-group relationships and norms of behaviour that create specific kinds of social capital with collective advantages.[187]

Communities with better social networks may have a higher level of well-being and just as social interactions may increase or diminish economic capacity, so they may be vital for the ability to fulfil non-economic and non-material needs. For instance, the "social networks and norms of reciprocity and trustworthiness"[188] that Putnam discusses are needed for a multitude of functions that strengthen community bonds and these norms are likely to be conducive to beneficial feelings and a positive sense of collective identity. An linked economic factor, outside the usual rationale, is that of cultural identity as a motivation. In Brittany, for example, some managers speak of their desire to create jobs and say that participating in Breton life is important to them.[189] This commitment is reinforced by networks that reach beyond work to include family, community and leisure.

The role of culture in social capital might be said to make it a commodity in the archaic sense of convenience and facility, where

184 *Ibid.*, p.109.
185 *Ibid.*, p. 98.
186 *Ibid.*, *op. cit.*, p.102.
187 *Ibid.*, p.100.
188 Robert D. Putnam (2000), p.19.
189 Comments by managers and engineers in ESOL classes.

it often refers to qualities like courtesy and thoughtfulness.[190] These could be said to be culturally-generated, cost-free ingredients for happy, socially-cohesive communities, recalling the popular wisdom, "politeness doesn't cost anything." Coleman and Putnam both discuss trustworthiness, a quality that links trust with worth (i.e. value) in a single word. This is said to "lubricate social life"[191] as an enabling characteristic, an awareness that shifts attention from the rational actor as an individualist to the collective community. Thus "a group within which there is extensive trustworthiness and extensive trust may accomplish much more than a comparable group without that trustworthiness and trust."[192] Unsurprisingly, social capital has interested a broad span of people (economists, sociologists, cultural analysts, health researchers) and has come to mean different things. Although implicitly rejected in Margaret Thatcher's infamous "There's no such thing as society", it has been a foundation for the Conservatives' discussions of the Big Society and "civic engagement". Its economic role has been accepted by the World Bank and neo-classical economists and it is a framework for analysing the usefulness of social relations and their bearing on economic outcomes, even within U.S. "political economics". The diverse uses share an awareness of relationships and community networking in establishing behaviours that impact economically and socially, and Coleman cites embeddedness in relation to how these produce social structures that have, "an independent effect on the functioning of economic systems".[193]

To recap, cultural practices and attitudes are part of what makes societies work or malfunction and contribute, through social capital, to well-being and fulfilment. The linked ideas of friendship, imagined kinship, neighbourliness, belonging, solidarity and so on, accord with collective action, social engagement and initiative. Mutual aid, reciprocity, obligation, trust and word-of-mouth information-sharing are all related norms that favour expectations and behaviours which potentially enable people in less affluent communities to live pleasant, satisfying lives despite hardship. It has even been suggested

190 Latin *commoditas*, via French *commodité*.
191 Robert D. Putnam (2000), *op. cit.*, p. 21.
192 James Coleman (1988), *op. cit.*, p.101.
193 James Coleman (1988), *op. cit.* pp.97-98.

that Cornwall's housing problems might have been mitigated by friendship and kinship networks, reducing homelessness[194] and other research has suggested an underlying, historic family structure that favours multi-generational households.[195] Social capital may be thought of as held by groups, rather than residing in individuals and it may be understood to have cultural underpinnings. Awareness of belonging to a an "imagined community"[196] may motivate people to pursue its interests, while culture itself supports the relationships that produce social cohesion. Coleman criticizes economists for ignoring the reality that:

'persons' actions are shaped, redirected, constrained by the social context' [where] 'norms, interpersonal trust, social networks, and social organization are important in the functioning not only of the society but also of the economy.'[197]

For a more social focus, we may to turn to Bourdieu's analysis of how power is exercised through exterior signs of status. Privilege is supported by verbal and visual discourses that allow members of dominant groups to "impose" their status through, "signes de richesse, destinés à être crus ou obéis."[198] Thus Bourdieu does not imagine a simple class structure based on wealth alone but outlines complex, multiple relationships where status is produced by many variables. The concept of capital is extended to include a range of resources, including cultural attributes and knowledge. Whereas Coleman has neo-liberal presumptions, Bourdieu comes from a post-Marxist tradition, yet despite being couched differently, their analyses broadly agree. Bourdieu emphasises the role of "cultural

194 Mary Buck, Malcolm Williams and Lyn Bryant, "Housing the Cornish: Containing the Crisis", in P.J.Payton (ed.), *Cornish Studies*, no. 1, pp.97-108.

195 Gilles Duranton, Andrés Rodríguez-Pose and Richard Sandall, "Family Types and the Persistence of Regional Disparities in Europe", in *Economic Geography*, vol. 85, issue 1, (January 2009) pp. 23-14.

196 Benedict Anderson (1991), *op. cit.*

197 *Ibid.*

198 Pierre Bourdieu (1982), *Ce que parler veut dire – L'économie des échanges linguistiques*, Paris: Éditions Fayard.

capital"—with which his name is synonymous—to consider how culture affects status and life chances, identifying four forms of capital. Each form may be converted into one of the others:

economic capital—money, wealth, property, land, income and so on.

cultural capital—knowledge and skills, notably acquired in socialization and education.

social capital—resources from relationships which are important in exercising power.

symbolic capital—represented and/or understood symbolically, in knowledge-based relationships and educational qualifications .[199]

Cultural capital leads to economic capital when it helps get a well-paid job and social capital may provide the contacts and credibility needed for opportunities. Bourdieu considers how differences of cultural practices, values, tastes, knowledge and competence are involved in socio-economic inequalities but notes that each form of capital may be involved in "social struggles" independently.[200] Cultural capital depends upon the acknowledged currency of attributes and their acquisition, physically through the body, materially as things, educationally as knowledge and symbolically.[201] It becomes part of who someone *is*, not just what they have and is considered to exist in three forms or states.[202] The first is the "embodied state" of "lasting dispositions of mind and body" which involves ways of moving, behaving and presenting and constructing the body which interact with feelings. It is thus related to well-being and how group members are recognized.

---

199 Pierre Bourdieu, "Les 3 états du capital culturel", in *Actes de la recherch en sciences sociales*, vol. 30, (November 1979), L'Institution Scolaire, pp. 3-6.

200 Cf. Mike Crang and Nigel Thrift (2000), *Thinking Space*, London: Routledge, p. 244.

201 Pierre Bourdieu (1984,1988), *Homo Academicus*, trans. Peter Collier, Cambridge: Polity Press; Bourdieu (1979), *La Distinction*, op. cit.

202 Pierre Bourdieu, *Les 3 états du capital culturel*, 1979, op. cit.

L'hexis corporel est la mythologie politique réalisée, incorporée, devenue disposition permanente, manière durable de se tenir, de parler, de marcher, et, par là, de sentir et de penser.[203]

Much of cultural capital is thus embodied visibly.[204] Some*body's* social place is inscribed in and on the body, "incorporated" or made flesh, so that body language, shape, size, weight, gestures, stance, bearing and complexion all connote status. Most people will be familiar with how one person may look working-class and another "posh" even when identically dressed. Although this seems natural, it is acquired and is hard to strip away, whatever the bearer's fortunes. Life experiences are ingrained as "lasting attitudes" which may be as simple as a way of walking, having a particular demeanour, or smiling, sitting or eating in a certain way.[205] The second form of cultural capital is the "objectified state"[206] where cultural goods have relationships with legitimate knowledge as props that relate to wealth. Finally, in the third or "institutionalized state" capital is institutionally underwritten and guaranteed, by academic qualifications for example.

Cultural and social capital give people varying social weight or currency as a kind of credibility which influences how seriously they are taken in particular contexts. This involves networks, mutual recognition and relationships (friendships, acquaintances, work contacts and obligations)[207] that require unconscious or conscious social investment,[208] including participation in practices that bring people with shared economic and social interests together, reinforce group membership and favour or disfavour the acquisition of all

---

203 Pierre Bourdieu (1980), *Le sens pratique*, (coll.) *Le sens commun*, Paris: Éditions de Minuit, p. 117.

204 Pierre Bourdieu (1979), "Les 3 états du capital culturel", *op. cit.*, p.3: "Most properties of cultural capital may result from the fact that it is linked to the body and supposes embodiment", Trans. N. Kennedy.

205 See Mike Featherstone, (1995), *Undoing Culture: Globalization, Postmodernism and Identity*, London and Newbury Park, California: Sage, pp. 22-23.

206 Pierre Bourdieu (1979), *Les 3 états du capital culturel*, p.5.

207 Alain Accardo and Phillipe Corcuff (1989), *La Sociologie de Bourdieu*, Bordeaux: Le Mascaret, p.94.

208 Cf. Stéphane Chevallier and Christine Chauvre (2010), *op. cit.* p.19.

forms of capital. Symbolic capital works by alterity where each component depends upon differing from a specific Other. Status is thus signified by visible or audible "distinction"—Bourdieu's term for attributes that mark social differences and contribute to the phenomenon of *habitus*. This is explored in relation to Cornishness in the next chapter so for now, it is enough to understand it as a social construction within which members broadly share identifying attitudes and dispositions without which symbolic capital has no currency, and to appreciate that all forms of capital may work symbolically.[209]

Intervention for One and All[210]

There are two connected areas that cultural intervention might address—social capital, with its implications for capacity and combined cultural and symbolic capital with their relationships to status and self-worth. The perceived decline of social capital in developed societies produces concern, such as complaints about inconsiderate behaviour, the isolation experienced when neighbours do not speak to each other and the difficulty of getting people involved in community life.[211] In Cornwall, it is also common for older natives to associate a perceived decline in friendliness and solidarity with weakened and displaced communities and this is a recurrent conversational refrain.

> I don't know a living sole here I can ask to fetch me home a bit of shopping.
>
> People we got here now living would soon as knock you down as look at you. Nobody speaks! Years ago we looked after each other and you never had to worry.[212]

209 Pierre Bourdieu (1997), *Méditations pascaliennes*, coll. Liber, Paris: Editions du Seuil, p.285; cf. Bridget Fowler (1997), *Pierre Bourdieu and Cultural Theory: Critical Investigations*, London: Sage, p.20.

210 *"Onen hag Oll"* 'One and All' is the Cornish motto.

211 Robert D. Putnam, "Tuning in, tuning out: the strange disappearance of social capital in America", *Political Science and Politics*, no. 28, (1995), pp. 664-83.

212 Remarks by elderly locals at the Prince of Wales Pier, Falmouth, 14 August 2011.

Yet, decline is not irreversible and we can envisage projects to "restore communities".[213] An underlying theme here is speculation about how useable culture might nurture the ingredients of social capital and give better outcomes—which is not unconnected to boosting cultural and symbolic capital. It is important to remember that interdependencies and mutual benefits need not extend to everyone. Putnam discusses "bridging social capital"[214] whereby networks "link substantial sectors of the community and span underlying social cleavages"[215] and this may combine with the "bonding social capital" or "sociological superglue"[216] of groups, reaching across fractions in society to create cohesion. As suggested in relation to civic identity, we can envisage using Cornish cultures to this end, spreading bonding and bridging functions across class, gender, ethnic and generational boundaries while promoting Cornishness, nurturing and spreading networks around activities.

The Cornish Movement's contestations may both require and contribute to social capital, which may be mobilized in "moving from individual protest to organized revolt".[217] Bourdieu discusses rule-breaking as requiring a "denunciation of [a] tacit subscription contract which defined the original doxa". It thus "presupposes a cognitive subversion, a conversion of world view."[218] Since symbolic and cultural capital rely upon arbitrary markers which have no independent existence, the status of cultures and groups is contestable and the weaponry available for re-evaluating status is cultural.[219]

Bourdieu's perspectives have already been fruitfully extended to study contestation in situations involving class, gender and ethnicity. Flux and instability is a theme in Derek Wynne's work on social mobility and the "new middle class" in Cheshire. This describes how undermining traditional hierarchies involves forms of capital in

---

213 R. Putnam and L. Fieldstein (2003), *Better Together: Restoring the American Community*, Simon and Shuster: New York.

214 Robert Putnam (2000), p. 23.

215 Robert Putnam (1995)

216 Robert Putnam (2000), p. 23.

217 James Coleman, *op. cit.* p.101.

218 Pierre Bourdieu, (1982, 2001), *Langue et Pouvoir, op. cit.*, pp.187-198, trans. N. Kennedy.

219 *Ibid.* "engagé comme arme et comme enjeu dans les luttes dont les champs de production culturelle…"

active struggles whereby social classes produce their own distinguishing cultures and achieve their own legitimacy. Wynne argues that this can change what is thought legitimate,[220] and this is what the Cornish Movement attempts by asserting the worth and geographically rooted legitimacy of Cornishness. Still in North-West England, Beverley Skeggs[221] has applied cultural capital to women's attitudes to class, taste and femininity, considering their identifications and dis-identifications with being working-class. Once more, this understands that arbitrary cultural distinctions operate within unstable hierarchies that can change. Collective interventions that combine culture with affirmation may challenge hierarchies and valorize previously illegitimate groups, and there are enough high-profile examples to show this possible, from feminisms, to gay rights and from anti-colonialisms to the "black is beautiful" campaigns of 1960s America. In such cases culture is, "the means by and through which various subordinate groups live and resist their subordination" [and] "the terrain on which hegemony is struggled for and established."[222] Wynne's account suggests the generation of an alternative order that is asserted by insiders and which may become widely accepted. Cultural capital is asserted within a contestable and unstable field of representation—much as advertisers intervene with demonstrable results. Post-structuralist semiotics views signs—such as Bourdieu's distinctions—as polysemous and considers how the "order of signification"[223] may be subverted. For the moment, we can note that challenges require "oppositional readings"[224] involving "heretical discourses"—a proposition that seems far more realistic, "if one knows the degree to which one may modify social reality by modifying the representation that agents make of it".[225]

220 Derek Wynne (1998), *Leisure, Lifestyle and the New Middle Class*, London: Routledge.

221 Beverley Skeggs (1997), *Formations of Class and Gender*, London: Sage.

222 Tim O'Sullivan, J. Hartley, D. Saunders, M. Montomery, J. Fiske (1994), *Key Concepts in Communication and Cultural Studies*, 2nd Edition, London: Routledge, p.71.

223 Roland Barthes (1982 [1957]), *Mythologies, op. cit.*

224 See Stuart Hall ([1973] 1980), "Encoding/decoding", in Centre for Contemporary Cultural Studies (ed.), *Culture, Media, Language: Working Papers in Cultural Studies*, 1972-79, London: Hutchinson, pp. 128-38.

225 Pierre Bourdieu, (1982, 2001) *Langage et Pouvoir Symbolique*, Editions Fayard et

Cornish myths and legends

A missing element of Cornish resilience is an aspirational social vision rooted in community narratives of the kind seen—amongst elites at least—in Brittany and Galicia. Essentially, this is about the views that people have of their communities, place and the wider world. It involves cultural signifiers—as capital—and may be related to Roland Barthes' idea of "mythology".[226] In his "second order of signification", signs carry cultural meanings or "myths" and operate through contextual connotations and readings which may come together in a "third order of signification" where they are organized and interpreted as mythology and/or ideology. This presents two challenges: identifying useful myths and developing supporting strategies. Mythologies need to connect with existing myths in order to interpellate people, which is why quasi-governmental agencies fail to mobilize identity. They are notable for lacking appeals to identity and for their reluctance to use the adjective Cornish. Ultimately their bureaucratic business-speak does not resonate with feeling or community aspiration.

Culture may be seen as made up of networks of socially constructed realities as imaginings and practices. Accordingly "useable culture" may accompany "useable histories" to convey mythologies through narrative discourse. Narratives may also be harmful, of course, and some Revivalist discourses partially accept and inadvertently reproduce ascribed versions, turning them into imaginings of identity that influence expectations and (in)actions. Some even support presumptions about the Cornish of the kind that were earlier attributed to outside decision-makers. For example, the idea that Celtic temperament prevents collaborative working is willingly taken up and becomes an excuse for disorganization and failure. Sometimes the same ascribed characteristics are cited as both negative and positive. Being "laid-back", for instance, and having a supposedly "slower pace of life" are presented either as agreeable aspects of life or as symptoms of being un-dynamic. They are also fictions projected onto the Cornish.

If aspirational intervention is to be attempted (by Cornwall Council and the Cornish Movement), specifically Cornish knowl-

Editions de Seuil, p.188, trans. N. Kennedy.
226 Roland Barthes (1982 [1957]), *Mythologies*, Paris: Le Seuil, pp.199-210.

edge needs to inform identification of useable components which are available and feasible. Choices are limited by realities as fostering myths that are wholly unfounded either in material fact or existing narratives would likely be doomed to failure as unbelievable; but myths may not need a "real" or proven existence in order to play a role. Wrecking and piracy, for example, are prominent in tourism despite having little, if any, grounding in history. To catch on narratives only have to be credible and appealing, and may influence people's ideas about their communities and cultures, how they behave and the realities they create. To pick an example, Cornwall has myths of egalitarianism and informality and it is often suggested that there are fewer hierarchies. This could be questioned on the basis of observable inequalities and social divisions but the myth works towards less divisive behaviours and an egalitarian ethos that is part of what many think of as Cornish. The point is that symbolically imagined norms may be useful. In this case, the myth may support a fairer, more democratic society by influencing behaviour, so thinking about what kinds of social capital Cornwall has already, or which narratives exist, might be a way to begin imagining a "third level of signification" or mythology. The following myths are sometimes claimed as positive features of Cornish society:

> egalitarianism, inbuilt democracy, informality, friendliness, strong families, confident women, extended community networks, a Celtic identity, a strong work ethic, enterprise (high levels of self-employment), past industrial prowess, a love of novelty, innovation and inventiveness, cultural creativity, musicality, international networks (transnationality), a outward-looking world view, independence and self-sufficiency (making do), low levels of materialism, participatory cultural activities, high involvement in charitable and voluntary work.

This list certainly provides fertile ground for mythologies if not outright boastfulness, but there is a downside, including these alleged and ascribed myths:

insularity, hostility to outsiders, ignorance, backwardness, nostalgia and living in the past, lack of ambition, resistance to change, stubbornness, nimbyism, individualism, disorganization, division, defeatism, apathy, laziness, semi-retirement, inbreeding and incest, stupidity.

All of these concern capital in its various forms and they inform the rest of the discussion.

Chapter 4

Cornish Cultural Hygienes
and Invented Tradition

In the cultural politics of the New Cornwall, the actors of the Cornish Movement, as campaigners, cultural innovators and performers, purport to represent and champion an imagined community and respond to its needs. This is the leitmotif of Revivalist musical scenes and the taken-for-granted motivation of Cornish language speakers and a multitude of engaged community advocates and political activists, but although most of these folk are Cornish, self-referencing discourses are sometimes distanced from a public whose cultural lights differ. In this respect, the activists resemble counterparts from other movements, from feminisms to trade unionism and minority rights, where having greater political awareness than most of the "represented" need not negate campaigns and projects but should demand reflection. Coupled with political motivation is a marked tendency towards cultural prescriptivism and grand narratives (Pan-Celticism, Cornish Nationalisms, Revivalism, Multi-Culturalism) that influence approaches in all areas from language planning (a preoccupation of Cornish revivalists) to selecting musical repertoires, visual representation and definitions of Cornish culture itself. The Cornish Movement is diverse but this chapter concentrates on Celtic Revivalism as a definable strand, recognizing that many in the Movement do not subscribe to all aspects of it. It also considers appropriations and departures from the Revivalist project. Distinctly Revivalist notions of cultural worth influence selections, production and innovation and involve prescriptions by people whose tastes and practices vary. These have implications for culture's "primary uses" and the usefulness and uptake of Cornish language learning and Revivalist activities for the purposes outlined.

The title of this chapter is inspired by Deborah Cameron's use of the term *Verbal Hygiene*[227] to discuss prescriptive approaches to language. Verbal hygiene encompasses

> all the normative metalinguistic practices through which people attempt to improve language or regulate its use in accordance with particular values, for instance: authenticity, beauty, truth, efficiency, logic, clarity, correctness, stability.[228]

Cameron discusses the supposed opposition between *descriptive* and *prescriptive* approaches and the turn away from judgmental notions of correct language towards relativist positions from which all forms are seen as valid. This leads linguists to describe language as they find it rather than holding up idealized forms as correct and better. This linguistic relativism involves taking a dim view of prescriptivism and the term is widely used to describe conservative and elitist applications of arbitrarily defined correct language. Thus, "the term 'prescriptivism' has a particular value attached to it, a negative connotation that is almost impossible to avoid."[229]

Cameron's verbal hygiene is complex and is not a straightforward synonym for prescriptivism. Her concept also embraces non-conservative, values and motives for attempting to control and shape language, including some that are anti-elitist, counter-hegemonic and innovative. In other words, verbal hygiene does not have to be bad. On the contrary, it can be involved in struggles against inequalities and injustices. To demonstrate non-conservative motivations, Cameron discusses feminist and anti-racist interventions (political correctness) which have successfully altered the everyday norms of English. She also cites Plain English campaigns which seek inclusiveness, artificial languages like Esperanto which are inspired by universalism, and language revitalization projects with aesthetic and counter-hegemonic motives. Cameron shows that practices of

227 Deborah Cameron (1995), *Verbal Hygiene*, London: Routledge.
228 Deborah Cameron, "The one, the many and the Other: representing mono/multiculturalism in post- 9/11 verbal hygiene", paper presented to "Multilingual 2,0?" Conference at the University of Arizona, 14 April 2012.
229 Deborah Cameron (1995), p.3.

verbal hygiene are always present in apparently natural, common-sense forms that define and police the boundaries of acceptable language, showing this to be essential for maintaining the integrity of a language as a functioning code with mutual intelligibility. This is obviously applicable to Cornish language planning but the concept may be extended to examine normative practices in Cornish culture as a whole. It is therefore proposed that "cultural hygiene" be coined as short-hand for all of the ways in which people attempt to delimit, shape and present culture. Understanding that cultural hygienes may have many motives avoids seeing it as a simple, one-way process and provides insights into the workings of cultural and symbolic capital which may inform intervention.

Cultural hygiene may be related to the idea that discourses arise and circulate in combinations that are specific to time and place.[230] These "discursive formations"[231] act as preconditions, largely shaping practices—including those of verbal and cultural hygiene—which then contribute to how discourse evolves. Foucault plays down the role of subjects as authors or initiators and regards them as operating within pre-existing discourses but nevertheless operating a kind of authorship function that contributes to further develop-ment. This applies to the ways in which participants in Cornish cultures—whether Revivalist or not—do not so much create discourses as sift through an available stock from within Cornish repertoires and from outside, variously reproducing, recombining and altering what they find. Discursive formations are not closed or static in other words.

Every discourse has a past and a trajectory which may be scrutinized using Foucault's closely connected methods of archae-ology and genealogy. Archaeology entails examining and describing the regularities, irregularities and changes in discourses, rather than interpreting and judging them and it does so by delving into the general system and available discourses within which practices operate.[232] Genealogy takes this a step further and uses the

---

230 Michel Foucault (1972), *The Archaeology of Knowledge*, London: Tavistock; Michel Foucault (1970), *The Order of Discourse: An Archaeology of the Human Sciences*, Tavistock: London.

231 *Ibid.*, pp. 31-39 and pp. 126-131.

232 *Ibid.*, p.130, cited in Gavin Kendall and Gary Wickham (1999), *Using Foucault's*

knowledge gained strategically to address difficulties. It identifies discursive practices and ongoing processes[233] to reveal otherwise hidden information about their roles and beginnings. The Revival has already received in-depth attention from the perspectives of the New Cornish Historiography so the next task is to use that work to develop a genealogical awareness of the Revivalist inheritance and grapple with its cultural hygienes and their outcomes.[234] The purpose is not historiographical though, nor is it to deconstruct myths for the sake of unsettling their adherents.

Cameron observes that verbal hygiene involves analogies between the "order of language and the larger social order"[235] where language may be a surrogate for other matters. In discussing Britain, she links a marked governmental turn against multilingualism and multiculturalism to fears about "domestic terrorism" following "7/7" and the belief—amplified by the 2008 financial crisis—that competing cultural loyalties fragment society. Like other cases of verbal hygiene this involves aspiration, desire, yearning, fear, worry, anger and so on, and is mirrored in culture. The Cornish Movement also responds emotionally to demographic, economic and social transformations and similarly makes culture a surrogate for concerns and a displacement activity. The interest of cultural hygiene is thus three-fold. Firstly, it is involved in rendering Cornishness illegitimate in respect to prevalent cultures—where many Cornish "distinctions"[236] arbitrarily connote low cultural and symbolic capital. Secondly, it operates within Cornishness when ideas of what Cornish culture *is* and *should be* are contested. A related contention is that some of the overseers of Revivalist cultures have oversights that devalue other versions of Cornishness, impacting upon the standing of differing constructions and the legitimacy of individuals as insiders and their sense of "belongingness". The third way in which cultural

---

Methods, London: Sage, p.25.

233 Gavin Kendall and Gary Wickham (1999), *Using Foucault's Methods*, London: Sage, p. 29-31; Foucault (1970, 1981), *The Order of Discourse*, in R. Young (ed.), *A Post-Structuralist Reader*, London: Routledge and Kegan Paul, pp.70-1.

234 Philip Payton (ed.), *Cornish Studies*, 2nd Series, vols. 1-20, *op. cit.*

235 Deborah Cameron, "The one, the many and the Other", *op. cit.*

236 Pierre Bourdieu (1979), *La Distinction, op. cit.*

hygiene is interesting is as part of selecting elements for intervention and the dissemination of preferred myths.[237]

Being Celts: A Revivalist Monopoly?

There is far more to Cornish Culture than Revivalism so taking the pro-position that Revivalism has useful ingredients should not mean slipping into the trap of thinking that there is nothing else. This marked tendency has repercussions for wider views of what comprises Cornish Culture and for perceptions of Revivalism itself. For example, Cornwall Council's "Green Paper for Culture" (circulated in 2010-11) took a fairly broad view of cultural activity but put Revivalism in a distinct category, giving the impression that it is detached from the mainstream and quirky but nevertheless intimating that it comprises Cornishness—affording it a kind of monopoly (This was partly rectified by the subsequent "White Paper", 2012.). Such approaches may be detrimental to more embedded practices that are overshadowed and overlooked—with the further danger that Cornishness may seem to be a side-show, colourfully ethnic but a redundant minority interest. Self-referencing Revivalist discourses spill over into academic work, notably from students who encounter obvious displays of Otherness (music and dance, visual symbols, language) but miss the fuller complexity of Cornishness. The word "revival" may be taken at face value so that Revivalism is thought more genuine than non-Revivalist Cornish activities which go unremarked. There are tendencies towards essentialism and purism whereby neo-traditions are treated as more authentic, as though Revivalists have stripped away an obscuring overburden to expose the cultural rock underneath.

A normally unspoken project of the Cornish Movement is the amplification of difference between Cornwall and England. This is a long-established motivation, already strong in the early twentieth-century but with growth and divergence, the Movement now encompasses popular responses to new circumstances that have little to do with the antiquarianism of the Revival's founders. In reacting to social and economic changes though, the most readily-available, off-the-shelf discourses and symbols are those inherited from

237 Roland Barthes (1982 [1957]), *Mythologies*, Paris: Le Seuil, pp.199-210.

Revivalism and mediated through pervasive networks. Its discursive formations therefore fuse with grass-roots concerns to shape how adherents frame their aspirations and, "It colours all our perceptions of Cornwall's past, and for many people it is the destination as well as the starting point of all discussion."[238] This ready-made framework offers great unifying benefits but also poses problems that are best understood genealogically. The Revival's early architects participated in, and helped shape, the truths of Pan-Celticism whereby Cornwall was measured against an Irish model (Romantic Ireland)[239] from the Gaelic Ireland Movement (c.1890-1930), informed by imaginings of the Celts. Although Celtic and indeed, Cornish, individuals contributed to ideas of shared identity and origins, many of these imaginings came from without, notably from England, France and Germany and connected with wider quests for otherness in Orientalism and Romanticism. Idealized versions of "Celtishness" assembled Irish, Breton, Welsh and Highland Scottish elements, favouring remote, rural imagery over modernity and in England, this allowed Englishness to be constructed in alterity. This means that there are parallels between *Celticism* and Edward Said's accounts of *Orientalism.*[240] The Celts were homogenized and ascribed generic characteristics whereby earlier views of them as hostile barbarians gave way to softer versions that saw them as free, imaginative, creative, fertile, passionate, spiritual, emotional, impulsive, unruly, natural and so on. As in Africa and Asia, the Other is feminized:

In short, the typical Celt appears to manifest those characteristics and to voice those concerns which a 19th-century middle-class Frenchman or Englishman would have considered appropriate in his wife.[241]

---

238 Tim Saunders "Cornish Symbol and Substance" in C. Ó Luain (ed.) (1983) *For a Celtic Future*, Dublin: The Celtic League. p.257.

239 W.B. Yates' poem appeared in *The Irish Times* on 8 September, 1913.

240 Edward Said (2003 [1978]), *Orientalism*, London: Penguin Books; Terence Brown (ed.) (1996), *Celticism*, Atlanta: Rodopi. .

241 Tim Saunders (1983), pp.255-6.

While some of the ascribed attributes are attractive, they may be arrayed in binary opposition to a privileged set of supposed male, English characteristics. Accordingly, Revivalists operate to an extent within dualistic schemes which cast Celtishness as inferior, despite having elected and negotiated the characteristics in question. Thus all of the following are common in Revivalist imaginings of Celtishness despite being opposed to potentially privileged alternatives:

wild, impulsive, natural, ancient, romantic, rural, imaginative, poetic, musical, mystical, spiritual, disorganized, spontaneous, disunited, colonized, oppressed.

In short, constructions of the Celts within Revivalism bring a great deal of baggage with them and connect, via early tourism and artists' colonies, with some of the disabling ascribed identities found in the discourses of regional development.[242] They have proved influential and lasting and are mirrored in Celtic Studies internationally, where Gaelic cultures occupy a privileged place at the peak of a hierarchy that relies on the requisite attributes of generic Celtishness. An inherent difficulty that this high-profile prescription poses is that its commanding components are essentially pre-industrial and pre-modern, in marked contrast to Cornwall's formative modern, industrial history. The corresponding heritage simply does not fit the model and Cornish culture is found wanting in some prerequisites, deficient in bagpipes, folk music, dance and traditional costume, all of which have been the subject of projects to fill the lack. At the same time, the Cornish language, as textually attested and communicated in place-names and dialect words, is found so embarrassingly Anglicized in vocabulary, pronunciation and spelling that it needs to be purged and re-spelt. Unlike post-industrial, largely Anglophone South Wales, which shares these perceived deficiencies, Cornwall is not part of a larger territory. There is no Llŷn Peninsula to conform more closely to the model, nor is Cornwall redeemed by national

242 Discussions, Malcolm Chapman (1992), *The Celts: The Construction of a Myth*, London: Macmillan; Amy Hale, "Foot in the Mouth, or Foot in the Door? Evaluating Chapman's *The Celts*", in P.J. Payton (ed.), *Cornish Studies*, no. 4, (1996), pp. 158-170; Simon James, (1999), *The Atlantic Celts - Ancient People or Modern Invention?*, London: British Museum Press.

institutions and a critical population mass. The Cornish are therefore slightly suspect, Cinderella Celts.

None of this would matter in the normal run of things but because Cornwall is small and a *de facto* part of England politically, the perceived need to establish Celtic credentials assumes exaggerated importance and opting out becomes tantamount to denying a non-English ethnicity. Insecurity about being thought Celtic has been a perpetual worry since Revivalists sought and achieved Cornwall's membership of the Celtic Congress in 1903.[243] The "recognition of Cornwall as a Celtic nation" (a common phrase)[244] is a longstanding desire which produces strenuous efforts to participate in inter-Celtic events on equal terms with Brittany, Wales, Ireland, The Isle of Man and Scotland, despite a lack of institutional backing and population size. The primacy of models can, however, be rejected and there are those inside the Movement who negotiate distinctly Cornish ways to be Celtic, the image of the "industrial Celt" being a prominent version that includes technological prowess.[245] In fact, Garry Tregidga identifies an alternative Cornu-Welsh model of Celtishness in nineteenth-century Cornish identifications rooted in industry, non-conformism and radical politics, and this current continues.[246] Yet for all these negotiations, there is a core strand that accepts and emulates so many ill-fitting prescriptions that dissonance sometimes emerges between Revivalism and the popular Cornishness explored in the next chapter. This occurs in a myriad of clashing and contradictory practices that do not quite fit. Although this is not a clear-cut matter, it involves an inherent conflict between ascribed

243 See Sharon Lowenna, "'Noscitur A Sociis': Jenner, Duncombe-Jewell and their Milieu", in P.J. Payton (ed.), *Cornish Studies*, no. 12, (2004), pp. 61-87; Amy Hale, "Genesis of the Celto-Cornish Revival? L. C. Duncombe-Jewell and the Cowethas Kelto-Kernuak", in P.J. Payton (ed.), Cornish Studies, no. 5, (1997), pp. 100-111; Alan Kent (2000), *The Literature of Cornwall, op. cit.* pp. 2000.

244 See Derek R. Williams, "'A Cornish Voice in the Celtic Orchestra': Robert Morton Nance and the Celtic Congress of 1926", *Cornish Studies* no. 16, pp. 104-125.

245 See Amy Hale, "Representing the Cornish: Contesting heritage interpretation in Cornwall", *op. cit.*

246 Garry Tregidga, "Celtic comparisons: Brittany and the Cornish Revivalist Movement", conference paper at, "Les rencontres, Bretagne/Monde Anglophone", Université de Bretagne Occidentale, Quimper, 29 June 2012.

attributes and Cornish myths of technical, innovative and concrete achievement. The latter, far from celebrating pre-modernity or the mystical, centre on matters that are modernizing, pragmatic, organized, "workish" and down-to-earth, if not literally underground and cutting-edge.

Bourdieu, whose parents incidentally spoke Béarnese Occitan, saw "symbolic violence" in the discontinuities between the values of home and school and between legitimate and illegitimate culture. From Revivalist perspectives this can only refer to the reductionist opposition of Cornish (subaltern) and English (dominant) cultures but this overlooks the possibility that some Revivalist cultural hygienes themselves risk symbolic violence by contradicting traditional Cornish forms that are already weakened and marginalized. Embrace of discordant Celtic models could even be said to involve Revivalists' in a kind of do-it-unto-thyself symbolic violence where elements are foregrounded and constructed to comply, even if they jar with the awkwardly ill-fitting realities of their own Cornish backgrounds. In Foucauldian terms, their discursive selections create, rather than discover, the truth and include silences or omissions. Broadly speaking, non-folkloric, Cornu-English[247] and industrially modern elements are left out of the script.

Romantic versions may interpellate insiders even—and perhaps especially—if they do not correspond to everyday reality and invented traditions and enactments of Celtishness may allow them to valorize themselves as imaginative, creative and picturesque (commonly ascribed and elected Celtic features), as well as hard-done-by and victimized with a ready-made excuse for failure. Paradoxically, they may simultaneously accept de-valorizing ideas about their home culture, internalizing the idea that its distinctions are inferior both to prevalent English cultures and to Revivalism. Indeed, embracing neo-tradition can involve a negotiated personal reading of Cornishness that partially accepts the inferiority of a parental background .[248] Rejected elements can conveniently be branded "English", removing awareness of contradiction, betrayal or hypocrisy. For example, a neo-traditional musician told me he

247 *Cornu-English*: Forms of English traditionally spoken in Cornwall.
248 Stuart Hall (1980 [1973]), "Encoding/decoding", *op. cit.*

was, "fed up with pasties-and-cream, tea-and-bun culture",—an easily-understood reaction to domestic Cornishness, except that he also disparaged local men as "good old boys" and "pards" (an address introduced by miners returning from the American West), parodying their accents and alleged attachment to "boring old crap", which evidently meant everything that constituted their established Cornishness, including how they behaved, spoke and viewed the world.

Robert Morton Nance's "Cornish culture"

Revivalist and nationalist discourses distinguish between "culture in Cornwall" and "Cornish culture", a differentiation made by the language revivalist, artist and nautical historian, Robert Morton Nance (1873-1959)[249] who, as the Movement's most influential twentieth-century figure, looked forward to a "New Cornwall" where present-day tradition and past cultural elements would be fused with native creativity and imagination to build a reinvigorated culture with the Cornish language at its heart.[250] When Nance made this distinction he was essentially opposing a, "continuous tradition of culture that is natively Cornish",[251] to "English" cultures that enjoyed legitimacy and attention at its expense. He thus consolidated older discourses of nationality and laid down somewhat binary terms of reference by which Revivalism still operates. Nance believed that Cornish national consciousness needed to be reawakened and acknowledge kinship with the rest of the Celtic world. "Cornish culture" had to be rescued, championed and disseminated by, "a movement to keep the Cornishness of Cornwall".[252] In his keynote statement, "What We Stand For", Nance eschewed anti-Englishness and cited "snobbery" as the only enemy, revealing his wish to raise the common worth of the Cornish as an affirmative action. Here was

249 Robert Morton Nance, "Cornish Culture", in *The Cornish Review*, no.1, (April 1949), p.3; R.M. Nance, "What we stand for", in *Old Cornwall*, vol. 1, no. 1, (April 1925), pp. 3-6.

250 Cf. Peter W. Thomas and Derek R. Williams (eds.) (2007), *Setting Cornwall on its Feet: Robert Morton Nance, 1873-1959*, London: Francis Boutle Publishers, p.26.

251 Nance (1925), *op. cit.*

252 *Ibid.*

a democratic vision that envisaged "Cornish for All"[253] and valued down-to-earth culture (stories, recipes, songs, work practices, crafts etc.), that were to be gathered from ordinary folk who were the respected custodians of an oral tradition. The role of recording and retrieving this knowledge was undertaken by a newly-established *Federation of Old Cornwall Societies* whose motto, *"Cuntelleugh an brewyon us gesys na vo kellys travyth"* ('Gather the crumbs that are left that nothing be lost') expressed the purpose of just-in-time safe-guarding.[254] This was not to be latter-day antiquarianism or top-down salvage ethnography but had to "appeal to all sections of [...] people" and include "anything that brings Cornish people together".[255] "Gathering the crumbs" was the task of everyone and local "recorders" collated the information. Nance's networks, his contacts amongst fishermen and his prolific production of songs, plays, stories and language resources are all testimony to his inclusiveness and the project did indeed attract support. His artistic, proto-socialist outlook, close to the Arts and Crafts Movement,[256] led him to produce what Tim Saunder's calls the "Nancian Synthesis",[257] a marriage between the Cornishness of everyday life and romantic Celticism, "Between Henry Jenner's other-wordly vision, and the detailed recording of living conditions by A. K. Hamilton Jenkin".[258]

As an interventionalist foundation for "useable culture", Nance's project is notable for the way in which it envisages modern tradition, including much that was industrial, sitting comfortably alongside customs, folklore, language and the arts in a comprehensive

253 Robert Morton Nance (1958 [1929]), *Cornish for All: A Guide to Unified Cornish*, 3rd edition, Federation of Old Cornwall Societies.

254 The first Old Cornwall Society was established in St. Ives in 1920 and the Federation in 1925.

255 Robert Morton Nance, letter to the *St. Ives Times*, 30 January 1920, cited in Brian Coombes, "Keeping Cornwall Cornish: Robert Morton Nance and the Federation of Old Cornwall Societies" in P. W. Thomas and D. R. Williams (eds.) (2007), p. 226.

256 Discussions of Nance's milieu with Sharon Lowenna. See references to Walter Crane in, Peter W. Thomas and Derek R. Williams (eds.) (2007), *op. cit.*, p. 40 p. 306.

257 Tim Saunders (1983), *op. cit.*

258 *Ibid.* p. 257.

expression of Cornishness. There is recognition of the need to connect with lived experience and be relevant and appealing to a wide public. Thus, in addition to reviving Cornish, the emergent movement would, "include everybody [...] by means of Cornish dialect speech."[259] Nance's synthesis was meant to inform a national project of cultural renewal and inspire "conjectural restorations"[260] and creative inventions. In admitting past, present and newly-created, components from multiple sources, he recognized Cornishness as an evolving construction that had absorbed external influences, including English ones. Like present-day constructivists he saw "continuous tradition" as a work in progress with a future that could be shaped by conscious input to reinvigorate Cornishness and carry it onwards confidently.

The "Wrong Turn"

For all its democratic, forward-looking strengths, Nance's approach held contradictions and incoherences which may explain why Revivalism has not been more successful. He retained an interest in the ancient and the medieval and privileged folklore, facilitating a lingering antiquarianism. Faced with the "relics of a failed industrialism"[261] and presented with ready-made Celtic utopias, Nance and his associates reached into the pre-industrial past and overlooked much of the present. Not least of the problems was Nance's subscription to linguistic "corruption" as a value judgment that prepared the way for arguments perpetuated in present-day language planning, where the shaping of Cornish adheres to the concept. Nance's linguistic hygiene meant that he "withdraw into a remoter past for his standards of style and vocabulary",[262] a decision Bernard Deacon calls the "Wrong Turn" because of its negative impact on the relevance of the language to the public:

This [fifteenth-century styles] guarantees that the Cornish language remains just as obscure now to the bulk of the

259 Robert Morton Nance (1925), *op. cit.*
260 See Alan Kent in P.W. Thomas and D.R. Williams (eds.) (2007), pp. 96-152.
261 Bernard Deacon, "And shall Trelawney die? The Cornish identity", in P.J. Payton (ed.) (1993), *Cornwall Since the War, op. cit.* p. 206.
262 Tim Saunders (1983), *op. cit.* p.257.

population as it was back in the 1940s when Morton Nance was practicing his elvish script on the back of invitations from his stockbrokers to purchase shares.[263]

Nance founded his "Unified Cornish" (*Kernewek Unys*) on the fourteenth-century *Ordinalia* rather than later sources that would have shown more connectedness to place-names, surnames and traditional words and phrases, still common at the time. Instead of quickly producing a popular revival, Cornish became an arcane symbol, dragged out on rare ceremonial occasions for set performances. An opportunity had been lost to emulate the short-lived experiment in bottom-up language revitalization by the Reverend Lach-Szyrma who had earlier collaborated with people in Paul and Mousehole who knew traditional words and phrases. Nance's medievalism allowed him to imagine the past as more Cornish and Celtic but it made it harder to associate the language with the present-day and arguably rendered it esoteric and beyond reach for all but the intellectually-inclined. The impressively fluent speaker, John Pengilly, described Unified Cornish as:

> invented in the 1920s by middle-class hobbyists, it broke all links with genuine Cornish. [...] it was designed to look quaintly mediaeval on paper but it was utterly useless for learning the sounds [and] fits in with modern life about as well as would the mediaeval monks who wrote the plays on which it is based.[264]

Pengilly's remarks echo Saunders' criticism of "pseudo-archaism"[265] and the claim that Unified Cornish, "plays the part of an unrecoverable past through its own impenetrability."[266] The

---

263 Bernard Deacon, "The Unimportance of being Cornish in Cornwall", Address to the Institute of Cornish Studies, 24 November 2012.

264 John Pengilly, in *Cornish Scene* (1987), vol. 2, no. 4, p.24.

265 Tim Saunders cited in Philip Payton, "The Ideology of Language Revival in Modern Cornwall", in R. Black, W. Gillies & R. Ó Maolalaigh (eds.), *Celtic Connections: Proceedings of the Tenth International Congress of Celtic Studies*, vol.1, *Language, Literature, History, Culture*, Edinburgh, (1999), pp.395-424 (p.404).

266 Tim Saunders (1983), *op. cit.* p. 257.

allegation is that, "Nance succeeded in paralysing Cornish for over forty years".[267] In 1985, after sixty years of Unified Cornish, the number of competent speakers was below fifty and most Cornish people had never heard it spoken. In effect, Nance's selections stored up trouble, laying the foundations of "The Spelling Wars" that have raged since the 1980s. It is not the purpose to discuss the arguments here—because they have been well-rehearsed elsewhere—but briefly, the disagreements involve several markedly different visions of the language, more-or-less corresponding to discursive formations and differing ideas of identity.[268] Corresponding linguistic hygienes affect how well language activity accords with popular Cornish identifications and disagreements arouse passions that take them far beyond heated academic debate and reasoned argument to produce personal attacks, *ad hominem*. Acrimony undermines trust and friendship and weakens the bonds and networks needed to build a speech community and lasting division has been a common reason for not learning or for dropping out. Squabbles have spilt over into all areas of cultural and political activity and speakers have been diverted from learning, teaching and social engagement.

There is nevertheless much that is positive in this ferment. All of the challenges share the desire to render Cornish usable as a present-day language for anybody who wishes to learn. They come from pent-up frustrations with its "quaint and archaïc"[269] presentation and could only have emerged from a generation that had successfully battled through the hurdles and started to build a speech community. Ken George's "Common Cornish" (*Kernewek Kemmyn*) tried, with some success, to make the language easier to learn by putting the practical function of orthography—as a representation of pronunciation—before non-functional, aesthetic form. Unfortunately though, its over-reliance on this ignored symbolic meanings that can be connoted by form, thus obscuring connections with tradition. While it embraced modernity, it adhered to a medieval

267 *Ibid.*

268 See Philip Payton, "The Ideology of Language Revival in Modern Cornwall", *op. cit*, note 405; Nicholas Williams (2006), *Writings on Revived Cornish*, Westport, Co. Mayo: Evertype.

269 Nicholas Williams (2006), *Cornish Today: An Examination of the Revived Language*, Third edition. Westport, Co. Mayo: Evertype, p. xvii.

base and an intensified Celtic purism that largely rejected historical hybridity. The more restrained "Unified Cornish Revised" (*Kernowek Unys Amendys*) differed in adopting a sixteenth-century foundation and a descriptivist approach that accepted historic loanwords, but still did little to strengthen associations with tradition. Although most speakers use varieties based on Middle Cornish, the desire to reverse the "wrong turn" motivated a small group in the mid 1980s to turn to the early modern period (c.1620-1780) and codify "Revived Modern Cornish", , originally called "Late Cornish" by detractors, though now generally called "Revived Late Cornish" more neutrally. The project started again as though the revival to date had not taken place and it operated its own linguistic hygienes. Richard Gendall, its main researcher, argued that its closeness to place-names and survivals in Cornu-English linked to the present and he saw it as fitting the general tenure of Cornishness.[270] He proposed a "warts-and-all" embrace as, "no make-believe, theoretical or nostalgic pseudo-Celtic reconstruction but Cornish as it really was, as it was used by Cornish farmers, miners and fishermen."[271] These differing perspectives came together in the fraught "Process to produce a Standard Written Form", which, under the direction of Maga, engaged Cornish speakers of all persuasions and thrashed out a standard, issued in 2008—intended to be "an orthography that is fit for the twenty-first century".[272] This Standard Written Form (SWF) is the subject of continuing controversy[273] but has already facilitated new collaborations and allowed work in schools. The fact is though, that it has been achieved only after years of intense activity and effort, at the expense of limited resources and with the counsel and arbitration of a commission of outside linguists—all of which is fall-out from the "wrong turn". Even now, Nance's worthy intentions of an inclusive renaissance have only been partially realized.

270 e.g. Richard Gendall (1991), *A Student's Grammar of Modern Cornish*, Menheniot: Cornish Language Council, Preface.

271 Richard Gendall, in *Carn*, vol. 63, (1988), The Celtic League.

272 Communications between members of Maga Corpus Panel.

273 See "Problems with the Standard Written Form (SWF)" in Nicholas Williams (2016) *The Cornish Consonantal System: Implications for the Revival*. Portlaoise: Evertype. Errors and inconsistencies identified in the SWF were examined in 2008 by a group called "Spellyans", and resulted in a compatible but less "leaky" orthography known as Standard Cornish (*Kernowek Standard*).

Positively speaking, Nance's broad vision, beyond language, embraced much of the everyday culture that the Cornish in the first half of the twentieth century would have considered theirs and it has been developed by socially engaged strands that have widened participation and produced a diversified Movement with pervasive effects. Nearly all of the means by which an embattled Cornish community attempts to valorize, mobilize and articulate itself ultimately descend from Nance's project to some degree. Less positively, Nance's aesthetics have left an opening for others who are condescending about the popular Cornishness that he valued, seemingly seeing core features as antithetical to their cherished versions. This tendency may be symbolically traced to the far-right Henry Jenner, often cast with enormous overstatement as a patriarchal founder of the language revival. Jenner was hostile to the Methodist, egalitarian Cornishness he found on retiring to Cornwall, even suggesting in his late years that continental fascism might be needed if "King Labour" took root.[274] Although born at St Columb where his father was an Anglican curate, he had no Cornish family origins, only marrying the Cornish writer, Kitty Lee Rawlings, in later life. Before retiring to Hayle in 1909, he had worked in the Department of Ancient Manuscripts at the British Museum[275] and was a Tory, a Jacobite and staunch monarchist, and a converted Tridentine Catholic who speculated about Celtic Christian rites and druidism. In short, he could hardly have been further from the everyday concerns and culture of most people nor less in tune with Nance's inclusiveness. This is not to infer that a corresponding tradition took root but the attitudes of Jenner and some close associates, nevertheless influenced the tone, taken-for-granted wisdoms and centres of interest of a strand within Revivalism (e.g. ceremony, saints and archangels, and antiquities) and have left a mark, if not a stain, on current discourses.[276] Some perpetuate a presumption against much of everyday Cornish culture that

274 See Jenner's papers in The Courtney Library, Truro. Discussed with Sharon Lowenna. Jenner died in 1934.

275 Derek R. Williams (2004), *Henry and Katharine Jenner: A Celebration of Cornwall's Culture, Language and Identity*. Francis Boutle Publishers.

276 Sharon Lowenna (2004), *op. cit.*

sometimes leads to them being treated as not Celtic enough to be of worth.

Useful invented tradition

A feature of ethnic revitalization movements generally is that, like nation-building projects, they create new cultural forms and symbols which may endure as "invented traditions". Cornish Revivalism is no exception. Numerous new forms have been produced using combinations of old and new, indigenous and imported elements which are interpreted within the discursive formations of cultural restoration, Cornish nationalism and Pan-Celticism. Eric Hobsbawm has observed that, "Where the old ways are alive, traditions need be neither revived nor invented",[277] but the Cornish Revival has a further complication. Its inventiveness certainly responds to real loss of traditions and involves creative nostalgia, but in addition to losses that have a basis in fact, there is an imagined loss of elements that are needed for attainment of prescribed Celtic models. The productive imagination that Pan-Celticism engages inevitably leads to re-imagining a fictional past that leads Revivalists to invent and even to believe in forms with no earlier existence—at least, not as imagined. Some, like the "invented traditions" discussed by Eric Hobsbawm, Terrence Ranger and company,[278] have become so established that they seem to have always been there. Invented traditions can quickly seem timeless and spontaneous so that we overlook their origins and they usually serve an ideological purpose. Those of states convey supporting myths, including the idea of the nation itself, and may connote multiple ideas which coalesce to form ideologies or mythologies.[279] Some, like those surrounding national sport, monarchy, democratic government, work and military prowess, can also be part of Althusser's "ideological state apparatus" (I.S.A.)[280] and support hegemony. Earlier it was suggested that the Cornish Movement represents a counter-hegemonic, "ideological

277 Eric Hobsbawm and Terence Ranger (eds.) (1983, 1989), *The Invention of Tradition*, Cambridge: Cambridge University Press.
278 ibid.
279 Roland Barthes (1957), *Mythologies*, Paris: Editions de Seuil.
280 Louis Althusser (1971), "On Ideology and Ideological State Apparatuses", in *Lenin and Philosophy and Other Essays*, New York: Monthly Review Press.

state*less* apparatus" and accordingly, invented traditions contribute to it, maintaining and recreating mythologies that are not otherwise mediated because of a dearth of Cornish institutions. As Michael Billig demonstrates, the communication of national identities, unity and purpose may take the form of practices and representations that we may not notice but which contribute to "banal nationalism".[281] Cornish invented traditions—as intervention—similarly contribute to mythologies and discursive formations. Thus they either support or contradict particular narratives and contribute to or detract from collective cultural capital.

Over time inventions and revivals can come to be seen as more important than the pre-existing culture that inspired them and this is what appears to have happened amongst Revivalists. The language revival and (re)invented traditions and symbols came about because there was already a deeply-rooted identity and culture but now Revivalism itself has come to be seen as comprising Cornish culture. Caroline Vink notes that, invented tradition is employed to enhance ethnic claims and that, in time, elements of that tradition are defended as central and legitimate aspects of identity.[282] Less grounded invented Cornish traditions could be said to fit the derogatory designations, "fakelore", and "folklorismus" which were coined by the anthropologist and folklore specialist, Richard Dorson[283] to distinguish between "genuine" traditions and "ideologically driven" folkloric inventions. Such accusations have often been leveled at the easy target of Ernest Morton Nance's post-war invention of a Cornish National Tartan, a replacement for the black Cornish Kilt invented by the eccentric occultist, Louis Duncombe-Jewell (1866-1947).[284] Like other inventions based on

281 Michael Billig (1995), *Banal Nationalism*, London, Thousand Oaks, New Delhi: Sage.

282 Caroline Vink, *op. cit.* p113.

283 Richard Dorson, "Is Folklore a Discipline?", in *Folklore*, vol. 84, no. 3, (Autumn, 1973), pp 177-205, Taylor and Francis: www.jstor.org/stable/1259723 (Accessed 15 December 2011); R. Dorson (1976), "Folklore and Fakelore: Essays Toward a Discipline of Folk Studies", Cambridge, Mass: Harvard University Press.

284 See Sharon Lowenna (2004), *op. cit.*; Marion Löffler (2000), *A Book of Mad Celts: John Wickens and the Celtic Congress of Caernarfon 1904*, Llandysul: Gomer Press.

Celtic themes, it has been branded kitsch,[285] but for all their offence against prim taste and authenticity, widespread uses of Cornish tartanry show that instances of Kelto-kitsch can provide some of the most useful symbols for communicating identification. The wearing of Cornish tartan at weddings and rugby matches and in ubiquitous, everyday displays on ties, scarves, skirts and assorted hats is proof that an invented item can be adopted within a fairly short time. What is more, individuals do not have to believe they are real revivals in order for this to work, meaning that lack of historic authenticity does not always detract from symbolic usefulness. At Murdoch Day in Redruth, two brothers who wore kilts with heavy work boots and tee-shirts advertising their scaffolding firm knew they were an invention but had found a playful way to display their sentiment. Such uses are close to Umberto Eco's identification of "authentic fakes"[286] which appeal to the senses and the emotions without us having to believe they are traditional. While there is a qualitative difference between the conscious creations of ethnic projects and the intergenerational transmission of age-old practices, the distinction between "invented" and "genuine" is contestable and, in any case, items do not have to be traditional to be useable. So-called fakelore can complement pre-existing cultures and be fully incorporated with social benefits. Revivalist innovators point out that all traditions are made-up and ask why there should be "one rule for Cornish culture and another for English culture".[287] The principle may even be extended to the invention of new vocabulary in language planning:

> [E]very modern language is "made-up" to some extent: whenever a new concept appears in the world, it is necessary to have a word or phrase to denote it. Why should this process be in order for English and not for Cornish?[288]

285 See Jonathan Howlett, "Putting the Kitsch into Kernow", in P.J. Payton (ed.), *Cornish Studies*, vol.12, (2004), pp. 30-60.

286 See Umberto Eco (1986), *Travels in Hyperreality*, New York: Harcourt Brace Jovanovich; (or) (1987), *Faith in Fakes: Travels in Hyperreality*, Picador.

287 Merv Davy at the CAVA conference, Peran Porth, October 2010.

288 Ken George (1986), *The Pronunciation and Spelling of Revived Cornish*, Torpoint: Cornish language Board, p.37.

These are reasonable questions but there remains something suggestive of dishonesty when, instead of being up-front about invention, some involved are not quite frank and cloud the waters so we cannot distinguish old from new. The intention may not be to hoodwink us but we may still be misled, as shown by this comment on the conjecturally reconstructed "Cornish bagpipes":

The pipes have likely been played in Kernow/Cornwall for at least 2000 years. I am sorry to disappoint anyone who believes incorrectly that they are a recent invention or have been 'made up'.[289]

An answer to the above questions could be that it is different for Cornish culture because ethno-cultural claims are already subject to scepticism and derision, unlike institutionalized national identities. That means that anything made-up or overly reconstructed is seized upon as proof that Cornish ethnicity is spurious, or at least that Revivalist constructions are. Even neo-Cornish, not an invented tradition, can then be assumed to be fake: "Made-up from Welsh by inbred hobbits."[290] Hostile reactions of the type, "You're just making it up to be different", and "What's wrong with being English?", are symptomatic of suspicions that there is something wilful going on that conceals the absence of a real identity. Add commodification and invented traditions start to look very much like Dorson's "commercially driven" cases of fake-lore and may give rise to greater scepticism. Jane Korey even goes as far as to speculate that Revivalists might be involved in as a post-modern exercise in consciously inventing an identity.[291]

The classic case of an invented tradition becoming central is *Gorseth Kernow*—The Gorsedd of Cornwall, the main institution of the Revivalist project. Through its honours system of bardships, it assembles a large body of cultural practitioners and community figures who comprise a high proportion of the Cornish Movement's leaders and innovators. Gorseth Kernow is thus one of very few

289 The Cornubian, accessed 3 January 2012. www.youtube.com/ watch?v=25MfD_2w3vk&feature=related,
290 Comments by a shopkeeper in Lostwithiel, August 2011.
291 Jane Korey (1992), *op. cit.*

specifically Cornish cultural institutions with far-reaching community networks and a degree of gravitas. Despite criticisms from
within the Movement, it quickly springs to mind when Revivalists
are asked to think of bodies that represent Cornishness and appears
to be very much part of the "stateless ideological apparatus"
suggested, relaying the idea of a Cornish nation:

> The Gorsedd is not political or anti-English, but we want to
> foster the self-respect of the Cornish people by making them
> regard themselves as one of the Celtic nations.[292]

Founded in 1928 to, "promote the Cornish language" and
"uphold the Celtic traditions of Cornwall", the Gorseth—with the
Old Cornwall Societies—has given rise, directly or indirectly, to the
plethora of bodies that exist for these purposes today. It has come to
be viewed by many as a tradition in its own right, as important, if
not more so, than those that first inspired its project to "maintain
the national Celtic spirit of Cornwall" and the institution and its
ceremonies are preoccupations. It derives from Edward Williams'
(alias Iolo Morganwg) invention of the Welsh Gorsedd at the end of
the eighteenth century[293] and its bards are similarly clothed in robes
inspired by imaginings of the druids and classical and orientalist
imagery. Bardic dress combines a sky-blue Romano-Greek toga and
Arab ghutra-style headdress adorned with the three-rayed *awen*
symbol invented by Williams to represent inspiration. The neo-
druidic and Arthurian repertoire is completed by beaten copper
plastrons inspired by Bronze and Iron Age torcs, a throne-like bardic
chair, a ceremonial sword representing *Calesvol* ('Excalibur'),[294] a
harp and a horn which summons the four cardinal points of the
compass: "*Kernow an Howlsedhes, eus cres?*" ('West Cornwall, is there
peace?'). Robed bards stand in a circle, matching romantic
portrayals of the druids and a "Lady of Cornwall" in quasi-medieval
garb bears the Grand Bard a bouquet.

292 Robert Morton Nance, *The Western Morning News*, 21 September 1928.
293 See Prys Morgan, "From a Death to a View: The Hunt for the Welsh Past in
    the Romantic Period", in Hobsbawm and Ranger (eds.) (1983, 1989), *op. cit.*
294 So spelt in *Bewnans Ke* (The Life of Kea.), c.1560. (NLW MS 23849D).

All of the imagery corresponds to the romantic period of Celtic revivalism and may connote mystical, natural, imaginative and creative Celtishness, thus supporting the ascribed models identified as problematic, and the scope for controversial readings does not stop there. The ceremony has often been taken to be neo-pagan, esoteric and in keeping with a magical, spiritual Cornwall traversed by lay-lines and the flight paths of witches and fairy folk. When a small Gorsedd was held at a Cornish gathering in the American Mid-West, bystanders reportedly compared it to the Klu-Klux Klan.[295] Some of the wording and musical content was created by Jenner's associates and reflects preferences which, despite modifications, produce the feeling of high church liturgy. Gorseth Kernow's invented origins are well-known but there is still insistence on revival:

This tradition, following that of Wales, was revived in Cornwall in 1928 at a Gorsedd, or meeting of Bards, at Boscawen-un [sic].[296]

The claim is founded on the Welsh Triads'[297] reference to "Beisgawen" in Dumnonia as the site of one of the *Gorsesddau* of Britain, and it permits statements that are sparing of recorded fact:

In ancient Celtic times, Bards […] had places of high honour at important assemblies regularly held at venerated sites throughout Britain, one of which was the stone circle at Boscawen-un…[298]

This emphasis on revival infers that there is something wrong with honest invention and recalls observations by the accomplished Cornish language writer, Peggy Pollard in 1947, that, "There are those who pretend to take a poor view of the Cornish Gorseth

295 Discussed with Amy Hale.
296 www.gorsethkernow.org.uk/english/history.htm (Accessed 3 Spetember 2012); The usual place-name spelling is Boscawen-Ûn.
297 Rachel Bromwich (ed. Trans.) (2006), *Trioedd Ynys Prydein: The Welsh Triads*, 3rd Edition, Cardiff: University of Wales Press.
298 *Ibid.*

because it was inaugurated in 1928 A.D. instead of B.C. [...] All things must have a beginning."[299] As Hobsbawm and Ranger show, many successful traditions are consciously invented, so perhaps Charles Thomas was right fifty years ago when he argued that the Gorsedd served a useful purpose:

> The uninformed regard the entire Old Cornwall and Gorsedd movement as a waste of time, bogus to the core and simply an excuse for an annual escapist junket of picturesque appearance. [...] the business of the movement is to see that the uninformed become the informed...[300]

In other words, the benefits of a body that promotes Cornish culture outweigh any negative visual connotations. When Thomas made his remarks, all things seemed possible. After all, the Cornish project needed institutions and the Gorseth could have risen to the occasion and developed its work in any number of useful directions. In the event, it has had an immeasurable effect but most of this has been indirect, resulting from informal networks and motivations that spring from it, rather than works that it has undertaken as an organization. Its imagery does, despite everything, inspire a body of Cornish people, inviting the suggestion that all it needs to be more widely relevant is a sophisticated, visual overhaul and a stronger sense of proactive engagement.

Invented traditions may be treated as more Cornish than Cornish. I witnessed a striking occurrence in a pub at Four Lanes near Redruth when a musician, irritated by noisy indifference to his "Celtic jazz fusion", snapped, "I'm giving you your fucking culture here". In reality, it was not their culture since they had never heard anything like it and were clearly not enthralled, so what he should have said is, "I'm giving you what I think your culture ought to be". Occasionally the Revival's players score home goals in pursuit of cultural hygiene. For instance, a grouping of cultural organizations declined an application from representatives of Cornish rugby on the grounds that it is "not indigenous culture", despite being at the

299 Peggy Pollard, *Cornwall*, 1947.
300 Charles Thomas, "An Dasserghyans Kernewek", at the Celtic Congress, 16-20 April, 1963, in *Old Cornwall*, vol. 6, no. 5.

core of popular ideas of what is Cornish. This baffling tactical failure demonstrates how Celtic models can get in the way. Trelawny's Army, the supporters' club, already makes assertive, symbolic uses of the Cornish language and Revivalist symbols and in 1989, 1991 and 1992, the county finals at Twickenham produced the largest ever Cornish gatherings for any purpose, in what took on the proportions of an epic pilgrimage and briefly turned rugby into the main channel for an outpouring of pent-up frustration and solidarity. As journalists observed, the supporters turned rugby into, "a statement, if not of Celtic nationhood, then at least of their distinct identity."[301] Rugby football, brought to Cornwall by returning public school boys c.1900, was quickly transformed as the levelling sport of miners, farm labourers and the middle-classes alike, coming to embody egalitarianism as a core Cornish value.[302] For a prescriptive set of Revivalists, however, the fact that it was introduced disqualifies it from being "indigenous" while innovations that conform to generic Celtishness, but have far less basis in tradition, are enthusiastically embraced.

The fact that Cornish tradition has long acquired outside elements and re-defined them, is widely understood and has been communicated by academics and informed practitioners who note the ongoing incorporation of new elements as a healthy sign of dynamism. The ongoing incorporation of practices was noted by Andrew George in the 1980s with the example of majorette bands in village carnivals, where the distinctions of those involved and the social context ensured that the activity became immediately Cornish.[303] We might question whether the same can be said of samba bands in more recent carnivals but in principal there is really nothing to stop such exotic practices becoming re-defined by Cornish people. Some innovators accordingly speak about eclecticism and point to examples as proof of growing confidence:

---

301 *The Independent*, 3 April 1989.
302 See Tom Salmon (1983), *The First Hundred Years: The Story of Rugby Football in Cornwall*, Illogan: Cornwall RFU; Kenneth Pelmear (1960), *Rugby in the Duchy, An Official History of the Game in Cornwall*, Falmouth: Cornwall RFU.
303 In B. Deacon, A. George and R. Perry (1987), *op. cit.*, p. 153.

A few years ago, people would never have done this but the young people have grown up with it [Cornish dancing] and they feel confident enough to interpret it. It's taken on a real life of its own [...] The new generation is taking it forward on its own terms.[304]

In practice, the picture is more complicated. Uninhibited eclecticism in some parts of the Revival sits alongside a kind of narrow-spectrum gathering of components in others. The admission criteria are shaped by enduring prescriptions and, just as importantly, by the tastes of participants. What this means is that activities serve to filter recruits, attracting people who share a set of tastes that corresponds to relatively stable aesthetics that they shape further. Constructivist arguments are advanced for the eclecticism of pioneers who have assembled an impressive canon of neo-Cornish dances and tunes by variously collecting, reconstructing and composing them. Some might not have ultimate origins in Cornwall, they acknowledge, but this does not mean they did not become Cornish and change in context. They cite examples from "other Celtic counties", such as the transformation of French quadrilles into Kerry sets or of English step dancing into distinctly Irish forms, and the argument is extended to new dances. This is all very open and permissive so it comes as a jolt when some of the same individuals exercise rigid prescriptivism, even falling out over the interpretation of dances that have been codified in the last thirty years and objecting to developments that have "just gone too far".[305] As with languages, participants police individual expressions (*parole*) so as to maintain the integrity of the code (*langue*)—but here the code itself is new and still being defined with reference to Pan-Celtic models. Some allegedly deviant expressions rejected may have the potential to embed neo-tradition in everyday life.

Re-symbolization: A second wrong turn?

Certain Revivalist activities, including community celebrations and revived customs, accord with overlapping counter-urban utopias,

---

304 Comments at Lowender Peran, 2010.
305 Comments directed at *Nos Lowen* dancing.

rural idylls and quests for alternative life-styles,[306] fitting aesthetics and centres of interest associated with the Cultural Turn.[307] They are not wholly informed by insider narratives and their appeal is not restricted to the indigenous Cornish. They may be (mis)appropriated and rendered more amenable to the lifestyles of some in-migrants than to the lives of most Cornish people. Preferred aesthetics and narratives within Revivalism enmesh with those of variously interested outsiders who imbue "Celtic Cornwall" and the Cornish with qualities of Otherness and interact with them in shaping culture. Some of the most pronounced imaginings come from a myriad of English "Celtophiles" for whom Cornwall is "a place of pilgrimage"[308] and the antithesis of consumer culture and modernity. For some, "Cornwall has come almost to represent a British Tibet; distinct, valued by others and threatened by an occupying territory..."[309] Discourses of Otherness support notions of traditionality, as though Celts, like Native Americans and the Sami, cease to be authentic when they innovate or embrace mass culture and modernity. What, for example, can be made of the recently invented traditions of Allantide in St Ives or the Montol Festival in Penzance? Both are conceived as community events and involve a mix of Cornish people and in-comers who broadly share a playful folkloric aesthetic. At Allantide (Halloween, All Saints), a carnival troop of masked musicians in raggle-taggle, fancy dress and hats, bedecked with greenery and ribbons, parades through St Ives with an invented 'obby 'oss, Penglaz, topped with a horse's skull. At Montol, similarly masked musicians process at night with lanterns, accompanied by "guise dancers"[310] and a magnificently presented *Arluth Muskok* or

306 E.g. C. Tims and S. Wright, DEMOS Report (2006), *op. cit.* note 34.

307 Frederick Jameson (1988), *The Cultural Turn : Selected Writings on the Postmodern 1983-1988*, London & New York: Version; cf. Peter Jackson, "Mapping Culture", in Alisdair Rogers and Heather Viles (eds.) (2003), *The Student's Companion to Geography*, 2nd Edition, Oxford: Blackwell.

308 Amy Hale, "Selling Celtic Cornwall: Challenging Markets and Meanings?", in Kevin Meethan *et al.* (eds.) (2006), *Tourism, Consumption and Representation: Narratives of Place and Self*, Wallingford Oxon and Cambridge MA: C.A.B.I. International.

309 John Lowerson cited in Amy Hale (2006), *op. cit.*

310 Alfred Kenneth Hamilton Jenkin (1934), *Cornish Homes and Customs*, London: J.M. Dent; William Botterell (1873), *Traditions and Hearthside Stories of West*

"Lord of Misrule". Both occasions provide enjoyable experiences and spectacles but they also conform to expectations of a remote but accessible Cornwall with slightly pagan traditions and a carefree lifestyle. They could not happen without imaginative recourse to recorded ingredients from Cornwall's past; Allantide was an eighteenth-century observance that involved gifts of apples, and guise dancing, masks, decked hats and finery were all involved in Advent traditions, some of which were "like an Italian carnival"[311]—so, to that degree, these events are faithful to the record. Even Montol, an attested Cornish word for the winter solstice, is probably a reasonable name for a new pre-Christmas festival. The notion of revival underpins the inventions while "fake-lore" is also present.

Authenticity and invention are not the concerns here though. What matters is that, for the first time, Revivalist production is involved in competing sets of meaning that have an enormous bearing on whether or not events of this kind will prove useable for revitalizing Cornishness in the longer term. They might well but the alternative is that they will be appropriated in a subcultural *bricolage*[312] that is not part of Nance's project to strengthen a "cultural tradition that is definably Cornish". These and other activities could go either way, either becoming more connected with a wider Cornish community and the Cornish Movement's core project or becoming part of a counter-urban lifestyle. Such events also illustrate that Cornish people sometimes share counter-urban tastes and lifestyle aspirations making it hard to differentiate between how undisputed insiders imagine and value cultural items and how outsiders do so. They are another reminder that insider and outsider discourses are not tidily opposed but are entangled, interrelated and nuanced by gender, age, social class and individual experience. There are many ways to be an insider and there are degrees of insideness. Pick-and-mix innovations, as post-modern *bricolage* bring natives and in-migrants together constructively in creating leisure activities and lifestyles from multiple Cornish and Non-Cornish elements which may acquire new meanings and social uses. All of this said, there are, nevertheless, distinctly Cornish discursive

Cornwall, Penzance.

311 A.K. Hamilton Jenkin: op cit., mentioned by individuals involved.

312 cf. Dick Hebdidge (1979), *Subculture: The Meaning of Style*, London: Routledge.

formations that have hitherto defined Revivalist priorities and allowed deeply-felt sentiments, which are not always articulated verbally, to find emotional outlets. A suspicion, for further exploration, is that these have been undergoing rapid transformations since the 1980s, bringing about a re-symbolization of elements that may detract from their relevance, accessibility and social usefulness for some sections of society while making them appealing as pastimes for others. One of the things that appears to be happening is that activities that were created for Revivalist motives in the second half of the twentieth century are being re-shaped by the "alternative", counter-urban and leisure-orientated motives of the "New Cornish" who constitute a growing proportion of participants. At the same time, indigenous Cornish participants may now be less likely to relate activities symbolically to political nationalism or social concerns and more likely to emphasize the value of the activities themselves. It is suggested that this is facilitated by Revivalists' efforts to make activities seem safe, respectable and inclusive, rather than dangerous, extreme and exclusive. A possibility is that certain scenes have become distanced from typically Cornish "structures of feeling" and that a "Second Wrong Turn" is underway. Some neo-traditions are, in effect, ceasing to be Revivalist in any meaningful sense, becoming simple leisure pursuits that are subcultural rather than ethnocultural. Activities that represent *past times* for some are—instead or as well—*pastimes* for others who are less concerned by maintaining a Cornish community. At many events involving neo-traditional music, in-migrants outnumber Cornish people and conversations reveal that the activities are important to them, yet there is an indefinable quality to discussions that recalls other part-time, subcultural activities. Although the scene holds the promise of becoming embedded in an indigenous social context and allowing non-Cornish recruits to become immersed in wider Cornish culture, it risks becoming compartmentalized as a counter-urban leisure pursuit. Indeed some events wholly lack the behavioural and embodied distinctions—acquired through culturalization—that characterize traditional Cornishness.

The suspicion must be that some Revivalist activities fit the picturesque expectations that drive tourism and counter-urbanization, supplying folkloric traditions to support urban imaginings of country life. Some offer safe, easily-acquired and superficial performances of Cornishness as a substitute for the deeper acquisitions of insiders. In this respect they contrast with the comprehensive cultural acquisitions encountered amongst working-class in-migrants who have engaged intimately and less self-consciously with Cornish people in their places of work and leisure. Surface-deep, subcultural acquisition does not embrace these traditional distinctions with their potential to cast individuals as uneducated, rustic and working-class. Thus, "wanna-be Celts" can build a social life around invented traditions without further engagement. In Brittany I heard the expression "celtes de cœur"[313] and saw how outsiders can dip into Breton dancing and traditional music without adapting further to the culture of the community. To gain membership of Cornwall's burgeoning neo-traditional music scene, it similarly suffices to learn a few dances and tunes and navigational references are to festivals, in-scene figures and groups, not inter-generational stories and knowledge.

New activities may be defined by specific groups before they are embedded in community practice, thus establishing customary meanings that restrict subsequent participation, at least in the short term. An example is *nos lowen* dancing, created in the late 1990s. Far from being fake-lore, the *nos lowen* ('happy night') was conceived as an upfront innovation. Neo-traditional dancing had, until then, been exclusively presented in the *troyl* format, modeled in the 1970s on the lines of the Scottish céilidh and Irish céilí. The inventors of the *nos lowen* braved criticisms from adherents to the self-referential norms of "Cornish Dancing" and found inspiration in creative fusions of traditional music with rock, jazz and other influences in Brittany. There, the similarly named *fest noz* is a widespread feature of life which, in December 2012, was inscribed on UNESCO's list of "Intangible Cultural Heritage". The aim of *nos lowen* was to create a similarly accessible and socially pervasive activity and attract a youthful public. The architects hoped it would be positively associated with non-Revivalist dynamics such as surfing, gig rowing and

---

313 Cf., Marion Bowman, "Cardiac Celts: images of the Celts in contemporary British paganism", in Graham Harvey and Charlotte Hardman (eds.), *Paganism Today*, London: Thorsons, pp. 242-251.

mainstream dance cultures. By good fortune, it came in the wake of rave and trance and coincided with a fashion for "world music". The Afro Celt Sound System had launched its first album (1996) fusing Irish and African music in electronic dance rhythms so the *nos lowen* concept was timely. Its music was punchy and rhythmically insistent and serpent-like dances with simple neo-traditional steps were devised for ease. Poster designs reflected contemporary youth cultures and in next to no time there was a regular following. So how successful has it become, some twenty or so years later? That depends upon which criteria are applied. *Nosow lowen* now happen all over Cornwall and new bands have emerged. The name has entered the vocabulary of Revivalists and some events are well attended. For all this success though, it has yet to become embedded within the popular culture of the Cornish, young or otherwise. A partial and controversial explanation is that the initial following was disproportionately middle-aged, non-Cornish and "arty", lacking social networks that reached into the native working class. The dispositions and attitudes of participants shaped the scene visually and socially so that it was defined, not as a cool space for the young Cornish, fresh from a day of surfing, but as part of an identifiably "alternative", leisure-orientated lifestyle. Such accounts appear to contradict the pro-position/proposition that conscious Cornish cultures may be employed for community resilience but the difficulties highlighted relate to context and discourse, not to the activities themselves. Targeting the problems is about reflecting with the understanding that context can be changed. Thus, neo-traditions like *nos lowen* may be actively steered in preferred directions.

It is hypothesized that where the usefulness of practice is reduced, this is sometimes because of tenets and aesthetics that circulate discursively and produce discordant cultural hygienes. Where these clash with popular Cornishness, the frequently-stated aim of "promoting Cornish Culture"—part of Revivalist rhetoric—risks further devaluing identities that do not have reference to the Revivalist project. Generic Celtic models may lead to activities being presented as "the real thing" before having the embedded context and participation that would afford grass-roots endorsement. Prescription can, furthermore, lead to reactions, such as those of a

Cornish decorator in his forties who described some participants at the Golowan festival as "Corn-wallies" or of a St Just barman who thought performers at Lafrowda Day were, "play-actors who think they're more Cornish". Prescriptions can indeed be imposed as better-than-Cornish, underlining the perceived inferiority of Cornish cultures that, because the indigenous middle-class is reduced, are associated with the working-class. This risks a double illegitimacy whereby not only do Cornish people have low cultural capital in respect to the prevalent/dominant culture (homogenized as "English" in reductionist accounts), but in addition they are not properly Cornish because they do not act out the Celtic script of cultural hygienes. For young adults involved in Revivalism, the back reference is not necessarily to the near, known culture of parents— Nance's "continuous tradition"[314]—but to histories of a distant past as semi-fictional post-memory. Imagining identity is thus relatively unbound by inter-generational narratives that are anchored in the facts (real or idealized) of the past and this leaves a vacant stage upon which the supposed ethnic culture of unknown predecessors may be performed. Some of the acts are unrecognizable to the inconvenient memory of elders but they are wishfully and sincerely upheld as having had a former existence. Many conform to ascribed versions of Celtishness as pre-modern, imaginative, intuitive, emotional, spiritual and disorganized.

In raising the above concerns it is easy to forget to underline the numerous instances of strong community engagement within the same scenes and activities. *Bagas Crowd* (Fiddle Group) is a large group of people of mixed ages and backgrounds who gather at well-organized and attended (around 35 participants at any one time) fortnightly work-shops for fiddlers and other neo-traditional musicians. The leader, Frances Bennett, aims to spread music in the wider community and works hard to make this happen. Sessions are held in rooms at Threemilestone Methodist Church so that musicians rub shoulders with people at a regular coffee morning. The "New Cornish" by far outnumber natives and have a similar profile to the musicians of English folk clubs but this does not stop the Cornish present from viewing the activity as theirs. Just as

314 Robert Morton Nance (1925), *op. cit.*

importantly, the participants of all backgrounds take the music out into the community where it supports a wide range of events that bring people together in friendship. They are also likely to have been inspired by neo-traditional dance-based events such as the troyl and nos lowen. The yearly Tom Bawcock's Eve (23rd December) in Mousehole is another such occasion. This community celebration was elaborated during the 1980s and 90s from low-key festivities which had already been reshaped by early Revivalists, building upon a fading tradition[315] by recycling and adding elements, including an old wedding march with new Cornu-English words by Nance.[316] Recent innovations have taken this further, creating a high-profile event where new elements sit comfortably alongside older ones. A lantern parade, in the style of the locally-based Kneehigh Theatre, has been added with processional music from multiple sources played in a folk style and traditional Cornish carols (*Hark the Glad Sound, Lo the Eastern Sages Rise, Hark what Music…*) are sung on the quay with the participation of local choirs. Mousehole's celebrated Christmas Lights—a spectacular display depicting boats and seasonal themes—provides a back-drop. What had been a fading local story about a fisherman saving Mousehole from starvation has thus become assured as a participatory festival. Alan Kent cites sceptical older locals who believe that the celebrations have been invented by incomers[317] but in reality its architects were mainly Cornish, even if some were not from Mousehole, and their desire was to reinvigorate community life. It involves the school, local choirs, the RNLI, clubs and a broad cross-section of the population, bringing natives and in-migrants together in a pre-Christmas bonding exercise that supports collective memory. Of course, individuals imagine the event differently and tourism cashes in, but it contributes to solidarity and shows that innovation can enhance tradition and respond to change.

---

315 Robert Morton Nance, *Old Cornwall*, (1927)

316 Song published in Ralph Dunstan, *Cornish Dialect and Folk Songs*, (1932).

317 Alan Kent, "From Ingraine to Callin' 'ome Mouzel: Two Paradigms of Memory, Language and Literature in Cornwall", (Prepublication copy: 2012); Discussion with Alan Kent (April, 2012)

Chapter 5

"Proper Cornish": Revivalism and Residual Tradition

It has been suggested that there is discordance between certain Revivalist cultural hygienes and traditional identity constructions that renders the latter doubly illegitimate, firstly in relation to prevalent/dominant cultures and secondly with regard to prescribed ideas of Celtishness. One purpose of this chapter is therefore to further explore this incongruence and consider whether it is possible to fuse Revivalist and non-Revivalist strands usefully. It has also been proposed that Revivalist cultures are undergoing re-symbolization as part of a subcultural, counter-urban lifestyle. The discussion accordingly has an eye to whether the "wrong turn" of earlier Revivalists and the "second wrong turn" identified can be addressed so that the inclusive, grass-roots aspects of Nance's project may be salvaged and made more relevant and effective for the social and emotional uses discussed. The notion of *habitus* is proposed as a framework for relating the uses of culture to multiple forms of capital and to a multidimensional group identity.

Without an ethnographic foundation and a sense of history it is hard to elaborate discussion or consider intervention, so this chapter begins with a brief sketch of a non-Revivalist cultural continuum that, internal heterogeneity notwithstanding, has hitherto constituted widely recognized ideas of Cornishness. Its past trajectory is described using perspectives from Cornish historiography allowing tentative suggestions to be made about the present context. This cultural continuum encompasses received and common-sense notions of Cornishness which are referred to variously as "popular", "grass-roots", "proper", "old-style", "working-class", "fitty",[318] "genuine" and "traditional" by insiders. These problematic names

318 Cornu-English *fitty* means, "appropriate", "fitting".

all identify a changing, far from uniform culture that nevertheless carries with it a sense of continuity and unity with a long past. It is a construction that, for all its earlier origins and subsequent developments, "was transformed in the crucible of industrialization",[319] so appropriately it is in describing the vigorous industrial society of the mid nineteenth century that Philip Payton coined the name "Classic Cornishness"[320] to describe what he reasonably views as its historic zenith, a period defined by confidence, innovation and the creation of institutions. Although it would be inaccurate to give precise dates for an evolving construction, it can be said to have provided a coherent, continuous and defined culture from c.1800 until the 1950s, despite the boom and bust of mining fortunes and the emergence of Celticism.[321] By the beginning of this period, a "first wave" of what Bernard Deacon calls "Methodist-mining culture" had taken shape in West Cornwall and this developed further in a "second wave" of change from c.1870 to 1920s.[322] In the 1950s its features still marked the lives of most Cornish people in a form that we could reasonably call Late Classic Cornishness. Throughout this period it formed a cultural identity that was easily recognized by others (notably by visitors and in the overseas destinations of emigrants) as well as by the Cornish themselves and was described by commentators, even emerging in novels by native writers and in Australian newspaper cartoons.[323] It retained much that was rural and agricultural and incorporated earlier elements, including those centuries-old traditions that appeal to Revivalists, such as Cornish

319 Bernard Deacon, "'The Hollow Jarring of the Distant Steam Engine': Images of Cornwall between West Barbary and Delectable Duchy", in E. Westland (ed.)(1997), *Cornwall, The Cultural Construction of Place.*

320 Philip Payton (1992) *op. cit.*; cf. Bernard Deacon (2004), *The Cornish Family*, p.189.

321 See Bernard Deacon (1997) *op. cit.*

322 Bernard Deacon (1993), "And shall Trelawney die? The Cornish identity", in P.J. Payton (ed.), *Cornwall Since the War: The Contemporary History of a European Region*, Redruth: Dyllansow Truran and Institute of Cornish Studies, p. 205.

323 See Alan M. Kent (2002), *Pulp Methodism: The Lives and Literature of Silas, Joseph and Salome Hocking, Three Cornish Novelists*, St. Austell: Cornish Hillside; Edward Bosenketh, Tin, London, 1888; Cartoons by Oswald Pryor (1881-1971) appeared in Australian magazines and newspapers, adb.anu.edu.au/biography/pryor-oswald-8127 (Accessed 2 January 2012.)

wrestling, saint's day parish feasts, crying the neck, trigging, hurling, hedge-building, festivals and survivals from Cornish;[324] but, for all that, it was modern and had technical progress and a strong work ethic at its core. While distinctly Cornish, it was connected to a wider industrial culture and came to share features with other mining areas so that it was, "by the 1900s closer in form to that in South Wales and parts of Northern England".[325] This was the period in which rows of terraced houses, non-conformist chapels, industrial buildings (Cornish engine houses), working men's institutes, public reading rooms and acres of mineral waste (tailings) became ubiquitous features of the landscape of these areas and when respectable working-class activities included choirs, brass and silver bands, team sports and self-improvement through education.[326]

Although, in its earliest phase, this industrial culture was restricted to parts of West Cornwall, it came to define Cornishness everywhere. Most parishes, even the most rural, have had mines or quarries at one time or another in the last two hundred years and this along with the importance of the associated population and new institutions, meant that this "classical popular Cornish culture"[327] spread throughout Cornwall to a greater or lesser extent. The particular combination of old and new elements and the narratives of an ethnic history accompanying it, gave it continuity with long-standing traditions of identity and it was further distinguished by the global dimension of Cornish mining, overseas working and migration. One result was that already democratic, egalitarian and self-sufficient attitudes and manners were reinforced by experience in North America. Tastes, attitudes and even cultural items were incorporated seamlessly so that some remain today and are thought of as thoroughly Cornish. What is more, there is still lingering awareness and memories of transnationality in the first half of the

---

324 *Cornish wrestling*: Popular until 1920s. Similar to Breton and Cumberland wrestling; *Crying the neck*: Former harvest custom; *Trigging*: Collecting shelf-fish at low tide; *Hurling*: Sport widely practiced in the 18th century but now confined as a "custom" to St.Colomb and St.Ives.

325 Bernard Deacon (1993), p. 205.

326 Cornwall has a higher proportion of industrial wasteland than any English or Welsh county.

327 B. Deacon, A. George and R. Perry (1987), *op. cit.*, p. 152.

twentieth century. For example, a retired mining engineer, Alan Trevarthen, remembers returning miners and growing up with the idea that America was an extension of home, almost to the point of feeling American and this had predisposed him to his own international career. A small illustration in local folklore is the nickname "Goss Moor Yanks" for people from the Clay District, still understood by middle-aged locals as an affectionate reference to supposedly working-class American manners and tastes in an area with past traditions of working in the U.S.A.[328] So, to caricature Late Classic Cornishness for the uninitiated, it would be reasonable to say that it was semi-rural, shared certain practices and forms with the English coalfields and industrial South Wales and combined democratic manners, tastes and speech patterns that vaguely recalled the American Mid West. As renewed exchanges reveal, it is also with derivatives of Classic Cornishness that many in the Cornish diaspora identify and this is evidenced in the content of overseas Cornish festivals in Australia, The U.S.A. and Mexico and by the centres of interest of visiting "cousin Jacks and Jennies".[329] It therefore supports reinvigorated transnational networks that have:

> an important part to play in the on-going project to build a mature Cornish identity for the twenty-first century: outward-looking but secure and confident about its past; assured of its uniqueness, but with a capacity for inclusiveness; an historical European region, but one with real global associations.[330]

From Classic Cornishness to Proper Cornish

Deacon and Payton have both charted the decline and fossilization of Classic Cornishness.[331] In his work on the collapse of mining and

328 Discussion with supporters of the St. Dennis Anti-Incinerator Group (November, 2011).

329 Discussions with Philip Hosken of the Trevithick Society. See Philip Hosken, "The Cornish Overseas" in S. Parker (ed.), Cornwall Marches On!: Keskerth Kernow 500, Truro, (1998) pp. 129-136.

330 Bernard Deacon *et al.* (2004), *The Cornish Family: The Roots of Our Future*, Cornwall Editions: Fowey, p.14

331 Philip Payton (1992), p.119.

the "Great Emigration" that accompanied it, Payton calls Cornwall's socio-cultural and economic predicament in the late nineteenth and early twentieth centuries, "The Great Paralysis",[332] and he considers that "the effects upon Cornish society and its culture were inevitably traumatic."[333] The Cornish could no longer think of themselves with (over)confidence and pick-wielding swagger as supplying a global elite of mining engineers and therefore sank into nostalgic uncertainty and inertia.[334] Deacon writes that, "The classical popular Methodist culture began to weaken and the debris of a shattered economy became the site of a fossilised culture as the popular culture ceased to change and develop."[335] These accounts describes a condition in which Cornish society lost its collective sense of purpose and worth, leading to a generalized stagnation in economic, cultural, social and political life and to a redefined peripherality that was to prove lasting.[336] Writing in the 1990s, Jane Korey observed that the symbols of fading occupational cultures no longer carried clear connotations, creating a "semantic vacuum"[337] into which other signifiers, namely those of tourism and Revivalism, could come.

To qualify this story though, we may observe that although the paralysis was certainly "great" and "traumatic", it was far from complete and did not, after all, bring Classic Cornishness to a shuddering end or wholly erase its narratives. Certainly it lost its erstwhile dynamism and features became redundant or vulnerable but they did not disappear altogether. Cornish identity continued to be transmitted by a now moribund culture that provided sentimental motivations for the late twentieth-century expansion of language learning and invented traditions. A new generation felt passionately enough about Cornishness to respond culturally and politically when it was threatened and, more often than not, the innovators behind the more successful efforts to popularize the language, develop neo-traditional music and dance and engage politically were close to Late

332 *Ibid.*, p.119-138; Payton (1996), p.248.

333 *Ibid.*, p.128.

334 *Ibid.*

335 Bernard Deacon, "Cornish Culture or the Culture of the Cornish", *Cornish Banner*, November, 1986.

336 See Philip Payton (1992), *op. cit.*, Chapter Eight, pp.167-191.

337 Jane Korey (1992), *op. cit.*

Classic Cornishness, whether they embraced it unconditionally or sought negotiated ways to move on.

Only twenty-five years ago, Jane Korey observed that, "all the elements people in Pendeen identify as typically 'Cornish'— originated in its period of industrialization."[338] Such a bold statement would be exaggeration today but it would not be wholly unfounded. Despite the loss of its industrial basis, many people still relate Cornishness to a low-profile, low-status, popular culture that is derived in part from the Classic construction. Even if they do not personally engage in its obvious practices or have close familiarity with its cultural forms, they symbolically refer to it, often obliquely, as representing a recent past that was more Cornish, and a present-day range of features descends from Late Classic Cornishness genealogically. For this reason the familiar expression, "Proper Cornish", is taken as a catch-all category and applied to the past, present and possible future trajectories of a loose assemblage of practices and identifications. This has the disadvantage of sounding, and often being, prescriptive but the advantage is that it is widely understood, so much so in fact that it names at least one business, occurs on tee-shirts and car stickers and crops up regularly in online social networks.

Just mentioning "Proper Cornish" to young adults is sometimes enough to elicit personal identifications with behaviours, attitudes and practices that partly derive from Classic Cornishness, even if that is not immediately obvious. This is interesting because there is a paradox in the reality that young adults have fewer traditional markers of Cornishness (notably accent), while often voicing identities that are constructed in alterity to Englishness (by which they evidently refer to privileged versions rather than Englishness in general). A material factor might be that sufficient numbers believe they have experienced economic and social marginalization but this cannot be the main reason. A more plausible explanation is that established identity narratives have been passed on within intimate, family and community-based networks despite breaks in the transmission of cultural form which depend more on external factors, like institutional presence and collective cultural capital. Today's

338 Jane Korey (1991), *op. cit.*

young adults are the children of a consciously Cornish generation, influenced by nationalisms, Revivalism and community campaigns, and this parental generation appears to have communicated attitudes and sentiments but few specific practices. While, outwardly and materially, young adults are less distinctive than former generations, their identities are shaped by home narratives and sharpened by experience. Thus, a student at Falmouth University, attributes her Cornish feelings to, "growing up here and listening to my Mum and Dad and going round my Gran's on Sundays and just ordinary things really", but she is also annoyed by "the way we get ripped off" and "disrespected" and feels, "more and more Cornish". Will, a twenty-seven year-old Truro College student echoes historical egalitarianism, informality and non-subservience:

> Cornishness is a different mentality.
> We are less serious about ourselves and less pompous.
> Everybody is on the same level.
> It's a more honest—less to do with appearances.
> People are disobedient and break the rules.[339]

His account reflects the new circumstances in suggesting that "Cornish is mainly working-class" and he relates attitudes to "the influence of trades around you", citing work situations:—building, fishing, garages, shops and a clothes factory. His account and those of other young adults re-filters vestiges of Classic Cornishness, merging them with nuanced subcultural influences (local experiences of wider phenomena), Revivalism ("The language is vital.") and the alternative lifestyles of counter-urbanization. He has encountered the Cornish Movement's histories ("The 1497 Rebellion", "what the miners achieved") and campaigns (The cross-Tamar constituencies, second-homes). An HND student, Liz, thinks that:

> It's partly about work—finding some if you can, getting stuck in… Cornish people do all sorts to make a living and they have to work hard, no turning your nose up […] We've

---

339 *Non verbatim.*

always had to do that […] the miners and the farmers in the old days…

She adds that Cornishness involves, "not looking down on people because of what job they do and not looking up to them either [laughs]". The Cornish speaker, Elizabeth Stewart, also identifies traits associated with Proper Cornishness as "strengths" (human and social capital) and alludes to traditions of work, endurance and making-do. Her contemporaries are, "hardy and resourceful… survivors… adaptable and reliable" and far from enjoying a "slower pace of life" some of them, "get up at the crack of dawn—have two or three jobs—and are always rushing about doing things." In numerous conversations with young adults and in social media, long established narratives are detectable and merge with the Cornish Movement's discourses, despite the low profile of both in traditional media and mainstream education (Common complaints of activists).

Unsurprisingly, "Proper Cornishness" shares much with other post-industrial areas, as I was reminded by a Cornish steam enthusiast at Trevithick Day (28.4.11), and by a trade unionist, originally from near Sheffield, who described Camborne as "home from home". Cornish people are sometimes aware of this. A woman from Stithians had supported holidays for Durham miners' children during the 1980s coal strike, adding that her grandfather had been a tin miner and that she had grown up near a quarry. Yet even without these conscious identifications, which probably concern few people, it is clear that there are shared post-industrial features. One aspect is the continuance of recreational activities associated with industry. These result in exchanges of choirs, bands and rugby teams (core symbols) that probably involve more people than the exchanges of Celtic Festivals. For instance, Cornwall International Male Voice Choir Festival (27th April to 2nd May, 2011) hosted choirs from former industrial areas and Cornwall Youth Brass Band attends festivals with musicians from similar areas. But these obvious activities are only part of the picture. Far more important are the qualitative aspects of post-industrial conditions—the forms of social capital engendered, the emotional responses and enduring tastes. At a meeting in St Dennis Working Men's Club (2011), members of St

Dennis Anti-Incinerator Group were aware of having things in common with other areas. One said that, "The Clay villages are a bit like the old coal fields, really," and in an oblique reference to social organization, another added, "We've got a similar set-up". An organizer was in contact with an anti-incinerator group in Hull and said, "It's just like here in the Clay. They get dumped on, just the same". Others from the area, including the writer, teacher and academic Alan Kent, confirm qualified recognition of similarities and supply anecdotal accounts of social organization and attitudes.

At first sight there is a problem with the argument that "Proper Cornishness" is significantly derived from Classic Cornishness. That is because the activities so far cited and the involvement of a minority of young people is not enough to constitute a general continuity between generations, even allowing for surprising levels of participation. Many practices that defined Cornish culture a generation ago have declined to the point that young adults have little experience or knowledge of them. Even middle-aged people who relate to them are likely to do so nostalgically and symbolically rather than as aspects of daily life and they sometimes do so through second-hand memories from parents and grand-parents. This moves them into the realm of remembered difference, if not post-memory and a sense of collective experience that is founded on things that nobody can actually remember. There are, however, less tangible ways in which present-day cultures have been shaped by Classic Cornishness and there are qualitative continuities that relate to its "structures of feeling"[340] in a modified, post-industrial form. Thus passed-on social norms, emotional responses and reflexes are the basis of "Proper Cornishness". Bourdieu describes "tastes of necessity" whereby the characteristic preferences within social groups—and therefore cultural capital—are related to economic means.[341] In the Cornish case, enduring tastes and attitudes, shaped by past economic constraints, might be said to predispose people to the new selections that they make and even to influence their preferences of diet, leisure pursuits, dress and music. In this way, Late Classic Cornishness has shaped the space into which new, but

340 See Raymond Williams (1988), *Keywords: A Vocabulary of Culture and Society*, London: Fontana.

341 E.g. Pierre Bourdieu (1979), *La Distinction*, *op. cit.*

not particularly distinctive, aspects of mass culture are adopted. The result corresponds to a phenomenon that Alan Kent calls "residual Cornishness" and which he celebrates in his novels. Asked if it is viable, he answers, "It has to be because it's all there is… We have to take it from where it is now." In other words, it is the appropriate place from which to innovate and build so as to valorize what Kent also connects to "working-class Cornishness" and distances from contradictory aspects of Revivalism. This suggests a people-centred approach, and the view that "residual Cornishness" is relevant is apparently shared by others who represent it in their work, such as film-makers associated with Awen and Cornish National Cinema.

To sum up, it seems that there are still significant continuities in the heterogeneous, identities of many young adults and that they have more to do with taste, attitudes and human relationships than defined activities. The multi-generational aspects of this may be experienced at Trevithick Day in Camborne, one of Cornwall's largest community events, held each year at the end of April and conceived as a celebration of Cornishness, motivated by community concerns. Many components are drawn from the post-industrial culture of the immediate area and relatively few come from Revivalism as such, despite prominent uses of its symbols and the presence of buskers playing neo-Cornish folk. A procession of steam engines is accompanied by the predominantly young Camborne Town Band and there are street performances by choirs. Musical performances and competitions, although eclectic in content (classical and operatic recitals, popular song, film music, jazz etc.), follow in a tradition of musicianship that stems from industrial culture and they take place in the chapels and halls it created. The inclusion of rock bands, percussion groups, country and western dance, samba, disco, mime artists, stilt-walkers and assorted elements of wider, popular cultures simply emphasizes the extent to which the area's everyday culture is typically post-industrial. Mobile hamburger and hot-dog stands complete the picture.

An Dasserghyans

It has been argued, convincingly, that the earlier Revival—*An Dasserghyans*—responded to paralysis and offered ways to move on,

107

producing a dynamic "resurgence" or "cultural renaissance" that re-imagines identity and reaches back into a pre-modern past for inspiration.[342] It has also been suggested that Revivalism has developed in response to new circumstances and it certainly provides spaces in which Cornish interests (economic, social, cultural, environmental etc.) are discussed. Past members of a language group based on social activity recall that it gave them a place where they could "be with other people that feel the same" and "say what we really think" (recalling 1970s-80s women's groups). One person had probably been motivated to become a school governor and Cornwall councillor "because of learning Cornish". Someone who attended dance practices at Carnon Downs said, "It's the one time when I can talk about Cornish things and just gossip." Such spaces contribute to the Cornish Movement's networks and thus to campaigns and initiatives. We nevertheless need to be cautious about positive assessments and consider whether there are problems in some of the relationships this "renaissance" has with Proper Cornishness. Revivalist ideas inspire creativity but it is not sure how much of this benefits or even reaches disadvantaged people whose families and communities bear the greatest inheritance of Payton's "Great Paralysis". What if some people have indeed embraced Revivalism and moved on but left others worse off than they would have been otherwise? Conscious and symbolic expressions have certainly multiplied and spread and new activities have emerged, changing the cultural landscape, but it is not at all sure that Cornish culture as a whole has evolved as creatively and dynamically as sometimes claimed. The Revivalist repertoire may not adequately fill the further semantic vacuum left by the last round of industrial and agricultural job losses in the 1980s and 90s. Another possibility for sections of the population is that described in the 1980s by David Penhaligon M.P. when he claimed that Cornwall had "never recovered"[343] from the consequences of industrial decline. Instead parts of the community have arguably experienced a second-stage paralysis brought on by the socio-economic marginalization that results from tourism-led in-migration and a reduced native middle-

342 Bernard Deacon (2007), p.216; Philip Payton (1989), p.239.
343 David Penhaligon, M.P. Speech in Camborne, September 1986.

class. Alongside the Revival's creativity and popular uptake of its symbolic repertoire (flags, Cornish tartan, Cornish names, music…), there is a relatively stagnant, post-industrial culture where activities from Classic Cornishness continue with diminished energy, participation and achievement. It is this assemblage that has been left behind by the pursuit of Celtic models and undermined by material and demographic realities. The consequences are that, with notably exceptions, it has not developed imaginatively to give relevant, contemporary forms. That would be all right if communities had really moved on to embrace new practices and found a source of esteem within them but some sections have limited access to core Revivalism and few benefits from any cultural capital it accrues. The fact that they neither participate nor gain status by indirect association suggests that Revivalist innovations have not always been grafted onto Proper Cornishness, despite Nance's attempted synthesis, previously discussed. Some of the Revival's middle-class and "arty" developments are somewhat removed from typical "tastes of necessity"[344] and cultures of making do (a feature of present-day culture with late 19th century foundations)[345] that are naturalized within the worst-off fractions of Cornish society.

Cornishness is not socially homogenous, despite egalitarian myths and an often-remarked lack of class demarcation. In practice, there are constellations of middle-class taste and attitudes that some Cornish people share with others throughout Britain and these shape Revivalist cultural hygienes disproportionately. A difficulty is that activities framed by these tastes can render them, not so much inaccessible but unappealing and uncomfortable to sections of society and they do not, on the face of it, valorize forms of Cornishness that are closely associated with the working-class, despite being imagined as more legitimately Cornish. For example, after an all-too-typical Cornish language event that included neo-traditional dance and lengthy discussions of comparative Celtic linguistics, two "down-to-earth" learners who I had talked into coming, described it as "a bit of a weird night". This, their first taste of a social event in Cornish, had been one of mild culture shock and

---

344 Bourdieu's term, e.g. Pierre Bourdieu (1979), *La Distinction*, *op. cit.*
345 See Bernard Deacon, (1993), p. 205.

bewilderment. Cornish appealed to them and they were learning in a friend's home but had this specific scene been their first encounter they might not have started. A week later, one of them told me it had been his first experience of "full-on Cornish music". He had not liked it but assumed it must represent something more Cornish that he was not part of. Frequent clashes between pretty displays of Celtishness and non-Revivalist Cornishness could explain why some scenes do not attract more working-class people, yet for Revivalism to produce optimum benefits for community resilience and well-being it needs to provide symbolic identifications for less advantaged sections of society, whether or not they take part. The issue was neatly identified by a student film-maker at a screening in Falmouth Polytechnic who whispered, "What would they make of this crap up Pengegon?", a reference to one of Britain's poorest districts where fifty-eight percent of children live in poverty.[346] If Cornishness is narrowly and prescriptively taken to be the Proper Cornish spectrum, there may be a paradoxical anti-Cornishness within some strands of Revivalism. Cath Camps has noted, for instance, that emphasis on the Cornish language may be coupled with a disrespect for Cornu-English that renders the latter more illegitimate and stigmatizing than it might be otherwise.[347] While it has been used for humour and short stories, there has been no assertive revaluing of accent and dialect of the kind seen in Yorkshire, Durham and Northumberland.[348] I pointedly asked Revivalists about this and while I heard many positive affirmations, there were also comments of the type: "We don't speak like that anymore." and "It makes us sound like yokels." Some were glad that others had local accents but had little trace of one themselves. Strangely, for people who are resurrecting a language, several Cornish enthusiasts were dismissive. A woman at a "Yeth an Werin" conversation group said that she missed hearing dialect but could not envisage using it and thought it was, "*re dhewedhes ha heb poynt*" ('too late and pointless'), to try saving it. Far better, she thought, to concentrate on, "*agan tavas gwir, in le a rannyêth Sowsnek*" ('our true language, instead of an English dialect').

346 "Deprivation and Child Poverty", Cornwall Council (2011).
347 Cath Camps, Silencing the voice of the Cornish, unpublished Cert.Ed. assignment for Cornwall College [n.d.].
348 Although maintained in Gorseth Kernow competitions.

A strand within Revivalism ignores or romantically reinvents the post-industrial present and community memory of industrial triumphs to fit Celtic models. Cultural websites illustrate this, listing exclusively folkloric events but almost nothing from the Proper Cornish spectrum. The widespread view that early twentieth-century Revivalists saved and restored the remnants of an authentic Celtic culture overlooks the fact that the Cornish of their day already had a distinctive culture—that of Late Classic Cornishness—the outcome, not of failure to be conservatively pre-modern but rather the successful and adventurous embrace of modernity and innovation. Activities that overlook the Classic Cornish inheritance may nevertheless be motivated by the feelings that Proper Cornishness generates. The full picture of Revivalism is complicated but what seems to be happening is an internal struggle for meaning and ownership of which few protagonists are aware. Proper Cornish motivations and meanings compete with the re-symbolization previously described and there are re-negotiations of Celtic prescriptions. If Revivalism were wholly inaccessible and disconnected from working-class lives there would be little point in looking to it as useable culture for community resilience but aspects have been enthusiastically adopted and incorporated into ongoing constructions of Proper Cornishness, a trend noted by Deacon who observed the uptake of symbols in the 1990s when, "At last, the gulf between popular and Revivalist culture seemed to have been bridged with this co-mingling of cultural symbols. Popular culture, Celticity and history were merging."[349]

This sounds as though the Nancian Synthesis has started to come about but even if that is so, these developments could be threatened by re-signification. Revivalism produces both ways to champion, re-invent and perpetuate Proper Cornishness as well as acts which undermine it, and all kinds of permutation and negotiated relationship exist, as two examples will illustrate.

The first example is the Holman-Climax Male Voice Choir, which was established in 1940 at the Climax Rock-Drill and Engineering Works that manufactured mining and industrial equipment until the

---

349 Bernard Deacon (1993), op. cit., p. 207.

1990s.[350] The factory was the focus of community struggles and demonstrations[351] in the 1980s and the choir, now a focus of nostalgia, is emblematic of fading industrial memory and economic woes. Nearly everybody in the choir has a Cornish accent and only a few members are under sixty years of age. Although exclusively male it involves wider family and community networks. The visual presentation (blazers and ties…) and style of singing has not changed greatly in decades. Attending social events with the choir, I nevertheless noted Revivalist influences and a desire to transmit singing to the young. At an informal party some members sang Cornish translations of the popular songs, "The White Rose" and "Going up Camborne Hill"[352] and two younger members shouted "Kernow bys vycken!" ('Cornwall for ever!') at the end of the patriotic song "Hail to the Homeland", itself a Revivalist-inspired anthem by the late Carharrack composer, Kenneth Pelmear. Others wore Revivalist symbols, including a base-ball cap with the bilingual slogan "Ober dâ—Proper Job" and a St. Piran's flag. At least two singers had been made bards of the Gorsedd for "services to Cornish culture" and had taken part in festivals alongside neo-Cornish musicians and dancers, including some in America. Members and their families talked about maintaining communities using the language of activists and occasionally mentioning some of them by name. A couple spoke about adapting the repertoire and involving younger people, switching to talk about the financial exclusion of Cornish people from St Ives. At a performance in Brittany, choir member David Oates took trouble to explain Cornish identity in French and emphasize links with "our Breton cousins". All considered, the choir is now an expression of the Cornish Movement but has little Revivalist content. This is a case of an activity from Late Classic Cornishness absorbing useable symbolic elements and discourses which help to articulate identity through the familiar.

350 The final closure was in 2003. Camborne developed as a sizeable town as a result of these engineering works.

351 Notably in September 1986 when tens of thousands of people attended a rally.

352 "The White Rose" was made popular by miners returning from America and was translated into Cornish by Julyan Holmes. "Going up Camborne Hill" recounts Richard Trevithick's invention of a steam-driven road vehicle.

The second example is a situation which is somewhat different in the unambiguously Revivalist activity of "Cornish dancing", having its origins in 1970s Pan-Celtic exchanges. Although this might be expected to follow ascribed Celtic models closely, it is not that straightforward. The urge to create the scene certainly included a sense of lack with regard to other Celtic countries but that is not the only motive. Recent developments have underlined a specific Cornish context and consciously incorporated elements from mining history, including the dress worn by bal-maidens (female surface workers). Methodist tea treat tunes[353] and popular dances are re-arranged and there is even a dance which mimics the rhythmic sound of "tin stamps", the machines that crushed ore.[354] These items celebrate the same industrial heritage that produced the previous example but whereas the choir is embedded in a popular, social and cultural context by virtue of its beginnings, trajectory and insider participation, Cornish dance is still "up for grabs" as far as meanings and participation are concerned. Everything, from the music to the dances and to the costumes and styles of presentation is largely unanchored by customary meanings. Thus the example of using nineteenth-century dress may be part of re-telling important community narratives but the costumes may alternatively be read as folkloric equivalents of the Breton costumes seen at Pan-Celtic festivals, a point not lost on sceptics:

> but Cornwall's no Brittany.
> *Coiffes* are no Gooks, Perranporth's no Lorient,
> the Hurlers are no Carnac...[355]

Any number of paths is available to Cornish dancing. It may be grafted onto Proper Cornishness as a new poetic and sentimental expression and recast as a popular culture but it may also be isolated as a prescriptive scene. It may also be stripped of its political connotations so that it becomes a cosy local equivalent of country

353 Discussions with Frances Bennett, Hilary Coleman-Davy, Neil Coleman-Davy.
354 Performed, for example, at Goldsithney Charter Fayre, 2011, at Mazey Day, Penzance, 2011.
355 Alan M. Kent, "Cross-Channel Envy" in, *Love and Seaweed*, St.Austell: Lyonesse Press, 2002 p.53.

dancing, suitable for festivals and village fetes but not for asserting Cornishness. In just over thirty years of existence, Cornish dancing has grown and diversified impressively and it is arguably the most dynamic area of Revivalist culture.[356] There are cases of it being fully integrated in community life as well as interpretations that uncomprehendingly fail to engage with Proper Cornishness. As with other activities, this variation reflects the differing interests, tastes, behaviours and identifications of participants, rather than any intrinsic aspect of the dances themselves.

A Common Cornish Habitus

Proper Cornishness is a basis of identity for much of the population so its stagnation and low status may psychologically reduce community resilience. It was sustained symbolically by late twentieth-century industries but even these are fading into the recent past leaving related identifications even more prone to redundancy. Proper Cornishness appears to be in stasis, rather than paralysis, now a durable, liminal state[357] with a naturalized air of permanence. The old-fashioned, out-of-date feel of associated activities has taken on the air of being an essential ingredient of being Cornish, often perceived as something comfortingly familiar and rooted to come home to but hardly dynamic or exciting. As a whole, its cultural forms are widely seen as "stuck in a groove", "fossilized", "old-fashioned" and are written off as doomed. Few see them as a tradition to reinvigorate and diversify.[358] Its musical tradition is failing to translate itself into dynamic forms like those sometimes produced in other former mining areas and has given way, not so much to Revivalist creativity, but to generalized popular cultures, albeit with local nuances. By association, Proper Cornishness, as a way of being and persona, is something to abandon and move on from. For the purposes of approaching Proper Cornishness in the

356 Merv Davey, "'As is the manner and the custom'; folk tradition and identity in Cornwall", unpublished Ph.D thesis, University of Exeter.

357 Cf. Bjørn Thomassen, "The Uses and Meanings of Liminality" in *International Political Anthropology*, no.3, (2010). www.politicalanthropology.org/component/search/?searchword=liminality&ordering=&searchphrase=all (Accessed 5 May 2011.)

358 Vocabulary from conversations.

wider sense—beyond cultural form—it is useful to turn to Bourdieu's elaboration of *habitus*[359] which is central to social, cultural and symbolic capital and thus to group status. Bourdieu used this concept to analyse inequalities, mainly in respect to class, but while class requires habitus, habitus does not require class as such (since social divisions do not automatically lead to class formation) and may be applied more broadly and related to ethnicity, gender, geography and other variables. It allows us to get beyond a limited focus on either ethnicity or social class, without abandoning either and since it is close to notions of culture as "a whole way of life" and to Raymond Williams' "structures of feeling",[360] it is a ready framework for thinking about cultural usefulness and how groups and their cultures are perceived and valued.

So what is habitus? Firstly, it is not a synonym for socialization or the "ensemble of everyday routines" as sometimes imagined and it is not social class either.[361] It is rather the whole set of acquired tastes, behaviours, practices, values and ways of thinking, doing and being that locate individuals within social structures and practices. A habitus comes about through collective experience and it is the socio-cultural space within which individuals learn lasting, common-sense ideas, truths and systems of values that are broadly common to others of the same *habitus*. It is where they make sense of the world and develop in-group tastes, preferences and lifestyles. It is where members acquire their world views:

Les conditionnements associés à une classe particulière de conditions d'existence produisent des *habitus*, systèmes de *dispositions* durables et transposables foncionnant comme principes générateurs et organisations de pratiques et de represéentations...[362]

359 Bourdieu elaborated the idea over time, notably in *An Outline of a Theory of Practice* (1972) and Le sens pratique (1980); cf. John Lechte (1994), p.48; John Thompson in P. Bourdieu (2001), p.26.

360 See Raymond Williams, "The Analysis of Culture" in J. Storey (ed.) (2006), *Cultural Theory and Popular Culture, A Reader*, London: Pearson, p. 37.

361 See John Lechte (1994), p.47; Mike Featherstone (1995), pp.31-32. Critics include Richard Jenkins (1992) *op. cit.*

362 Pierre Bourdieu (1980), *Le Sens Pratique, op. cit.* pp.88-89.

Habitus involves "dispositions", a term (with an echo of "position") that conveys the idea that individuals acquire attitudes, aptitudes and predispositions towards certain behaviours which typify the social group. Agents (Bourdieu's usual term) operate within prevalent "schemas of perception" (*schémas de perceptions*)[363] so that they respond to events, including unexpected and novel ones, according to principles, values and ways of doing things that are internalized and ingrained as reasonable and self-evident. Unlike ethics, these may be banal, not requiring conscious aim in order to attain particular ends.[364] Without agents having to be aware, the adaptable, "principes générateurs et organisations de pratiques et de représentations",[365] of habitus produce an apparent regularity which is, "collectivement orchestrées sans être le produit de l'action organisatrice d'un chef d'orchestre."[366] These practices and representations play a part in group belonging and where we position ourselves and are placed by others (Stuart Hall's "ascribed" and "elected" identities). Individual, but more-or-less typical, group attributes work semiotically as "distinctions". The role of acquired tastes in the construction of Proper Cornishness has already been mentioned and their arbitrary construction is an aspect of habitus:

> particular constellations of taste, consumption preferences and lifestyle practices are associated with specific occupation and class fractions, making it possible to map the universe of taste and lifestyles with all its structured oppositions and finely graded distinctions…[367]

Identifying, judging and revealing taste to others, as seemingly natural "distinction", produces cultural capital. Thus cultural consumption, participation and production act out status and group

---

363 Pierre Bourdieu (1984), p.171; Stéphane Chevallier & Christiane Chauviré (2010) pp.132-137.

364 See *Le Sens Pratique*, coll. *Le sens commun*, Editions de Minuit, Paris, 1980 p88-89). P. Bourdieu, 1980:88-89 *op. cit.*

365 *Ibid*. Trans. N. Kennedy: "generative principles and organizations of practices and representations."

366 Pierre Bourdieu (1980), *op. cit.*: "collectively orchestrated without being produced by a conductor", Trans. N. Kennedy.

367 Mike Featherstone (1995), p.22.

membership. Bourdieu calls the choices involved "discrimination", recalling multiple uses of the word to mean either "good judgement" or "unequal treatment". There is, in other words, a connection between identifying taste and values and the determination of what and who is legitimate. Passing on tastes, values and behaviours to the next generation is one way in which the habitus is reproduced, determining membership of groups.

Bourdieu stresses that the habitus is reproduced and transmitted as lasting dispositions which—individuality notwithstanding—are shared by people who have had same conditioning and material conditions.[368] Some relate to embodied cultural capital through what Bourdieu calls the bodily hexis (*hexis corporelle*) and this provides some of the non-verbal means by which people are identified. Bodily postures, gestures, ways of moving, mannerisms and physical dispositions produce, "the non-verbal cues and sign-reading operations that are significant in personal encounters in which people discern the relative social significance and position of individuals."[369] Both "distinctions", as group markers, and systems of dispositions are amplified when ethnicity is a feature of a habitus. Furthermore, ethnic groups, in so far as they are constructs and cultural creations, involve conditioning and members are identified by distinctions, much as happens with habitus and class. Indeed tacit awareness of distinctions feeds essentialist imaginings of ethnic identities because they seem to have existed for ever and be immutable or congenital. Thus, although ethnicity and habitus are flexible and potentially changeable, they may not seem so.

It is proposed that Proper Cornishness is connected to a "Common Cornish Habitus" which is characterized by dispositions, attitudes, shared knowledge and tacit understandings that come together as "structures of feeling".[370] Habitus may outlast cultural changes and remain quite stable even when "objective" and material aspects of a culture disappear or change; so, rather than thinking of Proper Cornishness as an array of activities, it may be better—instead or as

---

368 Pierre Bourdieu (2000 [1972]) p.282.

369 Simon Charlesworth (2005), "Understanding Social Suffering: A Phenomenological Investigation of the Experience of Inequality", *Journal of Community and Applied Social Psychology*, no. 15 (2005) pp. 296-312 (p.300).

370 Raymond Williams (1988) *op. cit.*

well—to think of it as comprising the ways of being summed up by the Cornu-English expression, "as we belong to", which conveys both a sense of what is customary and of what is appropriate and legitimate for insiders—in order to belong.[371] The items associated with Cornish culture, like structuralist *parole*, may be regarded as ephemeral signifiers of lasting dispositions which compose a code, somewhat like structuralist *langue*.[372] They may come and go while habitus and the atmosphere it generates stays, even surviving language shift, migration or economic transformations. This is missed when concern with practices themselves (e.g. dance, cuisine, sports, festivals, ceremonies) disregards social relationships and who takes part. At Bolster Day in St Agnes, a participant complained that there was "no Cornish vibe", revealing tacit awareness of dispositions and attitudes that locate performance socially.[373] An event that is labelled Cornish may not feel so if these ingredients are absent while an activity that is common outside Cornwall may do so if they are present. Thus, the practice sessions of the dance group *Ros Keltek* (established in 1980) have been a context in which features of the habitus are clearly perceptible because of who takes part even though some of the dances come from "the other Celtic countries". Exactly the same activities involving some other groups may not seem Cornish because the typical dispositions and attitudes of the habitus are absent. Even more strikingly, the locally reputed Smokey Joe's Café near Redruth, something of cross between a British transport café and an American diner, is identified as a Proper Cornish space within which the democratic, informal behaviours and attitudes of the habitus are tangible but where no specifically Cornish activity is identifiable.

Habitus helps understand why practices need not spring from conscious constructions of Cornishness or be traditional in order to be drawn into diffused identity discourses. Everything from flower-arranging to motor-bike scrambling and from gardening to tattooing may be defined by the feelings of habitus and serve as an occasion

---

371 Cornu-English "We belong to…" means "We usually…", "We habitually…" but may also mean "We ought to…".

372 Ferdinand de Saussure (1967 [1915]), *Cours de Linguistique Générale*, Paris: Payot. Chapter 2.

373 Bolster Day, St. Agnes, 2 May 2011.

to express Cornish sentiment. This was apparent at two gigs where a metal band called *Kernuyck* played to largely Cornish pub audiences. None of the songs referred to Cornwall but the event felt Cornish because the public made it so and this was not lost on the band and its supporters, an impression reinforced by Revivalist symbols (a flag, badges, tattoos, tee-shirts) and the band's name which is based on *Kernowek* ('Cornish'). At Wadebridge, another band played standard indie rock and covers but one song touched on affording somewhere to live and "staying put" and the band dedicated it to "everyone who keeps St. Piran's flag flying on the North Coast". Locals said the evening was "really Cornish" because of "the atmosphere" and "people who turn up from miles around", "a regular Cornish crew". It is the character of habitus that creates a Cornish feeling in these examples while the Cornish Movement and Revivalism furnish discourses and symbols that help articulate it as an identity.

Habitus concerns slippery, indefinable aspects of identity that insiders struggle to describe but know tacitly. They allow them to recognize one another and be identified, often unconsciously or without quite realizing how. In Yorkshire, Simon Charlesworth mentions students who recognize others by means of what one person called "posh-radar"[374] or unconscious "scoping". Similarly, in answer to the question, "How do you know somebody is Cornish?" insiders often speak vaguely of "being able to tell" and "just knowing". Some who are more conscious of identity dare to cite humour, mannerisms, body language and so on—things which they cannot describe precisely but know.[375] Speaking about prominent people who return after careers "away", a middle-aged woman commented that the opera singer Benjamin Luxon was "just as Cornish as he's always been", obliquely citing distinctions that I was expected to recognize. In the same vein, a teacher who had met the writer Don Thomas assured me that, "You pick up he's Cornish straight away." Most respondents had given little previous thought to how they recognized insiders beyond accent but their tacit awareness of non-verbal cues emerged and was emphasized:

374 Simon Charlesworth (2000), *A Phenomenology of Working Class Experience*, Cambridge: Cambridge University Press.
375 See a discussion in B. Deacon, A. George & R. Perry (1987), *op. cit.*, p. 153.

"It's easier to understand each other and it's more relaxed."

"We go about things a bit differently."

"It's instinctive… You can pick up on it."

"I suppose it's little things, like how you laugh or whatever."

A lecturer said she adjusted instinctively, choosing between her intragroup and intergroup personas in a chameleon-like exercise of code switching that involves both verbal (accent, shared references) and non-verbal cues. At an academic seminar, the proceedings started stiffly with everybody using standard, RP-influenced English but once all were aware—consciously or not—that almost everyone was Cornish their accents strengthened, they relaxed and insider references punctuated the discussion.

The suggestion is not that all Cornish people are positioned within a uniform habitus, though. It is rather that customary notions of what it is to be Proper Cornish refer to a more or less common range of distinctions, even though the reality is complex and contradictory. Many Cornish people, for one reason or another, do not operate within the norms of this habitus but when they do not and when they have no corresponding cultural markers, they are sometimes said to be "not very Cornish". The sub-text is that they are "Cornish but you would hardly think so" and that "being Cornish is not good enough for them". For example, a television presenter who reported on St Piran's day was said to be "ashamed to be Cornish" and "about as Cornish as Phil off Eastenders". Combinations of prescription and scepticism are common in (minority) identities and, in this case, conflate habitus, class and ethnicity to exclude contradictory distinctions. At the same time, a person who has the distinctions of habitus will be considered an insider regardless of economic status and occupation and usually irrespective of parentage and ethnicity.[376] This means that there are degrees of "insideness" according to the extent to which individuals conform. In the New Cornwall, there is interaction between the multiple cultures of Cornish people and in-migrants and there is assimilation

---

376 See a brief discussion in B. Deacon, A. George and R. Perry (1987), *op. cit.*, p.154.

and adaptation in all directions, rendering distinctions consequential for status and belonging. Native participants in any given activity, be it gymnastics, film-making, rock music, car maintenance or knitting, may have more in common with in-migrants who share their interests, (sub)cultural references and social backgrounds (class, gender, age, occupation…) than with Cornish people who do not.

To summarize, habitus is multi-dimensional and overlapping, involving distinctions that have arbitrary and negotiable currency. The contention, nevertheless, is that an identifiable Cornish habitus spans socio-economic differences within an indigenous, self-identifying community and that, for historic reasons, this traditional feature is linked to social capital through norms of egalitarianism, informality, self-dependency, social cohesiveness and other attitudes. In keeping with egalitarianism, the distinctions that mark internal inequalities are not very pronounced and are less important symbolically than overarching group markers. Bourdieu's notion deals with inequalities of cultural, symbolic and social capital and distinctions between habituses, so if this Common Cornish Habitus has attitudes and dispositions that are common to people of differing socio-economic circumstances, is it a habitus at all? The temptation might be to see it as a set of local traits but it distinguishes itself as habitus within the greater, British hierarchy of class, with its complex, fluctuating nuances of gender, ethnicity and regionality. Much of the "distinctiveness" of daily life then reveals itself as "distinction" in Bourdieu's sense and Cornishness, like other regional, national, class and ethnic identities, is homogenized, working as a single, multi-dimensional and low-profile habitus.

Emotional Capital

Habitus has been applied in research concerning emotional well-being in other post-industrial areas. Diane Reay has explored the indeterminacies of social status and developed an approach through "emotional capital", turning to habitus during her analysis because using cultural capital alone was not enough to "capture the complexities" of people's lives.[377] Reay discusses the physiological

377 Diane Reay, "Gendering Bourdieu's concept of capitals? Emotional capital, women and social class", in Lisa Adkins and Beverley Skeggs (eds.), *Feminism after Bourdieu, The Sociological Review*, vol. 52, Issue Supplement, (October 2004),

consequences of inferiority and the "biology of chronic stress" that occurs as "human beings are confronted feelingly by the meanings to which [they are] submitted from the first", and she cites Bourdieu in seeing this as "inert violence" that inferiors deal with everyday.[378] The amount of honour and esteem they feel influences their quality of life and involves collective and individual prestige. This fits with the proposition that the collective status of the Cornish is important for morale and that intervention may combat feelings of inferiority and marginalization by recourse to culture's primary uses. Simon Charlesworth takes habitus as a "distinct way of being" and "the socially constituted principle of perception and appreciation of the social world we acquire in a particular context"[379] and has applied it in his hometown of Rotherham[380] which shares (post)industrial experiences and cultural influences with parts of Cornwall. This informs consideration of how major economic changes (deindustrialization) have eroded "traditional forms of solidarity" leading directly to "disturbance"—in a broad psychological sense—amongst disadvantaged sections of South Yorkshire's working-class. Charlesworth examines low individual and collective worth and confidence as felt emotionally and he develops an idea of "emotional prosperity" akin to Reay's "emotional capital". He argues that accounts of class "give no sense of what it is like to be working class; how it feels or what it means" because they ignore the "experience of subordinates".[381] Testimony is therefore used to examine the "constitution of social space" and explore how status is felt personally within the "social-psychological framework" that emerges in conversation as largely "unreflective experience".[382] Feelings of inferiority and powerlessness, as sources of dissatisfaction and stress, are related to social standing. Charlesworth cites Bourdieu's, "truly metaphysical wretchedness of men and women who have no social reason for being, who are abandoned to insignificance".[383] This can

---

pp. 57-74.

378 *Ibid.*

379 Simon Charlesworth (2000), p.29.

380 Simon Charlesworth (2000), (2005) *op. cit.*

381 Simon Charlesworth (2005), p. 297.

382 *Ibid.*, p.299, p.297.

383 Pierre Bourdieu (2000), cited in Charlesworth (2005) p.240.

entail having to regularly defer to social superiors, for instance, or feeling excluded and Charlesworth argues that a "sense of injustice" and "worthlessness" may lead to angst and feelings that undermine well-being and relate to "social pathologies" which involve:

> the physiologically consequential effects of being dispossessed of the very grounds of self-respect and self-authority; of the capacity to be perceived and perceive oneself as competent and of worth.[384]

There are several potential contributors to such feelings in Cornwall. Firstly, ethnicity and social class are popularly conflated in seeing the Cornish as necessarily working-class so that their distinctions are associated with low status. This correlation reflects the nature of in-migration which has meant that, "the Cornish are under-represented in high status and over-represented in low status jobs".[385] The recent phase of deindustrialization has also sapped self-esteem and morale. Occupationally-linked attributes that formerly engendered pride may be devalued, even stigmatized, so that they mark social inferiority without being redeemed by suggesting working capability. Connected feelings are translated consensually into the acceptance and assumption of disentitlement. In Bourdieu's accounts, people are not barred from doing things but they may nevertheless be impossible materially and psychologically. Actions may seem, or really be, unachievable or so unlikely that it is not worth investing energy and time to pursue them. Charlesworth relates this to the difficulties "subordinates" have in mustering enough determination and confidence to achieve some goals and he mentions a person who felt unable to be a justice of the peace because it meant mixing with "posh" people. This accords with observations that Cornish people exclude themselves because of their own felt lack of entitlement. Expectations are linked to agency and choice within, "limits set by the historically and socially situated conditions of the habitus",[386] and since habitus is normative and

384 Simon Charlesworth (2005), p. 301.

385 See Bernard Deacon (1999), *The Cornish and the Council of Europe Framework Convention for the Protection of National Minorities*, Rowntree Reform Trust, p.21

386 Pierre Bourdieu (1990), *Distinction: A Social Critique of the Judgement of Taste*,

likely to produce sanctions for irregular behaviours, it "tends to exclude all 'extravagances' ('not for the likes of us') [...that are...] incompatible with the objective conditions".[387] Limits and norms may lower or raise aspirations, open or close doors to opportunities and increase or reduce all forms of capital as people restrict or expand their options accordingly, and the status of the habitus has the potential to shape lives by affecting whether individuals are taken seriously and take themselves seriously.

Redeeming Nance's Project

Much of the Revival's energy is devoted to maintaining traditions, customs and innovations as objective culture but this discussion is about how useable culture can address community needs. This emphasizes the whole culture so that instead of simply being evaluated for their own sake, cultural items are considered for usefulness to community well-being and continuity. Habitus is the most stable part of Cornwall's cultural continuity, identified here as the context for interventions to increase emotional prosperity through cultural, social and symbolic capital. The Revival's heterogeneity and struggles for meaning might be said to offer a "mixed bag of tricks", some of which point the way forward confidently while others are out of kilter with the tenure of Cornish habitus. Awareness of this allows us to understand that who takes part is more important to the continuity of Cornishness and well-being than the form and content of practices. The suggestion of a Common Cornish Habitus helps to recognize that the social and aesthetic framing of activities may either connect them with insiders or unwittingly raise barriers. Habitus may explain why some Revivalists are upbeat about Cornish culture making progress while others subscribe to despondent "end of Cornwall narratives". The former appear to conflate Revivalist neo-traditions with Cornishness while the latter are more often insiders, closer to weakening practices and less likely to identify with contexts which do not feel Cornish. Thus enactments of ascribed identities may prosper in detached scenes even while identities that are bound to ethnically-nuanced habitus decline.

Cambridge: Cambridge University Press. p.55.

387 *Ibid.*, p. 55-56.

Since cultural items do not have a fixed meaning as signifiers, there is no in-built discordance between any Revivalist activity and the habitus or cultures of Proper Cornishness and where there are clashes this does not necessarily stop activities from having potential. Intervention therefore means trying to anchor "preferred readings"[388] and consider likely connotations. Achieving compatibility could depend upon whose dispositions, attitudes and tastes define activities and the discursive formations within which they are performed. As there is nothing inherently incompatible or compatible in most activities—speaking Cornish or dancing at a *troyl*, for example—preferred meanings that accord with Proper Cornishness may be actively sought. This offers a way to redeem them so that instead of dismissing them as irredeemably irrelevant (to "the young", to "the working-class" and so on), they may be reinvented and reinterpreted.

Encouragingly, there is an emerging turn against received wisdoms that detract from Proper Cornishness and it is noticeable in the changing rhetoric of Revivalists and in initiatives to build upon traditional foundations. In Cornish language spheres where popular strands have existed for decades there are renewed efforts to graft Cornish onto rugby, gig-racing, popular music and a range of other pursuits. Neo-Cornish musicians and dancers are starting to develop close-harmony singing in new contexts[389] and are working with rock musicians and brass and silver bands. The "Horners" project, for example, aimed to "build up a whole network of brass, reed and percussion players across Cornwall" and took, "the Celtic music of Cornwall, combined it with the popularity of brass instruments [and] some wild percussion", to produce "brash and uplifting music".[390] Likewise, Picrous night in Luxulyan, billed as combining "twiddly Cornish music" and "proper Cornish carol singing", is a successful initiative to bring revivals and invented traditions into an accessible context:

---

388 Cf. Stuart Hall ([1973] 1980) *op. cit.*
389 See: Hilary Coleman and Sally Burley (2015), *Shout Kernow: Celebrating Cornwall's Pub Songs*, London: Francis Boutle.
390 Publicity.

It is not about 'performance' it's about 'participation'—no-one is in charge or sets any agenda, it's just about using Cornish cultural elements as a tool-kit for celebration.[391]

A valorizing, renegotiation of the relationships between Revivalism and Proper Cornishness may be getting underway—even if a parallel re-symbolization threatens it. Achieving compatibility with popular Cornishness is absolutely necessary whether the aim is to find social usefulness or to promote activities for their own sake. If the Cornish language is not bound to widespread identifications, for instance, and if its social activity does not reflect ways of being that let Cornish people feel at home, it will not serve a useful purpose and will not recruit and prosper. Much the same might be said for any activities, but what makes Revivalist practices different from say, roller-skating or samba dancing, is that they are labelled "Cornish" and designed as deliberate displays that are meant to voice the identity of a whole community. They offer people who already have cultural identities an interpretation of what their culture could or should be, so it is vital that they support and do not undermine them.

---

391 Comments by Will Coleman, 10 December 2012.

Chapter 6

Cool Cornubia:
Branding Celtic Cornwall

During my inquiry, as I broached the subject of "useable culture", most people assumed that I must mean branding. They discussed cultural tourism and packaging in the food and drink sector where using the Cornish language and cultural symbolism were thought to offer "added value" in the form of "regional distinctiveness". For a few Cornwall Council officers and councillors, using culture in branding is, however, understood to be a potential part of wider strategies, yet undeveloped, to "brand the region" and "put Cornwall on the map", with implications for inward investment and external decision-making. Accordingly, some within the Cornish Movement argue that Cornishness itself is a commercial asset and "powerful marketing tool",[392] and they use this to support the case for the language:

> If you're looking at Cornwall's distinctiveness, its brand in the future world of trade and so forth, having something that distinguishes and defies our brand like a living language is very important.[393]

Yet even these perspectives risk missing the roles that cultural branding could have as an intervention to boost the forms of capital discussed and to help shape and assure important mythologies of Cornish identity. Branding can be directly related to these questions using Barthes "three orders of signification", previously introduced. Thus, defining a desirable and useful "vision" of Cornwall and

392 Comments by Colin Roberts of Bewnans Kernow.
393 Bert Biscoe in "Fears for Cornish Language Partnership", BBC News, 13 April 2011, www.bbc.co.uk/news/uk-england-cornwall-13059389

Cornishness is about selecting a "third level" message as a useable mythology and effectively communicating it. In accordance with the discussion so far, this needs to connect with traditional identity narratives and with the attitudes and dispositions of the "Common Cornish habitus". Branding, as image-making, contributes to the wider field of representation, whether it seeks to promote a territory (region, country…) or simply one of its products, businesses or sectors. Some of the myths—in Barthes' sense—that could be socially and economically beneficial to community resilience are overwhelmed and subverted by contradictory, disabling and prejudicial messages so a coordinated public approach is essential to take sides in the conflicts of interest that concern emotional and economic prosperity and the survival of a Cornish tradition. In other words, an overall public vision is needed to replace piecemeal, contradictory branding exercises for specific sectors. The vision focused upon as a proposition here updates the established mythology of the Cornish as "Industrial Celts",[394] considering how to make this into a valorizing brand with corresponding social and cultural aspirations.

Although branding is usually discussed from the perspective of marketing products, services and destinations, it has further consequences for how a territory and its inhabitants are looked upon, not only by outsiders but also by insiders. It can be forgotten that residents are a home market and audience that may be susceptible to branding based on identity. They are more exposed to brand images of themselves than outsiders and may also generate them. Branding therefore involves the production and consumption of elected, negotiated and ascribed identities,[395] in much the same way as the Revivalist representations previously considered. The policy advisor Simon Anholt, something of an international guru on branding countries, observes that, "although the usual context of brand theory may be buying and selling and promoting consumer goods, this is a thin layer that covers some of the hardest philosophic questions…"[396] Amongst these he lists, "the mysteries of national

394 Amy Hale, "Representing the Cornish: Contesting heritage interpretation in Cornwall", (2001), *op. cit.*

395 Stuart Hall ([1973] 1980), *op. cit.*

396 Simon Anholt (2007), *Competitive Identity: the new brand management for nations, cities*

identity, leadership, culture and social cohesion." In other words, it is of paramount importance to all areas of this discussion and once non-commercial impacts are taken into account, it becomes misleading to define the point at which intervention in representation become branding.[397] In principle, branding is image-making for commercial motives but it may be impossible to separate it from the production of community narratives.

Branding and advertising are commercially, and often institutionally, driven and funded so their messages may be widely disseminated, and in Cornwall tourism ensures extremely high levels of public exposure. Several successive generations have negotiated and constructed identities against the background of intensifying promotion by tourism, but if this works to increase visitor numbers and change buying habits, it may also affect other behaviour, influence inside and outside views of Cornwall and the Cornish and join with other representations to favour attitudes that are conducive or not to given economic and social activities. It may thus interact with who Cornish people think they are, what they imagine they are like, what they think they can do and what they aspire to. In addition to direct commercial impacts, branding can thus indirectly influence the economy, for better or worse, by conveying narratives and myths that underpin or undermine human and social capital, self-image, motivation and expectation. This makes it too important to leave to chance because portrayals may colour residents' perceptions of which activities may reasonably be undertaken and their commitment to Cornwall. These matters are arguably more important than what outside target audiences think and they make branding another practice that contributes to the stories communities tell about themselves and have told about them.

Representing countries and regions is not like branding companies because they have complex cultural, ethnic and historical dimensions. While corporate identities may be commercially engineered, national and regional identities have insider versions that are lasting

and regions, Palgrave Macmillan, p.xii.

397 Cf. Simon Anholt (2010), "Definitions of place branding: Working towards a resolution", in *Place Branding and Public Diplomacy*, Palgrave. secure.palgrave-journals.com/pb/journal/v6/n1/full/pb20103a.html (Accessed 12 June 2011.)

and emotionally charged. Anholt observes that, "although nations and cities do have brand image, they can't usually be branded: at least not in the way that products, services or companies can",[398] yet the belief that they can, leads to

"a naïve and superficial interpretation [...] that is nothing more than standard product promotion, public relations and corporate identity, where the product just happens to be a country rather than a bank or a running shoe."[399]

In the branding exercises of imposed institutions, such superficial and corporate approaches, devoid of connections with Cornishness, contrast strikingly with what happens elsewhere in the Atlantic Arc where there are ethno-cultural claims. In Wales, there are ongoing public discussions with multidisciplinary input that consider culture and language as economic factors and consider how identities and stereotypes relate to image.[400] A component of the Welsh Assembly's "Wales Brand", is the, "Wales Nation brand, which represents Wales as a whole", and "brings to life all the characteristics of the people, place and culture that make us, us."[401] Instead of marketing Wales without reference to culture or community strengths, this vision presents it as "special" because of, "the people, the culture and the place" and "original ideas" that are related to them.[402] Distinct qualities are said to, "affect everything we do or say, because those values are who we are", and far from being a matter for insiders alone, Welsh identity is said to, "affect the way we tell people about tourism, business, studying and regions in Wales."[403] *Cymru Greadigol* ('Creative Wales') also acknowledges that for cultural tourism and

398 Simon Anholt (2007), *op. cit.*, p.5., cf. S. Anholt, Keynote Speech to the European Commission, 2011: www.youtube.com/watch?v=baxr9Ie0zqg (Accessed 25 November 2011.)

399 *Ibid.*, p.xii.

400 E.g. 4-6 March 2010, kaleidoscopicfest.org/programme/adapting-brand-wales/ (Accessed 15 February 2010.)

401 www.walesthebrand.com/Default.aspx (Accessed March 2011.)

402 *Ibid.*

403 *Ibid.*

culturally related businesses to mean anything there has to be, "living culture not just heritage".[404]

Although regions and countries have long had images and promoted themselves, globalization has made branding a worldwide phenomenon with the tendency to regard image as a market profile. In an age of heightened visual awareness and overload, consumerism and market competition, people are confronted by a bewildering array of products and choices of holiday destination. Identity, image and brand are conflated as the subject of intensified activity and branding countries, regions and cities has become so common that it is widely thought of as an expected role for government, spawning all manner of quasi-governmental bodies, advertising agencies and consultants. This is so at all levels from multi-state collaborations to national, regional and more local projects concerning, for example, individual cities and towns, tourist destinations and the production areas of foods and drinks. In order to reflect upon Cornwall's options we may turn to numerous European "regions"[405] where schemes have been developed to raise their profiles and support particular associations—and many have languages, ethno-cultural identities and constitutional aspirations which are mobilized to these ends.

Successful brands rely upon cultural elements as ingredients. Thus language, music, dance and customs feature alongside legends, cuisine and the human landscape, its architecture and monuments. Even stereotypes of temperament and physical appearance may be incorporated with often shallowly clichéd outcomes which serve an immediate commercial end while harming other economic interests and collective status. To start thinking about how two-dimensional clichés work, we have only to contemplate everyday advertising that presents Germany and Japan as technological and efficient, but reserved and humourless, or Italy as classical, stylish and passionate but, by implication, unreliable. Advertising invites us to come to laid-back Jamaica and soak up the reggae, visit passionate Andalucía and experience real flamenco or drink stout in authentic Irish pubs with jigs, reels and fun-loving locals who have "music in their voices".[406] As these examples recall, brands may draw upon and contribute to

404 Remarks by Julie Russel at the Bewnans Kernow conference, *op. cit.*
405 Here "region" and "regional" are used irrespectively of claims to nationhood.
406 Marketing of West Cork. vimeo.com/18624408 (Accessed December 2011.)

stereotypes where the things that are charming, picturesque and marketable imply incapacity in certain areas. They may contribute to identities, increasing perceptions of difference, without serving wider economic interests or enhancing status. Furthermore, the romanticism of incapacitating portrayals may appeal to insiders who then live them out. Representations from tourism confirm and reinforce constructions of inferiority and produce their own truths where the flip side to representing Cornwall as remote, rural and timeless and the Cornish as traditional is that modernity, dynamism, innovation, intellect, science and technology are excluded.[407] Moya Kneafsley makes similar points about the "type-casting of people as traditional" in other Celtic territories where this belies realities such as the fact that, "Brittany has one of the most productivist, tightly manicured and regulated agricultural landscapes in Europe" while portrayed as untamed and pre-modern.[408] Branding Cornwall as a "land of Celtic myths and legends" or "exclusive haven"[409] benefits tourism and property speculation but must hamper the knowledge economy and technological sectors.

The effects of tourism-orientated representations extend to empowered decision-makers who incorporate aspects into their work unreflectively.[410] To generalize, their interaction with the indigenous Cornish is negligible and some have next to no exposure to grass-roots counter-discourses or identity narratives, only knowing more deprived communities through remote professional contexts. This is hardly surprising and does not imply lack of concern but it does involve reproducing and entrenching matter-of-fact presumptions in favour of certain courses of actions and against others. Crudely speaking, it is as though tourists have been asked to decide policy. Institutionalized discourses are amongst the hardest obstacles to overcome and they impede intervention in policy generally. What is left out can be as important as what is included. For example, omitting supposedly unsightly and outmoded industrial representations that clash aesthetically with leisure and up-market

407 See Amy Hale, "Representing the Cornish: Contesting heritage interpretation in Cornwall", in *Tourist Studies*, Vol. 1 (2), pp. 185-196, (2001), London: Sage.
408 Moya Kneafsey in David Harvey *et al.*, (2002), *op. cit.*, p.131.
409 Visit Cornwall website (Accessed August 2011.)
410 Cf. Joanie Willett (2009), *op. cit.*

lifestyles renders certain economic activities inconceivable so that Cornwall is steered further towards tourism dependence and the vagaries of a service economy. Cornwall Council's Core Strategy (2012) has notably been criticized for further emphasis on "high end" tourism and speculative housing with little attention to traditional industries and agriculture.[411] The institutions of regeneration have also appeared to apply a narrow interpretation of "knowledge economy", keenly supporting infrastructure and clean and tidy activities, compatible with counter-urban lifestyles and tourism, but largely ignoring facilities such as Falmouth Docks. Mining and quarrying have been anathema. The reopening of South Crofty Mine was fiercely opposed by the now abolished R.D.A. which preferred to put retail chains, long-unoccupied business units and housing on land it partly obtained by a High Court battle for a Compulsory Purchase Order (October 2006). Decision-makers revealed crass disregard for the central symbolism of mining and ignored the view that reopening with ancillary activities would boost local morale and motivation. Thus it is despite regeneration agencies, rather than thanks to them, that Crofty continued development work. Service-orientated discourses view mining as part of a doomed industrial economy, rather than a spring-board for the knowledge economy and a symbol of technological tradition.

The conflicts of interest involved in image-making might come down to a contest between marketed leisure lifestyles and services on the one hand, and community continuity and economic diversity on the other. Of course this is an over-simplification but over the last two decades or more, tourism, the heritage industries and attendant development pressures have coalesced to produce the phenomenon introduced earlier as "Lifestyle Cornwall", a significant change in Cornwall's evolving image.[412] As a coalition of interests, it brings together diverse actors in shaping a brand that is firmly associated with up-market leisure and lifestyle choices. This "Lifestyle brand" reflects and largely defines a changing tourist gaze,[413] manufacturing

---

411 E.g.   coserginfo.wordpress.com/2012/01/20/falmouth-responses-to-core-strategy; www.facebook.com/pages/Cornwall-beyond-the-Crossroads-Bin-the-Core-Strategy/274653485930072; (Accessed 12 October 2012.

412 Bernard Deacon (2007), *Cornwall: A Concise History, op. cit.* p.227.

413 John Urry (1990), *The Tourist Gaze*, London: Sage.

desire for a new array of leisure options and potted difference that has acquired fashionable status. Its elements feature prominently in glossy magazines and travel programmes, producing an intensification of representation that supports Visit Cornwall's claim that, "In the last decade Cornwall has emerged as one of the World's iconic destinations."[414] Indeed this "destination" is one that fashion-conscious visitors now wish to be seen to have experienced. Moderately well-heeled tourists can now combine the established attractions of, "the dramatic coastline with its captivating fishing harbours, the spectacular beaches and the pounding surf",[415] with visits to prestigious galleries, museums, heritage sites and gardens. As *Invest in Cornwall* (a body ostensibly concerned with inward investment) reminds us, they can also indulge in "gastro-tourism",[416] sampling the menus of celebrity chefs and shopping for "excellent local produce" and "a fine range of locally-brewed beers". These will be found alongside shops selling craft objects and quality leisure wear that correspond to the tastes of middle-brow and middle-class visitors and residents—many of whom are former visitors. They may attend Rock Oyster Festival and watch polo on Watergate beach[417] and in Falmouth they may choose from Seasalt's well-fashioned nautical-style clothing, buy formulaic paintings of harbours and eat at Rick Stein's Seafood Bar, choosing from, "a sort of seafood tapas menu, with such things as Scallops with Guindillo Peppers and Chorizo, Creamed Leeks and Smoked Haddock on Toast and a Cornish Fish Stew".[418]

The Lifestyle brand is far removed from the classic seaside holidays that have typified tourism hitherto, or the family-based attractions

414 www.visitcornwall.com/about-cornwall (Accessed 10 July 2012).

415 www.visitcornwall.com/about-cornwall (Accessed 10 July 2012). Such descriptions abound, e.g. www.dailymail.co.uk/news/article-1373450/British-seaside-resort-St-Ives-Cornwall-beats-Spain-European-beach.html; www.cornwall-online.co.uk/restormel/newquay/newquay-beachguide.htm

416 www.investincornwall.com/key-business-sectors/food-drink/ (Accessed 10 July 2012)

417 www.visitcornwall.com/whats-on/rock-oyster-festival; www.visitcornwall.com/whats-on/north-cornwall/newquay/polo-on-beach (Accessed 6 January 2012.)

418 www.rickstein.com/Rick-Stein%E2%80%99s-Seafood-Bar,-Falmouth.html (Accessed 10 July 2012).

and theme-parks of the 1980s and 90s.[419] These are disparaged as "bucket and spade" and "fish and chip" tourism and there is an assumption that "high-end" facilities will generate more income, even though visitor surveys show that popular family holidays are still a staple and involve higher unit spending.[420] The suspicion must be that championing "quality tourism" and supporting related developments has more to do with cultural sensibilities and snobbery than economic rationale. Decision-makers reveal their own middle-brow tastes in associating cultural tourism with a "dynamic art scene"[421] comprising an array of artistic activities—from the innovative to the banal. They cite galleries, art studios, theatre, ceramics, music and literary festivals and historic gardens, demonstrating understandings of "cultural distinctiveness" that are far removed from the Revivalist's "indigenous Cornish culture" and further still from Proper Cornishness.

The implicit presumption in favour of socially selected tourists and corresponding lifestyle promotion might be expected to maximize side effects, disproportionately attracting those with the means to acquire "an exclusive range of local properties".[422] The brand thus promotes relocation, with all its attendant problems, not just holidays. As Malcolm Bell puts it: "Cornwall is such a great tourism product that people want to buy into it".[423] Lifestyle Cornwall has coincided with Objective One which, while not responsible, has nonetheless helped to fund "flagship attractions" that reinforce it. These are so central to the brand that it has been deemed appropriate to support some that are loss-making.[424] Attractions that have received public funding include: The Tate St Ives, The Eden Project, The National Maritime Museum, The Lost Gardens of

419 E.g. Flambards, Paradise Park, Poldark Mine, Land's End, Dairy Land.

420 Discussions of "Cornwall Visitor Survey, 2010" and "Cornwall Visitor Survey, 2008-9", The South West Research Company for Visit Cornwall.

421 www.visitcornwall.com/about-cornwall; www.visitcornwall.com/videos, (Accessed 11 July 2012.)

422 Estate agent's publicity.

423 Malcolm Bell head of Visit Cornwall in a film by John Howe and Richard Stevens, Digital Media students at UCF, 2010. www.youtube.com/watch?v=KPIGqCJWXpk

424 E.g. The Eden Project's 2 million pound losses in 2011 were written off by Cornwall Council.

Heligan, the Cornish Mining World Heritage Site and Heartlands.[425] Of these, the Eden Project has received the most media attention, even earning a knighthood for its founder,[426] and both enthusiasts and detractors identify it as emblematic of recent transformations. On opening, it quickly became Cornwall's answer to the London Eye, a "must-see" attraction that was soon better-known than most Cornish towns, including, "St Austell near the Eden Project". It joins a litany of, "iconic attractions such as St Michael's Mount, the Minack Theatre, Land's End, King Arthur's castle and the Eden Project."[427] Eden's situation in a former clay pit marks the ongoing demise of the kaolin industry and the ascendency of a form of gentrification that, if plans come to fruition, will see leisure developments at nearby Crinnis (Carlyon Bay), a marina—in place of cargo-handling—at Par and five thousand houses at "eco-villages". For critics, these are unsustainable trends in a part of Cornwall that saw 16 percent population growth between 2001 and 2011 and 21 percent growth in the 1990s and they conflict with maintaining Cornish communities and diversifying industry. Planners have nevertheless backed plans and the former R.D.A. wrote off loans of 1.8 million pounds to the Eden Project that "opened up the whole of the derelict Clay Country for an eco-town".[428]

Institutionally-driven projects to promote and brand Cornwall mesh so closely with the Lifestyle vision that the name "Lifestyle Cornwall" might be said to embrace them. The Cornish cultural and linguistic heritage that justified regional status with the European Union and Council of Europe is subverted so that references to "Cornwall's distinctive way of life" are reinterpreted as meaning green-washed, leisure lifestyles rather than anything to do with Cornish tradition. Joanie Willet identifies, "the notion that Cornwall is a lifestyle choice" and observes that "the cultural

---

425 See www.cornish-mining.org.uk/ (Accessed 10 July 2012.);
   www.heartlandscornwall.com/ (Accessed 26 July 2012.)
426 *The Western Morning News*, 14th December 2012.
427 www.visitcornwall.com/things-to-do (Accessed 11 July 2012). "Iconic" is a
   favoured word in current tourism promotion.
428 www.thisiscornwall.co.uk/Council-s-pound-1-8m-loan-Eden-Project-
   written/story-16238734-detail/story.html (Accessed 11 June 2012.)

distinctiveness used by policy neglects Cornish ethnicity and with it the helpful nature of local narrative based on cultural memory."[429] In a message intended to attract businesses, the "Invest in Cornwall" website emphasizes leisure pursuits, prominent attractions and environmental assets that are said to define, "the Cornish way of life" [and] "make the county a place where people are delighted to settle".[430] Not even a fleeting reference to indigenous culture and community purpose is made, nor is there any inference that investment and initiative might come from within. Instead the emphasis is on lifestyle-led in-migration as a source of improving human capital:

> "our highly regarded quality of life attracts high calibre people"
> [and there has been] "over 30 years of high inward migration."[431]

A page aimed at "business investors" is similarly dominated by holiday brochure spin:

> by being surrounded by some of Europe's most beautiful landscapes and beaches, having a variety of leisure activities to chose from, and attending some of the UK's most stimulating cultural venues, Cornwall is a continuous reminder of what is really important in life.[432]

The first statement contradicts studies which indicate that the educational profile of young and middle-aged in-migrants resembles that of out-migrants[433] and the second reads like an appeal to lotus-eating satisficers who might care to down-size and run a small

---

429 Joanie Willet (2009), p.6-7.

430 www.investincornwall.com/living-in-cornwall/ (Accessed 20 April 2012)

431 *Ibid.*

432 www.investincornwall.co.uk/relocate-to-cornwall/lifestyle.htm (Accessed 28 July 2012)

433 M. Williams, B. Cheal, P. Mitchell, L. Bryant, "Movers and Stayers; Population and Social Change in Cornwall", 1971–1991, Plymouth: Department of Sociology, University of Plymouth, 1995; See also, R. Perry *et al.* (1986), *op. cit.*

beachside café. What is not mentioned is the improved retention of qualified young people from Cornwall, a heartening feature of the last decade—but that would mean dispensing with assumptions.

A groundswell of criticism, informed by the Cornish Movement, is making connections between intensified building pressures and the Lifestyle brand, alleging that developers are carving up Cornwall and that institutions have a service-based vision that is just a new manifestation of tourism dependence. Planners are accused of helping to drive the agenda and of "collaborating with developers" to unlock funding for their departments,[434] and a spoof Cornwall Council Twitter account depicts them playing at covering Cornwall with Lego houses and devising absurd scams to build theme parks, displace St Michael's Mount and convert Truro Cathedral into luxury apartments.[435] The independent film-maker, Mark Jenkin observes that tourism in its new guise has reached the point where it excludes everything else. It is a vision that is, "driven by the outward appearance we give in an attempt to attract more people", and which suggests that, "we ... now live off tourism but in the past we were blood-thirsty savages". It thus manufactures an enthralling fiction that obscures reality: "What could be more attractive to a holiday-maker? Possibly truth but maybe not."[436] The dominance of the Lifestyle brand creates a need to counter "what we get bombarded with and how we're portrayed",[437] a point reinforced by Denzil Monk of *Awen Productions* who speaks of being obliged to make films about Cornish circumstances and themes, "as a response to the rubbish we get fed", and as, "a way of making sure we don't end up accepting it."[438] In articulating counter-discourses, "our culture and the language" are "what we've got available so we can stand up to it".[439] Despite continuing opposition though, a striking impression is of widespread resignation to the inevitability of trends:

---

434 Comments at a "Save Truro" protest, August 2012.
435 twitter.com/CornwallCouncil (Accessed 5 January 2013.)
436 Mark Jenkin (CNC film).
437 *Ibid.*
438 Remarks by film-maker, Denzil Monk at the Krowji.
439 *Ibid.*

"That's the way Cornwall's gone, like it or not. They' got the cash."

"There's plenty of money but who's got it? Nobody I know."[440]

"It was better when the place was less trendy but felt like home."[441]

Complaints about developments reveal dilemmas and contradictions and rarely identify Lifestyle Cornwall as a whole phenomenon. Pride in prestigious attractions and associations with quality co-exists with hostility to the accompanying social exclusivity and cost of living as though these are unconnected. A councillor noted that St Ives had become so expensive that, "none of us go out anymore", and another referred to parking places that sold for fifty thousand pounds each.[442] Others mentioned the exclusivity of Padstow, associating it with the celebrity chef Rick Stein, the television series *Doc Martin* and "posh" and "Hooray Henry" tourism in nearby Port Isaac, Rock and Constantine.[443] Revivalism has complex relationships with the lifestyle brand because it provides means for opposition at the same time as supplying elements that are re-symbolized for its promotion. A possibility already suggested is that Revivalists are unwittingly aiding and abetting harmful trends. They are sometimes involved in loose, unstated alliances with tourism where legitimizing and asserting nationhood seems to go hand-in-hand with branding that uses Cornish culture. They may be convinced that by collaborating they are helping to represent the Cornish as a nation, recalling early Revivalist cooperation with tourism when both shared an interest in portraying Cornwall as different, the former to assert Celtic credentials and the latter to attract visitors with a measured dose of exoticism.[444] The overall

440 Comments in a Falmouth optician's.

441 Remarks by a community nurse at Constantine. *Non verbatim.*

442 www.guardian.co.uk/money/2012/nov/28/st-ives-parking-spaces-auction (Accessed 29 November 2012.)

443 See *The Telegraph*, 23 June 2007: www.telegraph.co.uk/property/3358656/Rock-on.html

444 See Chris Thomas, "See Your Own Country First: The Geography of a Railway Landscape", in Ella Westland (ed.), *Cornwall, the Cultural Construction of*

impression is of struggles for meaning within a Movement that cannot quite define its position on Lifestyle Cornwall, variously torn between opposition to accompanying woes, fatalistic acquiescence and short-term opportunism.

Tourism offers Revivalists opportunities to present their messages to the outside world, as well as to the Cornish themselves. For example, volunteers who ran a work-shop were "quite cheered" after presenting the Cornish language and some "genuine Cornish culture" to "English holidaymakers" who were, "greatly interested and very supportive". Symbiotic collaboration between ethno-cultural activists and tourism is common elsewhere and the principal of communication is the same whether it happens on a Native American reservation or a Scottish island. Using tourism as a channel need not involve collaboration through. In Spain's "autonomous communities", I observed political messages that simply take advantage of tourists being there. Galician activists at *Día de Patria Galega* handed out leaflets in English, French and Italian, explaining demands for further support for their language and in the Basque Country banners across buildings and bridges proclaimed: "Welcome to the Basque Country", "You are not in France. You are not in Spain" and "Here we speak Basque."[445] The English slogans target outsiders but they also address Basques. The point is that in Cornwall, there might be unexpected ways of profiting from tourism and culture that neither the Cornish Movement nor public bodies have engaged with but which involve affective appeals.

The economic potential of culture was discussed at Bewnans Kernow's well-attended conference, "Cornish Identity—Good for Business" (12.2.11 at Lys Kernow).[446] Practitioners and campaigners from the Cornish Movement were brought together with representatives of business, local government officers and councillors to:[447]

Place, Penzance: Patten Press with the Institute of Cornish Studies.

445 I visited the areas in August 2010 and July 2011.

446 See www.businesscornwall.co.uk/news-categories/cornish-economy-news-categories/cornish-identity-good-for-business-123 (Accessed 6 July 2012)

447 Including Cornwall Council's chief executive Kevin Lavery, Visit Cornwall's Malcolm Bell, Cornwall - European Region of Culture's Julie Seyler, Jenefer Lowe of Maga and Stephen Gilbert M.P.

explore how competitive advantage can be gained by understanding and using Cornwall's inherent characteristics and how Cornish culture and identity and Cornish business can co-operate further in order to develop and maximize both economic potential and cultural distinctiveness.[448]

Achieving prosperity and respect for the whole community was a clear motive and discussions revealed intense awareness of Cornwall's "new circumstances" and the heightened concerns that accompany them. Some voiced these concerns strongly and emotionally, revealing frustration and alienation from institutions that were accused of being "part of the problem" and "making things worse". The objective of generating work to "let our young people stay here"[449] and allow "the Cornish way of life to carry on and prosper" was linked to hopes for the "Cornish language and culture" and issues around Cornwall's image and self-respect. Using the language of the Cornish Movement, Stephen Gilbert M.P. suggested, ambitiously, that the challenge was to, "get the best out of that identity, to make sure that we are able to promote Cornwall's culture and position ourselves as one of the twenty-first century's leading nations". The range of issues covered supports Anholt's observation that branding has multiple motives, not just immediate and *a priori* rational interests of commerce and profit. Unremarkably though, the main themes were branding and marketing for tourism, products and services and there was agreement on the need to "stand out from the rest" and "present a strong, distinct identity that everybody recognizes". Malcolm Bell of Visit Cornwall related this to "competitive identity", observing that:

> The last decade has seen an explosion of the use of the words [Cornwall and Cornish] to sell products and services [...] associating Cornwall and Cornish with the positive.

Others mentioned an increase in business names that include "Kernow" and the "Cornish culture" that most speakers wanted to

---

448 Colin Roberts, conference organizer, Press Release, February 2011.
449 A remark by Richard Angove.

validate was evidently the subset of Revivalist expressions that includes neo-traditional music and dance and the language. Several contributors focused on professionalizing and marketing cultural practice to allow people to make a direct living and spoke of struggling to get access to venues, funding and media exposure. The conference was not limited to commodification, though and several business chiefs emphasized feelings of belonging, saying that Cornish identity contributed to their motivation and gave their businesses distinct and advantageous profiles. These might be more fruitful areas to explore. For example, performers might be informal ambassadors for the whole economy, not just tourism. This is lost on public bodies and there is failure to grasp that audiences abroad may include potential business collaborators and supporters in all domains. At *Brest 2012*, Europe's largest maritime festival and an important showcase for maritime industries, just over a hundred miles away, Cornwall was almost the only Atlantic Arc region without a stall to promote trade and industry and sponsored performances and exhibitions. Similarly at the Lorient Interceltic Festival, year after year, a small Cornish Language stand is staffed by volunteers while funded performers from Asturias, Australia, Galicia, Ireland, the Isle of Man, New Brunswick, Scotland and Wales accompany professionally mounted exhibitions.[450] Audiences include business people, public representatives, politicians and journalists who share Pan-Celtic identifications which might pre-dispose them to work with Cornwall.

In particular, Cornwall appears to be missing a trick in not using culture and heritage to make explicit links between its industrial past and the technological present and future. This could boost morale by setting the identity myths of the globe-trotting, "Industrial Celt" in the here and now and it could support a realistic brand built around innovation, skill with the credibility that accrues from a demonstrable engineering pedigree. This connection is not made by regeneration bodies but the ingredients of industrial heritage and an industrially-motivated diaspora could be used to brand Cornwall differently. Cornwall's falteringly-transmitted narratives and myths are well suited to branding for technology. Requisites such as

450 festival-interceltique.com/ (Accessed 2 January 2013.)

dynamism, innovation, enterprise, imagination, efficiency, "workish-ness" and reliability may be claimed and asserted as aspects of an industrial attitude to combat Lifestyle Cornwall's "longed-for Cornish laid-back feel".[451] Cornish Studies students may recognize these attributes as resembling those ascribed to the Cornish in the late nineteenth century when such flattering adjectives as: fearless, enterprising, indomitable, industrious and independent, peppered accounts.[452] Joined-up institutional interventions might use heritage and culture strategically to tell a story of cultural and technological continuity that foregrounds industry, invention, connectedness and maritime potential. This would update narratives of past industrial prowess so that working in engineering and cutting-edge tech-nologies and developing international connections is presented as a natural succession. It might therefore be possible to support a community mythology that accords with a brand message that includes something like this:

> Cornwall's culture of engineering, mining and ship-building is being transformed into innovation in cutting-edge technologies and internationally connected businesses by a generation that is inspired by our history as a centre of world mining and invention.

UNESCO's designation of a Mining World Heritage Site (2006)[453] is opportune. It represents, "a significant but slightly mysterious sea change in the ways in which Cornwall's industrial heritage is viewed"[454] and could therefore be used for the kind of brand proposed above; but as some involved acknowledge, it has, "to date, been almost wholly linked to bolstering and diversifying [Cornwall's] leisure industry."[455] An important element is Heartlands in the middle of the Camborne-Redruth conurbation—a £30 million, Cornwall Council-led project close to South Crofty where a re-

451 www.visitcornwall.com/whats-on/rock-oyster-festival (Accessed 7 January 2013.)
452 Cf. Philip Payton (1992), p.110; P. J. Payton (1996), p.210-211.
453 www.cornish-mining.org.uk/ (Accessed 7 November 2012.)
454 E-mail exchanges with Adam Sharp of the Mining World Heritage Site.
455 *Ibid.*

launch of metal mining is underway. Heartlands is promoted as "A Brave New World Heritage Site" a "Cultural Playground" and "19 acres of eclectic fun"[456] which sceptics criticize as a sanitized theme-part that cleanses the industrial landscape and supports the Lifestyle brand. It is probably all of these things but there is also an opportunity to communicate an economic message, there being nothing inherent in a heritage site that precludes using it to brand non-leisure activities. On the contrary, public education is a traditional justification, but present uses for tourism push industry further into the past. Former miners spoken with dislike the statue of a nineteenth-century miner in Redruth, wondering why he could not have been from the late twentieth century and have a hydraulic rock drill, instead of being perched on a slab of Chinese granite in a vaguely comic stance. When raised with a heritage site manager, he thought that such an image would be "too recent", revealing an assumption that picturesque pastness is appropriate. Changing this would be one way to challenge the norm for decision-makers to ignore the recent scale of extractive industry, with accompanying cultural predispositions towards certain types of employment in sections of the community. In the mid to late 1980s around 9,000 people worked in China clay, more than 2,000 directly in tin mining and hundreds more in granite and slate quarrying, not to mention related and auxiliary industries, yet decision-makers and heritage managers overlook the fact that these combined as one of the most important sectors of the economy less than thirty years ago:

> Given the period of time which has elapsed since Cornwall's industrial sites were substantial contributors to its economic base, and also a major employer, a process of re-interpretation and re-evaluation will inevitably take place.[457]

Industrial heritage provides important symbolic references so raising its profile, valuing it and relating it to the quest for a dynamic future could contribute to emotional capital. In response to this suggestion, heritage management professionals agreed with varying

456 www.heartlandscornwall.com/ (Accessed 26 July 12.)
457 E-mail exchanges with managers of the World Heritage Site.

degrees of conviction but, interestingly, one thought that the benefits would apply most to the indigenous Cornish and "economically-deprived parts of the county".[458] It was recognized that heritage could raise the confidence and aspirations of young people through appeals to, "Cornish identity and an awareness that there is ample evidence that Cornwall could again play a larger role on the national and international stage if it had the opportunity..."[459] This is precisely where the World Heritage Site's contribution to "raising Cornwall's national and international profile" could be linked to, "the next stage—building a vibrant and innovative local economy".[460]

The traces of industry could put Cornwall in the same category as areas where new technologies are actively encouraged to replace old industries and build upon residual skills and attitudes. Even a degree of industrial grime and dereliction may suggest a serious setting for work, and visiting engineers and scientists may be attracted by past technology:

> Guess what, engineers like engineering and if they're into biomass or turbines or oil exploration or whatever, they get off on beam engines... When they come here to work, they're gob-smacked.[461]

A long mining and engineering tradition would therefore seem to be the perfect background for promoting emerging sectors (offshore exploration, renewable energy, marine engineering...) so as to profit from connections—as recognized by a former head of Camborne School of Mines:

> mining engineering and minerals processing education in particular are excellent backgrounds for a diverse range of careers and businesses [...] it is wonderful to have on our

458 *Ibid.*
459 *Ibid.*
460 *Ibid.*
461 Conversation at Pool, August 2011.

doorstep modern, high technology companies who are likely to employ our graduates.[462]

In the same vein, a cluster of businesses at Wheal Jane (a former mine) that build upon mining skills have been related to the knowledge economy:

[T]he technologies deployed in these businesses have evolved from the mining sciences which put Cornwall at the forefront of the industrial age and today these emerging businesses use cutting-edge technologies in environmental services and dot com applications to add value to our knowledge-based economy.[463]

The transferability of skills is also understood by students:

When I finish my degree, I don't know. I'll try and get a mine surveying job somewhere in the U.K. or go abroad for a bit but I could just as easily work in civil engineering or something else that uses the skills.[464]

A public project that grasps some of these issues is the "Cornwall Brand",[465] which is "primarily aimed at businesses which operate in the knowledge economy sectors". These are defined rather narrowly as, "environmental technology, aerospace, medical and I.T. sectors"[466] but Cornwall Brand's website includes a rare instance of the leisure image being identified as a problem:

Many still see Cornwall as just a beautiful holiday destination—a great place to relax, but not one that they

---

462 Keith Atkinson, Cornwall Provost University of Exeter and previously Chair of the Combined Universities in Cornwall Executive, former Head of Camborne School of Mines.

463 Carleen Kelemen, director of the Objective One Partnership, 14 June 2007, "Cutting rock to cutting edge" (unlocated document received).

464 A student at the C.S.M. Test Mine, November 2011.

465 www.cornwallbrand.co.uk/ (Accessed July 2012.)

466 *Ibid.*

associate with dynamic companies delivering state-of-the-art products and services that can compete with the best in the world.[467]

The website combats this "one-dimensional perception"[468] with technological images, vocabulary and news in order to, "Promote Cornwall's entrepreneurial expertise" and "represent a dynamic Cornwall". Absurdly though, Cornwall Brand is associated with Cornwall Development Company and funded by Objective One Convergence and Cornwall Council, meaning that it is institutionally and financially linked to bodies that send contradictory messages. In the absence of a global Council policy on Cornwall's image, closely related organizations offer competing messages that are financed by the same public sources. If conflicts of interest seem insurmountable, we may turn to countries and regions whose prevalent images impress us with capacity in multiple economic, social and cultural fields while being aesthetically and affectively appealing. Britons might think of New Zealand, Australia and Canada in this way, for instance and many Europeans think of the Catalan capital, Barcelona as economically and socially dynamic, culturally rich and blessed with a top football club. The point is that geographical locations can have positive, valorizing images which are diverse and which do not carry many negative caveats, so it might be possible to displace Cornwall's one-dimensional lifestyle brand with something less distorting. It is not enough to be liked because an image based wholly on the attractiveness of scenery and lifestyles, or even upon difference and likability, will not have ingredients for industry and business. Having a high profile that works for one economic sector is not the same thing as having the best brand. When it comes to building a strong, diverse economy, perceptions of capacity may be more important than media prominence, so somewhere that is seldom in the news may nevertheless have a brand that is suited to its needs. Cornwall's high-profile brand currently favours a small number of sectors and development interests at the expense of large swathes of its people so a public branding policy needs to ensure that

---

467 *Ibid.*
468 *Ibid.*

leisure does not exclude other sectors, including those which already contribute more economically.[469]

Anholt suggests that trying to, "contradict or erase long-standing negative perceptions that are deeply rooted in other countries",[470] can be counterproductive because, "Public opinion often remains strongly attached to negative perceptions about countries, just because they are deeply rooted and picturesque, and will resist even quite categorical proof against such views."[471] The foundations of Lifestyle Cornwall come into this category and include problematic images that have emerged from tourism, the arts and romantic novels over the last two hundred years. As Anholt remarks, "people will never voluntarily 'trade down' from an exciting and negative but incorrect perception to a boring and positive but correct one",[472] and those of Lifestyle Cornwall are so closely bound to escapist fictions and holidays that they would be hard to tackle head on with success. Anholt's advice is sobering but not defeatist and founded on the principle that it is easier to "direct a moving perception" than stable ideas. As a starting point he advocates concentrating on aspects of image that are easier to influence and suggests making links with opinion trends on wider issues (e.g. climate change, the global economic situation…).[473] Lifestyle Cornwall rearranges established ideas, adding new elements to create a still-developing image that, for all its problems, is dynamic and shifting, opening people's minds enough to offer an entry point for intervention. so it might be feasible to step in and steer a preferred course, adopting Anholt's strategy of identifying ideas that people are happy to drop or adopt. They may cling stubbornly to picturesque and romantic notions, for instance, while abandoning the idea that Cornwall is unconnected, behind the times and problem-free. Cornwall could

---

469 ONS figures in 2011 state that leisure-related industries represent about 11% of the economy.

470 Simon Anholt (2010), *Places, Identity, Image and Reputation*, Basingstoke and New York: Palgrave Macmillan, p.144.

471 *Ibid.*, p.146.

472 *Ibid.*

473 Simon Anholt, "Is this about me? – The critical issue of relevance", in *Place Branding and Public Diplomacy* (2009) 5, 253–259.

therefore seize the opportunity of being en vogue[474] to build a viable brand for the whole economy.

Tourism brings the opportunity for a joined-up strategy to address 4.5 to 5 million visitors each year. Visitors come from all walks of life, including prime ministers,[475] business leaders, journalists and civil servants so there is ample scope for altering perceptions and influencing decision-making. For example, Cornish cultural performance could inform visitors about Cornwall's international connections, highlight aspirations and spread awareness of social, economic and cultural issues. Technological and business innovations could be show-cased and associated with mining heritage. Visit Cornwall report that, "80% of visitors know we've got industrial history",[476] so this is really just a matter of continuing the story into the present. It is apparent that visitors are interested by encounters with working life. In Falmouth they stop to photograph dry docks and cranes and at Wheal Martyn China Clay Museum they view a working clay pit. This could mean building relationships with visitors and providing multi-faceted images of Cornwall and it could develop the affective phenomenon remarked upon at the Bewnans Kernow conference, leading former holiday-makers to buy Cornish produce and do business with Cornish firms.

The potential for building upon visitor experiences is also suggested by strategies in Brittany where cultural identity is used in domestic and external marketing. The label "Produit en Bretagne" brings together hundreds of companies and several thousand products, representing hundreds of thousands of jobs and it consciously valorizes Breton culture, extending a label that began with food and drink to include everything from companies that manufacture car parts and beds to geothermal energy and accountancy services. It builds upon partnerships between universities, cultural bodies and industry and it works because non-

---

474 So described by Will Hawkes in an article on beers and small breweries: blogs.independent.co.uk/2012/01/27/beer-cornwall-is-now-en-vogue/ (Accessed 10 July 2012.)

475 Regulars have included David Cameron, Margaret Thatcher and Harold Wilson.

476 Comments by Malcolm Bell of *Visit Cornwall* at the Bewnans Kernow conference, "Cornwall means Business", 12 February 2011.

commercial uses of culture generate solidarity amongst insiders that can be communicated to outsiders. Commercial uses thus depend upon Breton motivations, extending loyalty to wider markets as a kind of friendship. A publicity campaign combines images of the Breton flag at the head of a demonstration with the caption "*Génération Solidaire!*" and the slogan "*L'achat solidaire pour l'emploi*", and another advertisement uses the Breton phrase "*Plijadur penn da benn*" ('Pleasure from beginning to end'). The latter appears through-out France (in the Paris Metro, at the Stade de France and the Cannes Film Festival) where it appeals to people who are well-disposed towards Brittany, including thousands who appreciate Breton music. Once again culture benefits the economy indirectly instead of just being a commercial commodity and performers act as ambassadors. *Breizh*, the Breton name for Brittany, and its abbreviation *BZH* name everything from small businesses to estate agents and the highly successful Breizh Cola.

Private branding usually ignores wider social, economic and cultural considerations and does so for sound commercial reasons. A local brewery, for example, does not have to think about how the imagery it chooses contributes to perceptions of a region or country and doing so might even reduce its profits. It just has to sell beer and may exploit stereotypes or clichés to do so; but although private branding is a matter for individual enterprises, it is reasonable to expect public institutions to consider wider interests. This would be expected to lead all levels of government and their agencies to agree objectives and preferred images and to coordinate strategies. Even if this proves hard to extend to outside bodies, Cornwall Council might rise to the challenge on its own and develop a clear collective strategy which it is prepared to respect in its own work and assert in dealings with agencies, quangos, central government and business. This cannot be separated from strategic planning because it is bound up with desires for the future, questions of identity, economic controversies and political debates. At present though, officers and councillors confirm that there is no coordinated approach or policy, despite consideration at senior levels.[477] There is, however, a degree of frustration which bodes well: "There is a lot of good work going

---

477 Communications from the Chief Executive's Department (1st to 5th March 2012.)

on in Cornwall, within and without the council, yet to read the local press you would hardly know it."[478] Some at Lys Kernow wish to, "work with partners to develop more of a 'campaigning' style, for Cornwall, rather than any sectional interests",[479] but are thwarted by certain limitations. Isolated efforts are dissipated for want of coordination and political direction and relevant policies that are voted upon by councillors are not then translated into a purposeful strategy. For example, "supporting regional distinctiveness" is a policy intention but it is commonly subverted or ignored. Like policies on "sustainability", it has funding implications that can be reduced to box-ticking and an occasional nod to indigenous Cornish cultures, thus adding "Kernow-wash" to the "green-wash" of fake environmentalism.

The first stage in any coherent branding exercise is identifying aims and objectives, so it is proposed that Cornwall's institutions should unambiguously take sides in conflicts of interest and develop an image that supports community resilience, addresses disadvantage and maintains a Cornish tradition. Although it would be naïve to suppose that it is possible to implement a strategy with full success, the fact is that public bodies already intervene massively, expensively and inefficiently in image-making for multiple ends, such as attracting visitors, wooing new businesses and promoting themselves. An example was the commissioning of a Cornwall Council logo in 2008 at a cost of £476,000. The exercise underestimated widespread attachment to the symbolism of the former "County" Council arms and had to be abandoned in the face of protests about the cost and the design. This is just one example of matter-of-fact public branding and image-making being undertaken disjointedly without an overarching strategy or convincing consultation. Public bodies with differing agendas spend large sums on presenting Cornwall in conflicting ways so if public promotion is to continue, its compartmentalized activities should be replaced with a cohesive policy. Ironically, given the massive scale of public financing for selective images, Council officers say that it is conflicts of interest and political differences that make coherence difficult to achieve.[480]

478 *Ibid.*
479 *Ibid.*
480 Communications from Chief Executive's Office, Cornwall Council, 1 March

Without a clear political will, a worry is that proactive policy-making would leave officers open to charges of "spin doctoring" and favouring certain interests,[481] yet this is precisely what happens now. Supposed limitations do not stop piecemeal branding and publicity being undertaken by individual departments and by non-elected agencies. Some kinds of promotion, particularly those connected to tourism, are rendered banal, unremarkable and almost unquestionable so that economic discrimination passes unnoticed. The departmental organization of regional government reinforces disconnected and contradictory approaches which are further fragmented by creating companies and agencies for specific tasks. Departments and officers charged with specific objectives, such as attracting businesses, marketing heritage sites or boosting visitor numbers, currently have nothing to gain professionally by compromising them in the wider interest.

The need for common purpose is basic wisdom in the hard-headed world of branding and Anholt observes that regions and countries "will only get where they're going if they all agree what they want and who they are."[482] He makes analogies with corporate culture and discusses "brand purpose" using such vocabulary as:—"shared values", "spirit" and "common purpose".[483] This connects with linking image and brand management to strengthening and shaping a mythology built upon Cornish narratives and aspirations. Branding works best if accepted, relayed and lived out by the communities concerned, so to be useful Cornwall's public brand needs to connect convincingly to imagined identities and a desirable future that interpellates local people.[484] Imposed brands that fail to do this give rise to scepticism and may be rumbled as cynically motivated fictions.

2012.

481 *Ibid.*

482 Simon Anholt, Keynote speech to the E.U. (2011), www.youtube.com/watch?v=baxr9Ie0zqg (Accessed May 2011.); cf. S. Anholt, "Place branding: Is it marketing or isn't it?", in *Place Branding and Diplomacy* (2008) 4, 1-6. Palgrave Macmillan. secure.palgrave-journals.com/pb/journal/v4/n1/full/6000088a.html (Accessed 12 June 2012.)

483 Simon Anholt (2007), p.5.

484 Cf. Simon Anholt, "Is this about me? – The critical issue of relevance", *op. cit.*, pp. 253–259.

Chapter 7

Kernow or Kernowland?

This discussion began with the subjective pro-position that Cornish cultures are worth maintaining and it has explored ways to use them in working towards more resilient and inclusive communities following transformations that have shaken the very foundations of local identities. This has been shown to be far from straightforward, though. Circumstances have been exposed which have implications for how cultural practitioners undertake their work, as well as for policy and image-management. This chapter therefore includes warnings and recommendations to the Cornish Movement.

The term "Cornish Movement", normally applied to the organized activities of Celtic Revivalism and political nationalism, has been extended to a broader, more diffuse spectrum of cultural and political phenomena that result from the pervasive effects of nationalist discourses. These have been linked to everyday responses to new circumstances and trends that threaten the material and social foundations of a distinctly Cornish community. Although this has highlighted the oneness of the Movement as an assertion of identity and solidarity, it has also revealed its heterogeneity as a nebulous assemblage of responses that encompasses widely differing ideas about what constitutes Cornish culture, how that might best be maintained and transmitted and which purposes it should serve. Recognizing an underpinning unity has allowed the Movement to be considered as a focus for community organization and networking while considering its heterogeneity and that of Cornish society has made it possible to begin fleshing out complex issues that are often reduced to binary oppositions and an exclusive focus on ethnicity. The Movement has been identified, firstly as a set of discursive formations that challenge imposed representations and decisions, and secondly as a site of conflicting internal imaginings and cultural hygienes. It brings together agents who collectively offer the prospect of beneficial change but also risks being diverted and missing that vital opportunity.

The point has been made that in challenging ascribed representations, Cornish responses are themselves influenced by external discourses so that it is hard and ultimately misleading to clearly differentiate insider and outsider versions. Thus, although the Cornish Movement provides the discursive and symbolic means by which the Cornish—and affective allies—perceive and defend their collective interests and perpetuate a sense of group, it also allows unhelpful outside imaginings of Cornishness to be elected by insiders and incorporated into identity performances. Revivalist cultures are therefore at the centre of struggles for meaning that mirror the material conflicts between socially inclusive regeneration and a Lifestyle Cornwall of "exclusive" residential developments and leisure services that inhibits building a diverse economy. Some activities, created for militantly Revivalist, nationalist or community-strengthening purposes, appear to be undergoing re-signification within counter-urban lifestyles that depend upon imagining Cornwall, in one way or another, as an accessible, lightly "green-washed" rural escape with beaches, good schools, safe streets, middle-class cultural attributes and corresponding recreational facilities. Cornish symbols are being safely imported into marketing Cornwall as a consumable experience so that a revamped Revivalist package risks becoming part of an upgraded lifestyle offer. These dangers were brought starkly into focus by poorly-spelt but insightful comments on the news site, *This is Cornwall* where individuals allied to the Movement clashed in discussions with free-market opponents:

It is a source of great irritation for [name] and his handfull (*sic.*) of extremist fellow nationalists that the point of difference they worked so hard to manufacture, i.e. a seperate (*sic.*) identity, is the very thing that works against their miserable end goal. While Team Kernow carries on his lost battle the rest of us are getting rich on the marketing tool

he thought was his alone. It must really get up his nose…
lol.[485]

The correspondent's goading reveals something that Revivalists prefer not to acknowledge, namely that picturesque, invented and revived traditions are tailor-made for branding a counter-urban destination for visitors and one-off movers, perhaps fuelling the developments that threaten Cornishness itself, while paradoxically offering the means to resist them. They may contribute to the Lifestyle brand that "manufactures desire"[486] for repeat holidays (and second-homes) and sells Cornwall as a place to move to and enjoy the blissful promise of having a slower pace of life. Revivalist imagery is beginning to contribute to a safe and heavily commodified simulation of Cornishness that exists independently of any lived, ethno-cultural reality and its socio-economic conditions. Like those ersatz performances of Hawaiiana that continue in the near absence of indigenous Hawaiians, simulations need have no reference to the Cornish.

In Frederic Jameson's identification of "Late Capitalism"[487] or Jean Baudrillard's "hyper-reality",[488] culture takes the form of representation and cultural performance in the broadest sense and is consumed in the form of material and non-material products. Distinctions between art, culture and commerce have become increasingly unclear and the whole of everyday life is aesthetic and subject to the all-pervasive reach of commodification.[489] The consumption of signs as exchange-value may thus be considered to be what drives consumer capitalism and it leads us away from direct lived experience. In Baudrillard's account, this "seduction" involves us being "bombarded" by images and "saturated" by representation

485 www.thisiscornwall.co.uk/Devon-Cornwall-communities-left-scourge-second/story-17361766-detail/story.html, (Accessed 20 November 2012.)

486 See Arthur Asa Berger (2008 [1996]), *Manufacturing Desire: Media, Popular Culture, and Everyday Life*, New Brunswick and London: Transaction Publishers.

487 Frederic Jameson, "Postmodernism or the Cultural Logic of Late Capitalism", *New Left Left Review*, No. 46, (1984).

488 Jean Baudrillard (1983), *Simulacra and Simulations*, translated by Foss, New York: Semiotext(e).

489 Cf. Mike Featherstone (1991), *Consummer Culture and Postmodernism*, London and Newbury Park, California: Sage.

to the point that "authentic", first-hand cultural experience cannot be distinguished from aspects that are packaged and consumed. Baudrillard identifies four orders of simulation which are progressively removed from reality. In the first, "faithful copies" or images are generally believed while, in the second order, unfaithful copies distort reality but nevertheless refer to it. Then, in the third order of simulation, arbitrarily proposed images may obscure the absence of reality and masquerade as faithful copies, despite there being no original. Finally, in the fourth order of simulation, symbols and signs replace reality as *simulacra* that have either lost any reference to an original or which were never connected to reality in the first place. Cultural products need no longer pretend to be real because consumers' cultural lives are largely "artificial". What matters is the exchange-value of signs and their currency as cultural and symbolic capital. Instead of mediating or concealing reality, fourth order simulacra hide the extent to which reality has become irrelevant to how we make sense of society and everyday life. Simulacra, as copies without originals, construct perceived realities with the implication that cultural identities are also consumed as such in the same crowded and competitive market-place that has been discussed in relation to branding.[490] The magnitude and intensity of representations of Cornwall and the Cornish make this an extreme case[491] of an identity that is bombarded with commercially or romantically preferred themes that have been altered and amplified by a still evolving Lifestyle brand, leaving oppositional voices hoarsely shouting and gesturing against a semiological wall of sight and sound.

Baking a Cornish Pastiche

Lifestyle Cornwall is a stark example of cultural commodification in the form of consumable signs, including simulacra, which have little or no reference to "real" Cornishness. This might be bringing about the circumstances in which the distinction between a Cornish reality and its representation is disappearing for insiders and is unperceivable and irrelevant for visitors and in-migrants. Much of

490 Jean Baudrillard (1983), *op. cit.*
491 Cf. Neil Kennedy and Nigel Kingcome (1998), *op. cit.*

what Lifestyle Cornwall serves up could be described by the inevitable pun, "Cornish pastiche"[492] and related to Jameson's identification of pastiche in postmodern cultural production.[493] Basically, pastiche involves re-using existing cultural elements and may combine them with other characteristics of postmodern culture, namely eclecticism, fusion and *bricolage*, as well as reflecting scepticism and commercial cynicism. These characteristics manifest themselves to varying degrees within the phenomena that contribute to Lifestyle Cornwall but it is notable that appropriations of Cornish distinctiveness as saleable heritage, as marketable imagery and as the recyclable material of cultural production, often take the form of pastiche. Items from Cornish cultural pasts are cannibalized and presented in recycled, disembedded and distorted forms. Although there is usually no intended parody, neither is there any serious intent beyond the consumption of signs as ephemeral commodities with exchange-value. Commercial displays of Cornish history and commercial art forms often combine appeals to the past with shallow imitations or simulations that correspond to Jameson's characterization of pastiche as "blank parody".[494] Pastiche and simulation extend to the cultural industries where much of the arbitrarily tasteful production aimed at discerning, middle-class consumers reworks elements from Cornish heritage and earlier art forms. This is evidenced, for example, in numerous galleries that sell paintings that reuse elements from the work of the St Ives modernists and the naïve artists, Alfred Wallis and Bryan Pearce. These phenomena have not just happened overnight but have been present in the commodification of Cornwall's culture since the days of the 1960s plastic pisky, fisherman's smock and cream tea. Now though, they have intensified and extended into all aspects of culture.

All of the above forms of simulations and pastiche occur in Cornwall's burgeoning heritage industries and in practice it is impossible to distinguish clearly between the different registers of visitor "attraction" or theme-park, and serious, educational "site". Most notably, the heritage industries present fragments of history or

492 *Ibid.*
493 Frederic Jameson (1991), *op. cit.*
494 *Ibid.*

consumable images as "bombardments of 'perpetual' presents"[495] and recombine elements in much the same ways as sound-bites are reassembled to produce entertaining, but not necessarily informative, radio programmes. Sanitized presentations entrench a presumption against industry and favour leisure, creating further consumable experiences that are detached from working reality: "The paradox of the industrial museum movement is that it is ultimately anti-industrial…"[496] Thus instead of being used to present Cornwall as a place where technology and innovation can happen, industrial heritage sites are stripped of any connection to a working present and incorporated into the Lifestyle brand. This is one of the points at which the received discourses and reflex practices within regional governance (cf. Bourdieu's *doxa*, Barthes' *myth* and Foucault's *technique*)[497] may be exposed as having their origins in fictions and simulations that are removed from basic realities. Just as heritage industries misrepresent an industrial past, so tourism-linked simulations have overwritten modernity, achievement, geographical connections and technology to produce an obscuring palimpsest.

Kernowlond a'gas dynergh[498]

It is in the areas of pastiche and simulation that Lifestyle Cornwall interacts most with Revival's practices. Revivalism includes strands of political opposition to the trends that contribute to it but it is an opposition that is increasingly compromised by unwitting contributions to the brand itself. Whereas this sometimes involves intentional acts, promotion of the lifestyle phenomenon is unintentional and inadvertent. Revivalists furnish visual material for commercially motivated pastiche by others in tourism, leisure and branding and engage in pastiche themselves. Their cultural production resembles

495 Frederic Jameson (1988), *Post-Modernism and Consumer Society*, in A. Gray and J. McGuigan (eds.) (1997), *Studies in Culture: An Introductory Reader*, London: Arnold, pp. 192-205.

496 Robert Hewison (1987), *The Heritage Industry: Britain in a climate of decline*, London: Methuen, p. 104.

497 Approaches to "common-sense" application of discursively-produced "truths". cf, Chevallier and Chauviré (2010), *op. cit.* p.56; Gavin Kendall and Gary Wickham (1999), *op. cit.*; Barthes (1957), *op. cit.*

498 "*Welcome to Cornwall—Kernow a'gas dynergh* (sometimes *dynnargh*)" is the wording on current signs.

other postmodern practices in its intertextual recycling and recombination of elements and in re-imagining cultural pasts and trying to define the present. Revivals and (re)invented traditions rake through the ashes of the cultural past and are shaped discursively by cultural hygienes to produce simulacra of Cornwall which incorporate simulations of Celtishness from elsewhere. These simulate imagined ideals and attach meanings to them as signs and symbols, and in emphasizing ethnicity many appeal to sentimental, romantic, kitsch[499] and picturesque aesthetics. Much of this visual repertoire is a gift for marketing which can be used to brand products for insiders, connecting with the oppositional rallying calls of the Cornish Movement but it can also sell recreational experiences. The same polysemous elements may therefore name and brand everything from beer and free-range eggs to goat's cheese and holiday cottages. The ongoing re-signification of Revivalist items and the collaboration of some practitioners with commodification therefore raises the possibility that Lifestyle Cornwall is being complemented by a parallel "Kernowland"[500] that departs from the socially engaged and embedded project imagined by Nance and his politicized successors.

Kernowland shares characteristics of hyper-reality with Baudrillard's analysis of Disneyland where, "all the tangled orders of simulation" come together[501] and may be related to visitors' consumption of the "authenticity" of places, populations and cultures as commodities. Visitors' expectations have been shaped by what they have already seen and heard while, as the object of their interest (and consumers themselves), local people sometimes modify their behaviour and culture, either acting out ascribed roles with cynicism or believing in them. In much the same way as described by John Urry in *The Tourist Gaze*,[502] this involves evolving and multiple gazes, including those that uphold Cornwall as authentically Other. The latter have been found to get Revivalists unduly exited and hopeful that Cornish identity is being recognized. At last, they suggest, there

499 e.g. Jonathan Howelett, "Putting the Kitsch into Kernow", in P.J.Payton (ed.), *Cornish Studies*, no. 12, pp. 30-60.
500 Neil Kennedy and Nigel Kingcome (1998), *op. cit.*
501 Jean Baudrillard (1983), *op. cit.*, pp. 1-13 and 23-49.
502 John Urry (1990), *op. cit.*

is awareness that Cornwall has its own language and culture, yet just as cinema-goers do not have to believe in Tolkien's elves in order to watch *The Hobbit* (2012), visitors do not have to believe in Cornish difference in order to gaze upon it. The Cornish language may arouse interest without enjoying much more credibility than the tongues invented by Tolkien.

In Baudrillard's analysis, the *simulacrum* is removed from authenticity but may nevertheless be consumed as a sign in a willing suspension of disbelief that need not be lasting or deep. Visitors may consume identity performances as spectacle and sensual experience without being bothered by whether a reality exists behind the simulation. The Kernowland phenomenon may offer something to enjoy playfully, even humorously, but not an identity to believe in seriously once the performance is over. This may occur in the expanding use of Revivalist imagery and Cornish wording to label and name an impressively large range of quality beers. Some examples combine parodies with comic, naughty postcard-style cartoon imagery that recalls the work of Donald McGill. Cornish consumers may read them in a variety of ways that bring together a sense of fun with a sip of identity but one possibility, for visitors and locals alike, is that they connote a spurious, holiday playground Cornishness. Thus drinking culturally branded craft ale does not have to mean swallowing a real identity, even if it sometimes does. While simulacra, pastiche and parody may support insiders' feelings of difference and contribute to strong identities, they do not lead automatically to everybody having the conviction that it is really out there in homes and work places.

In keeping with Kernowland as a Disneyesque simulation, some suggestions for paid performances resemble the theme-park experiences that attract attention in heritage studies, or of those choreographed Massai dancers who entertain visitors to East Africa. They recall the objectified roles of ex-miners as guides at their former places of work and of actors dressed as cartoon characters at Disneyland. This already happens, at the former Geevor Mine for instance and in general interactions with tourists, but recent propositions raise the spectre of performers acting out hyper-real versions of a folkloric culture based on invented tradition with varying degrees of similitude as far as a pre-simulational reality is concerned. Like those Peruvian pan-pipe players who sell mass-produced Native American paraphernalia in towns and cities across Europe, they could peddle ephemeral Celtic performances and ersatz wares that audiences enjoy momentarily but do not really believe in. In other words, while embedded performances could communicate believable political messages about culture and identity, simulacra are just as likely to reinforce scepticism.

Performances of Cornishness have increased as the Cornish have diminished as a proportion of the population and felt the need to assert themselves. In a similar way, it seems likely that some commercial uses of Revivalist imagery and the Cornish language have only become feasible as the Cornish have become less visible and audible. Thus both insider awareness and commercial appropriations may occur in inverse proportion to the quantitative strength of the indigenous Cornish. The suggestion is not that the Cornish can be written off as an irrelevant minority but they could have dipped below an indefinable level that allows hyper-real simulations to be relatively unconstrained by contradictory realities. For all the displays of flags, car stickers and bilingual street-names, Cornish cultural distinctions have less impact on the everyday experiences of non-Cornish residents and visitors and must surely seem less connected to real people. Cornishness becomes unthreatening, in marked contrast to Welsh or Catalan equivalents where outsiders may even be perturbed by the audible presence of different languages, the imminent possibility of greater autonomy and encounters with imagined or real hostility to the English and Spanish respectively. By contrast, the Cornish may seem hardly more real and present than the spriggans, piskies and giants of legends.[503]

Even without the contributions of Revivalism, Lifestyle Cornwall includes stark examples of the commodification of culture as simulacra and might therefore be thought of as the triumph of processes that critics of tourism and its side-effects identified as "theme-park Cornwall" in the late 1980s.[504] This was criticized as a

---

503 Margaret Courtney (1890), *Cornish Feasts and Folklore*; Craig Weatherhill and Paul Devereux (1994), *Myths and Legends of Cornwall*, Wilmslow: Sigma Leisure.
504 Andrew George, "The Natives are revolting down in the Cornwall Theme-Park", *Cornish Scene*, (1986) Vol.2.2, p.3.

low-wage economy of non-Cornish-owned businesses where, instead of simply having attractions within it, Cornwall as a whole was becoming a playground. Developments like those at Land's End were "The First and Last Straw"[505] and Cornwall's image was said to reflect a "guide-book culture"[506] which was, "a heady concoction of Celtic Remains, Merlin's Magic Land, tales of smugglers and wreckers, ruined tin mines, pasties, pixies and cream."[507] In other words, theme-park Cornwall fed upon parody, pastiche and simulation of indigenous Cornish culture and in doing so it laid the foundation for its social-climbing successor, Lifestyle Cornwall.

Throughout the 1980s and 90s tourism operators sought to move from seasonal business towards "all-year-round facilities" that would maintain their incomes and create employment. A wide range of attractions was supported by public marketing strategies and new businesses catered to niche markets, targeting specific interests. This was the period in which emphasis was placed on "making the most of heritage"[508] financially and publicly owned sites were packaged and marketed with attention to profit-driven imperatives, often resorting to pastiche as "faction" or "edutainment"[509] in a substitute for rigorous public information. Cornish activists clashed with interpretations of history at sites managed by English Heritage, removing signs and picketing events—and a new charity, "Cornish Heritage", was created to keep other sites open to all and free from commercialization. The commodification and "interpretation" of heritage sites further added to the density of a tourist map which figured prominently in the imagination and appealed to the social groups ABC1 that Perry found to comprise a majority of in-migrants—and which still represent a majority of tourists.[510] The density of attractions was reflected in ubiquitous brown road-signs

---

505 Andrew Lanyon (1985), *The First and Last Straw*, [s.l.]: [s.n.]

506 B. Deacon, A. George and R. Perry, (1987), *Cornwall at the Crossroads, op. cit.* p.105-116.

507 *Ibid*, p.106.

508 "Tourism '87, Making the most of Heritage", Department of Employment (1987).

509 That is, combinations of "fact" and "fiction" and of "education" and "entertainment".

510 Visit Cornwall visitor survey, 2010, define these as the main social groups who visit.

for attractions, complete with the red Tudor rose of English tourism—provoking a long paint-daubing campaign and their replacement with a Cornish flag logo, c.1999. As part of the project to transform Cornwall from seasonal holiday destination to year-round leisure zone, some bodies turned to the explicit marketing of culture[511]—but instead of the culture of "the present-day Cornish"[512] this was that of the decision-makers and tourism operators themselves, the same middle-brow and metropolitan-orientated assemblage that Perry noted as typifying the largest section of in-migrants.[513] Indeed, these new residents made corresponding activities viable, leading to facilities such as the Sterts Theatre and Arts Centre near Liskeard, as well as bodies like the Cornwall Arts Centre Trust and events like the Daphne du Maurier and Three Spires Festivals which mainly involve residents, rather than tourists.[514] Against this background, Revivalists created their own festivals and events but in contrast to those that benefited from legitimate cultural capital, they did so with only rare instances of funding.[515] The *Lowender Peran* festival of music and dance involves hundreds of participants from other Celtic countries, filling hotels and guest houses and including outreach activities in schools and public spaces, all without significant support from the leaders of tourism or arts bodies. In the same way, working-class cultural heritage has received scant attention:

In Cornwall, unlike Liverpool or London, very few, if any, examples of working-class heritage are interpreted for the public or promoted by a national organization. Clay-work-ers' houses or Non-conformist chapels, for instance...[516]

511 See R. Perry *et al.* (1986), "The Economic Influence of the Arts and Crafts in Cornwall", Exeter: (A study sponsored by South West Arts and Cornwall Planners.)

512 B. Deacon, A. George and R. Perry, (1987), *Cornwall at the Crossroads, op. cit.*, p.113.

513 Ronald Perry *et al.* (1987), *Counterurbanization: International case studies of socio-economic change in the rural areas*, Norwich.

514 www.dumaurierfestival.co.uk/wp-content/uploads/2012/07/Customer-feedback-from-dMFS-Questionnaire-2012.pdf (Accessed 16 November 2012.)

515 Communications from Merv Davey, a founder.

516 Amy Hale, "Representing the Cornish..." (2001), *op. cit.*, p.191.

If these omissions are beginning to change, that is happening in ways that do not necessarily support the primary uses of culture discussed. The qualitative transformation of Theme-park Cornwall into Lifestyle Cornwall involves an evolution in the tourist gaze and corresponding changes in the aesthetics and emphasis of tourism that reflect changes in British cultures and lifestyles including, for instance, the heavily accessorized growth of outdoor, "designer" sports as signifiers of social standing and the "foody" trends of television cooking programmes, world cuisines and "artisan" bakeries.

When Revivalists contribute to Lifestyle Cornwall they implicitly resign themselves to the present direction of development. Some have been unwilling to challenge this unambiguously and have instead seized upon opportunities to get Cornish items included and to suggest, often tokenistic, modifications to projects that others in the Movement oppose. Gaining acceptance for symbols of national identity and ethnic distinctiveness has been a concern since the early days of the Revival so promoting examples like St Piran's flag and bilingual signs through commercial projects sometimes leads Revivalists to overlook the material impact. For example, an "exclusive" and controversial development of 3,750 houses by the Duchy of Cornwall near Newquay has been named Nansledan (broad valley) and has Cornish-only street names, kindly provided by the unpaid Cornish Signage Panel, but the housing itself generates and caters to outside demand, adding to the process that Bewnans Kernow and others criticize as destabilizing communities. Some Revivalists are so confirmed in the idea that English people— homogenized and *en masse*—are opposed to them that they cannot acknowledge that Cornish names might be a pull factor for well-intentioned in-migrants who find them interesting and attractive. The growth of invented traditions as leisure activities and social outlets also means that participants do not have to look beyond them to a wider, multidimensional Cornish culture, let alone to the nationalisms and social campaigns that inspired their creation. This is evidenced by the awkwardness that I meet from some Revivalists when controversies around development are raised. Whereas they would once have provoked lively comment and vociferous expressions of anger—and often still do—these issues now sometimes meet with embarrassed evasion or suggestions that the language, music and dance should be disconnected from political associations.

Revivalists commonly speak of "promoting" Cornish and Cornish culture, a choice of words that avoids defensive, preservationist vocabulary. Verbs such as "save", "defend" and "preserve" are thought to unhelpfully underline fragility and imply conservatism. It follows that they are self-fulfilling and settle for standinging still. Promotional language is, on the other hand, thought to convey confidence and a presumption in favour of recruitment where the Cornish language is "set to grow exponentially" and Revivalist music and dance have, "the makings of a vibrant youth culture". Discussions in Cornish customarily employ the verb *avonsya* (to advance, progress, promote) and Cornwall Council uses the horticultural-sounding buzz-word "grow". New strategies aim to, "grow indigenous Cornish culture" and "grow the language" with "professionalization of delivery".[517] These usages are accompanied by unrelentingly upbeat accounts of growth and the active communication of entitlement aimed at countering disentitlement and exclusion. Assertively "talking up" Cornish cultures like this can improve their image and doing it with conviction may raise morale and self-esteem,[518] convince others and produce the factor of "congeniality"[519] that recruits and retains.[520] Like some business practices, it is a puffer-fish strategy of bluff where, by feigning strength and self-confidence, Revivalists hope to be taken at face-value like successful gatecrashers: "If we don't seem confident they'll [funding bodies] think we're losers and we will be. We should just act like we expect some of our own taxes and money to come back to us."[521] It is a sound strategy but some instances appropriate the language of marketing ("promotion", "grow", "brand", "publicity",

517 Comments at MAGA conference, Lostwithiel, 1 October 2011.

518 Recalling Mauss' bodily technique. Marcel Mauss (1934), "Les Techniques du corps", in *Journal de Psychologie*, no. 32 (3-4), Paris.

519 Jane Korey (1992), *op. cit.* suggests that congeniality is the most important factor for success.

520 Cf. Bourdieu on bluff in relation to individuals and families, (1980), *Le sens pratique, op. cit.*

521 *Non verbatim* comments.

"exposure", "sell") and could facilitate a blurring of policy objectives. The advancement of culture and language is conflated with commercializing difference, which is then seized upon as an argument for institutional support. The assumptions and values of consumer culture may now be shaping and limiting the strategies considered while a culture of grant applications leads project leaders to apply the imposed criteria of funding bodies to their work. Parts of the Movement are now arguing for commercial routes that contribute to the Kernowland phenomenon in approaches to performance, heritage, tourism, signage and branding, and although it offers opportunities it also leads to potential problems. Firstly, the primary uses of culture are overlooked in a quest for profit that is motivated by a desire for status and the frustrations of "unpaid amateurs" and "struggling professionals". Activists argue for creative practices which are good enough to take the cultural high ground and, "dare to challenge in the interests of excellence" on the "world stage of regional cultures".[522] This is expected to reverse the abandonment of practices which suffer from perceptions of "low value".[523] Amateurs and professionals alike share the reasonable belief that value will accrue to performances in prestigious settings and venues but the extent to which activities are embedded in community cultures may be ignored.

Avoiding a Second Wrong Turn

The emergence of a Kernowland dimension is ironic given the longstanding opposition of the Cornish Movement to exploitative tourism and misrepresentation by the heritage industries[524] but, since the re-signification of Revivalist items is in its early stages it may be contested giving several possible outcomes. Positively, they could be part of the means by which some new residents identify with new communities and value something Cornish, even if it is a simulation. At the same time, though, it could be part of the means by which they act out superficially anti-consumerist and neo-rural styles, playing at being green country folk. Without those involved being aware, such a scenario could co-opt and distort the Movement's

522 Remarks by Bert Biscoe, 12 February 2011.
523 Cf. Ron Perry *et al.* (1986), *op. cit.* p.86.
524 Cf. Amy Hale, "Representing the Cornish..." (2001), *op. cit.*, Abstract.

discourses to support the idea of Cornwall as a counter-urban refuge from the realities of twenty-first century urban life, rather than as a forward-looking community with an ethno-cultural dimension. The suspicion must be that this is already underway and it fits distortions of nationalist rhetoric in marketing "an exclusive haven beyond the border of the Tamar"[525] and branding "Cornwall's distinctive lifestyle".

In the British countryside wealth works to sanitize gentrified enclaves by pricing poorer people out of housing and enabling affluent populations to oppose things that devalue their properties. Relatively inoffensive economic activities are already opposed while almost everything unsightly or noisy, like refuse dumps, recycling centres and waste incinerators, is thrust upon a small number of relatively disadvantaged areas like Gwennap and Goss Moor. Current trends, perhaps best symbolized by planned "eco-villages", could be an extension of this phenomenon, whereby the Tamar is transformed from historical ethnic border to the perimeter of simulational Kernowland that is one step away from a gated community. Some embraces of culture and symbolism may not be what they seem to Revivalists, in other words, but may instead be another form of hyper-real playfulness where the visitors have taken up residence in the theme-park and embraced a do-it-yourself subculture which involves "fourth order simulation" without reference to the lived cultures of the Cornish. The Kernowland phenomenon could therefore worsen the dissonance that makes Proper Cornishness more illegitimate and hamper efforts to bind Revivalist creativity to the Common Cornish Habitus discussed. At worst, it could mark the end of Nance's project to build a culture for all.

If re-signification through commodification, branding and market-ing is beginning to serve interests that are driving speculative building and migration trends, the Cornish Movement has arrived at a crucial turning point—somewhere on the wrong side of CoSERG's "crossroads"—and adherents need to respond with sophistication. In so far as it is possible, the movers and shakers within language revitalization and cultural projects need to become

---

525 Visit Cornwall, www.visitcornwall.com, *op. cit.*

aware of the ease with which the meanings that they attribute to cultural items may be intentionally or unintentionally subverted. Every aspect of culture, cultural landscape and language is open to diverse, unstable interpretations. Engaging actively with the proliferation of meanings and struggling to anchor readings that accord with the social, economic and political project of the Cornish Movement is therefore a prerequisite for employing them to strengthen communities. It is vital to not simply give in to simulation or sell out to short-term gains for individual activities as though revived and invented traditions were the end, rather than the means, to cultural resurgence.

Alongside Baudrillard's orders of simulation, it is possible to "keep it real" and maintain a degree of pre-simulational reality and primary use for human need. Cultural practitioners can, furthermore, sift through simulacra, picking out those which may carry useful myths. This does not have to mean rejecting all commercial uses of culture, nor taking a po-faced authenticist attitude to simulation in principle, but it does require wariness and selection. Care needs to be taken to avoid simply slipping into the logic that commodification is good so Revivalists need to rely less upon marketing-speak and exchange-value as justifications. They might wish, instead, to talk up primary uses and couch more of their work in the language of participation, referring more often to feelings, belonging, community ownership, embeddedness, fostering, nurturing, encouraging, enabling, communicating and sharing. Such an overarching vocabulary might be essential to maintaining ownership.

Signification is an unstable area of unpredictability and dilemma rather than of straightforward choice but the broad issue is of how to avoid collaborating in representations that fuel the processes the Movement has hitherto existed to oppose. Indeed, if the Cornish language and Revivalist activities are to be part of maintaining an indigenous tradition and contribute to emotional and social capital, their practitioners will have to engage unambiguously, tooth-and-nail, to fight those processes on all fronts. There are hard choices to make about how to present Cornish cultures and what to use them for and there are traps and temptations that offer the temporary illusion of progress. Making the wrong choices could compromise the scope for using the language, neo-traditional music and dance and (re)invented traditions and symbols to engage in community building for "one and all". In a short-sighted expedient that is likely to produce scepticism, some have presented their activities and the language as respectable, safe, unthreatening and compatible with the prevailing logic of commerce that underpins the processes marginalizing much of the community. This appears to detract from their transgressive potential and diminish their usefulness as an oppositional rallying point, since part of their appeal involves what might be called militant capital—a symbolic potential that conveys an alternative currency of cultural worth to that of legitimate cultural capital and carries connotations of resistance, solidarity and stoicism in the face of hardship. Where Cornish has been taken up at a grass-roots level, the motives are plainly oppositional and several *Kernowegoryon* (Cornish speakers) suggest that this is why advances were made during the 1980s and 90s when perceptions of exclusion and alienation fuelled learning and everyday use.

When it came to carving out an institutional place for Cornish, it was its symbolic associations with community concerns and the context of marginalization that counted—not meek collusion with lifestyle branding or the prospect of cultural tourism. The creation of Maga, the Cornish Language Partnership and its unfolding public projects in education and awareness-raising were entirely a product of this, as was the U.K. Government's inclusion of Cornish under the terms of the Council of Europe's "Charter for Regional for Minority Languages" in 2003.[526] When the charter was adopted in 2000-2001 it did not at first include Cornish and it was only after a seven-year campaign that this was achieved. This built upon support from councillors and officers, some of whom had attended Cornish classes and Cornwall Council produced a resolution:

This Council sees the Cornish language as a vital part of contemporary culture and welcomes the work being done to

---

[526] Signature for Cornish, 11 March 2003, registered 18 March. Recognition as an official language of UK 11 June 2003 (Parliamentary answer in House of Lords.). cf. Ken Mac Kinnon, "'As Cornish as Possible' – 'Not an Outcast Anymore': Speakers' and Learners' Opinions on Cornish", in P.J.Payton (ed.), *Cornish Studies*, no. 12, pp.249-267.

promote its wider usage and status. This Council will, where appropriate, encourage the use of the language for the naming of streets. (8 April 1997)

The campaign connected with a sense of struggle within the Cornish Movement and the wider community and was led by people who also campaigned for jobs, notably and symbolically during the "tin crisis" (1985-2000) and the *Keskerdh Kernow* march to London in 1997.[527] The issue united revivalists across the divides of the spelling disputes that had hampered development, quickly gaining the participation of Andrew George, M.P. and Robin Teverson, M.E.P. It also mobilized affective alliances between linguistic minorities, so that some of their politicians and civil servants argued Cornwall's case within British and European institutions,[528] much as happened during applications for European regional status and Objective One funding. As a result of unrelenting representations, the Government commissioned "An Independent Academic Study of Cornish",[529] and subsequently included Cornish under Part II of the Charter. For its part, Cornwall Council created the Cornish Language Partnership in 2005 and obtained funding for staff. Understandably, this successful outcome was felt as a hard-earned victory against Establishment opposition and left a sense of common purpose, despite continuing disagreements about orthography and language planning. Arguably then, the voyage has been more important than the destination, building precisely the kind of relationships, solidarity and morale that favour the capacity to get things done.

The Cornish language could become a key component of developing networks and strengthening communities. Some speakers have long recognized its symbolic and potentially unifying functions[530] and talked about them in ways that recall post-structuralist themes of symbolic subversion; but there are barriers to

527 Simon Parker (ed.) (1998), *Cornwall Marches On!*, Truro: Keskerdh Kernow 500.
528 E.g. Dafydd Wigley M.P. (Plaid Cymru).
529 Ken MacKinnon, *An Independent Academic Study on Cornish*, EKOS Ltd. & SGÙD for the Government Office of the South West, Plymouth, 2000.
530 E.g. Tim Saunders, in Cathal Ó Luain (ed.) (1983), *op. cit.*; cf. Pierre Bourdieu (2001), *Langue et pouvoir symbolique, op. cit.*; P. Bourdieu (1980). *Ce que parler veut dire…, op. cit.*

this happening, including the dissonance that has been related to social context and cultural hygienes. Some reactions to the language suggest that it can be perceived as part of an authentic Cornishness that "ordinary people" do not have experience of but which they think makes speakers more Cornish:

> "He speaks proper Cornish, not just the accent like we do."[531]
>
> "They speak Cornish, like real Kernowek. We can't because we lost it, but they're full-on Cornish Celts and they keep it going. [...] We haven't even got the proper accent like the old guys."[532]

This could be good news for language revitalization in that it offers an incentive to learn but it is more likely to be barrier to identification and it supports the proposition that some feel their everyday Cornishness to be inferior to Revivalist simulations. Maga have found that 24.2 percent of Cornish speakers have a higher degree and that a further 38.4 percent have a degree or equivalent while a third of fluent speakers live outside Cornwall.[533] These categories may be overrepresented in responses to questionnaires but if correct, the figures show unambiguously that Cornish is less available to disadvantaged sections of society and that there is still much to do, not just in learning and teaching, but also in developing socially comfortable and relevant settings with connections to Proper Cornishness. This can happen though and there are instances of teachers successfully working with representative groups of learners. Affirmative, grass-roots uses of words and phrases are increasing in everyday settings and in social media, showing that the language could be acquiring a useful symbolism for a growing number of people. For example, the comedian, "Kernow King" *tweets*, "Had a text earlier... Some of it was in Cornish and I replied a bit in Cornish! Sum proud!"[534] In the same vein, the comedy duo,

531 A woman from St. Ives who knew the then grand bard, Mick Paynter.

532 A man, about 23 years old, at Liskeard Station, August 2011.

533 Sally Burley, "A Report on the Cornish Language Survey Conducted by The Cornish Language Partnership", Truro: Maga, 2008.

534 A tweet from Edward Rowe, aka Kernow King, 31 December 2012.

"Cornish Oafs" incite visitors to their Facebook page to, "slip some Kernewek in too when you speak, to strengthen the language so it won't stay weak".[535]

Some ways in which fragments of Cornish are used resemble the affirmative aspects of similar projects in North America where groups like the Wampanoag, Ojibwe, and Yuchi are creating morale-boosting contexts for language revitalization that proclaim, "We still live here".[536] The value attributed to a language can have implications for all who belong to the group traditionally associated with it, not just its speakers so is there an emergent tendency to associate Cornish people with Cornish? The ongoing re-valorization of Cornish in public projects could unlock this potential and speakers already say they are witnessing a new respect which is a far cry from the situation where they were more often ridiculed. Demands for translation by non-Cornish businesses and individuals indicate that they expect the public to be pleased and it hints at growing prestige. All of this supports the idea that Cornish may be essential for achieving and maintaining self-respect and gaining respect from others. The Cornish may be able to develop in-group confidence and acquire the kind of consideration that makes it harder to do things like moving the fifth-century Tristan Stone to make way for a housing development.[537]

Figuring out a way to keep ahold of militant social capital might be more important than respectability. After all, being respectable or well-thought-of is not the same as having high status and its pursuit by Revivalists involves collective censorship to avoid controversy. Employing and deploying language and culture to strengthen community and cohesiveness is at odds with turning them into uncontroversial marketing assets. Such uses may sometimes help but culture's primary uses could be compromised if social and economic conflicts are avoided. Collaborating with Lifestyle Cornwall makes Revivalism toothless rather than uncontroversial

535 See www.facebook.com/CornishOafs (Accessed 7 January 2013.)

536 A film about the Wampanoag language, itvs.org/films/we-still-live-here (Accessed 7 January 2013.)

537 Widely covered in the press, e.g. www.dailymail.co.uk/news/article-2247020/Ancient-Tristan-Stone-moved-site-near-Fowey-Cornwalll-make-room-development.html (Accessed 14 December 2012.)

and less useful for communicating myths and building solidarity. Cornwall's new circumstances involve physical and symbolic displacements that make promoting Cornishness more a question of taking sides to tackle inequalities and social divisions than creating an illusion of harmony. The latter is rather like not making waves and claiming that everyone is in the same boat when they are not. Consequently, the key consideration might be how to put Cornish culture at the centre of articulate, mutually complementary agendas that mobilize community belonging positively. This might involve building upon a kind of motivated social capital based on cultural identification so as to develop networks of engaged action—as found in Brittany where informal circles and lobbies are evident in every sphere from education to food processing, car manufacture and banking. Leaving aside Cornwall's weaknesses (lack of institutions, a reduced native elite, poor access to traditional media, lack of access to economic capital, strong development lobbies), there are strengths that could help produce common purpose. Cornwall's relatively small size, group identity and sense of marginalization all favour unity. They produce intimacies of scale and tendencies towards informality which could be an advantage in networking across administrative, governmental, academic and voluntary bodies.

A Cornish Standpoint

The motive for this discussion has been to find ways in which Cornishness can be passed on meaningfully to future generations as a rooted/routed tradition and—at the same time—be used to address social divisions and integrate new residents. It has therefore started to argue for strategic intervention and has discussed strengthening and privileging certain intragroup narratives to negotiate and support a preferred Cornish "mythology" or vision through "useable cultures". These aspirations might sound inoffensively platitudinous, like the proverbial "motherhood and apple pie" served with a large dollop of Cornish cream, and they recall the banal references to sustainability and distinctiveness in policy documents and mission statements that are generally subverted or ignored.[538] What is proposed, though, is working to

538 For discussion of Brittany, see Jean Olivro (2010), *Projet Bretagne, op. cit.*, p. 75.

achieve a geographically and culturally grounded standpoint from which to explore, define and develop a coherent project that takes sides in conflicts of interest to address material and cultural inequalities and further the cause of an imagined Cornish community in all domains. Bernard Deacon has already suggested Cornish standpoints, similar to those developed by feminists, to advance the methodological development of "critical Cornish studies" through critical discourse analysis but the idea may be extended beyond academic circles.[539]

Feminist standpoint theories use women's experiences to construct perspectives from which to study and criticize a patriarchal order, sometimes extending this to challenge positivist notions of objectivity and truth.[540] They variously employ the notions of situated female imaginations and knowledge to argue for strategies that challenge androcentric knowledge by making use of insights that come from women's respective positions. Cornish standpoints, imagined from perspectives already available within the Cornish Movement, also offer off-centred subjectivities from which to critically consider institutionally and economically supported discourses that create the truths behind decision-making. This is not to suggest, naïvely and deterministically, that there is a "proper Cornish" standpoint or that Cornish people might share a single outlook, let alone one that is dualistically opposed to Establishment wisdoms. Instead, the principle is that subjects' knowledge, values, aspirations, cultural practices, political views and allegiances nevertheless have relationships to culture, social roles and habitus. By building affirmatively upon insider knowledge, such a standpoint (or in Cornish, *savla*) could be used to denaturalize and oust taken-for-granted discourses and alter cultural, social and material realities. This is very different from having a set agenda with the risk of inflexible prescriptions or grand narratives and it allows an ongoing, responsive search for changing local solutions as a component of resilience. Cornishness has historically been articulated within the paradigms and discourses of the particular age and in this respect

539 Bernard Deacon, "From 'Cornish Studies' to 'Critical Cornish Studies': reflections on methodology"; *Cornish Studies*, no. 12, (2005). pp. 13–29.

540 Sandra Harding (ed.) (2004), *The Feminist Standpoint Theory Reader: Intellectual and Political Controversies*, London: Routledge.

situated standpoints allow for continuous, critical sifting of discursive formations as they present themselves. Just like the propositions behind the Breton aspiration, "Bretagne belle, prospère, solidaire et ouverte sur le monde",[541] this approach means going beyond slogans or symbolism to address the conceptual gaps that exist when Cornish knowledge is absent and solutions are imposed by career-mobile decision-makers without ties to locality, community or culture. To compensate for a dearth of Cornish voices within governance, Cornwall needs to foster locally specific knowledge and translate it into action, a very different proposition to institutionally-driven interpretations of "transforming knowledge" and developing a "knowledge economy".

Taking sides involves exercising subaltern power according to Foucault's understanding of power, not as something people have, but as an exercise of relations which are rehearsed and re-established discursively:[542] "Discourse transmits and produces power; it reinforces it, but also undermines it and exposes it, renders it fragile and makes it possible to thwart it."[543] Bourdieu makes the complementary point that subverting representation can precede social changes: "La subversion hérétique expoite la possibilité de changer le monde sociale en changeant la représentation de ce monde."[544] This is pertinent to the idea that interventions in practice and representation can influence cultural and symbolic capital and enhance primary uses that are important for well-being, and it supports the possibility of upsetting strong discourses from Cornish standpoints. It fits strategies suggested by Guy Debord and Gil Wolman's *détournement*[545] and Umberto Eco's "semiological guerrilla

541 Jean Olivro (2010), *op. cit.*, p. 75.
542 Michel Foucault (1977), *Language, Counter-Memory, Practice*, (translated), Ithica: Cornell University Press, pp. 184-192.
543 Michel Foucault (1978), *The History of Sexuality: An Introduction*, Vol.1, Harmondsworth: Penguin, pp. 100-101 cited.
544 Cf. Pierre Bourdieu, (1982, 2001) *Langage et Pouvoir Symbolique*, Editions Fayard et Editions de Seuil, p.188: "heretical subversion expoites the possibility of changing the social world and changing the representation of that world", trans. N.Kennedy
545 Guy Debord and Gil Wolman, "Mode d'emploi du détournement" first published in *Les Lèvres Nues*, no.8 (May, 1956), in translation by Ken Knabb, "A User's Guide to Détournement" in *The Situationalist International Anthology*

warfare" whereby agents engage tactically as "cultural/semiological guerillas".[546] This can find expression in many ways but the expansion of "culture jamming" (notably to subvert neo-liberal and consumerist discourses in the media and advertising) offers a useful model for concerted bottom-up intervention as a positive practice of cultural hygiene. Intervention means venturing into the semantic and discursive battlegrounds that public relations agencies and advertisers deal with routinely and where even the most cleverly constructed messages are open to multiple readings. Those exposed to branding or other kinds of image-making need not accept the preferred reading and insiders may read portrayals of themselves oppositionally, sceptically or with negotiated acceptance—the positive aspect being that representations can be resisted.[547] Like other signs, those of branding are polysemous and the intended or unintended audiences interpret and reinterpret them subjectively. Therefore, instead of there being a straightforward cause and effect between representation and the image in people's minds, there is a less predictable range of possibilities.[548] Malcolm Bell makes the sobering observation that, "you can't police the brand" and that intended messages about Cornwall may be drowned by those over which public bodies have no influence.[549] Although Simon Anholt takes the same line, he stresses that while there may be no control over individual perceptions, it is possible to influence them by with a brand identity that is "clearly and distinctively expressed" using selected language and imagery.[550] This is one of the most important areas for the Cornish Movement to engage with by proactively and consciously grappling with signification.

(2006).

546 Umberto Eco (1986), *Towards a Semiological Guerilla Warfare*, Harcourt Inc.; See also, Umberto Eco (1986), *Travels in Hyperreality*, New York: Harcourt Brace Jovanovich; (or) (1987), *Faith in Fakes: Travels in Hyperreality*, Picador. Eco employs both terms.

547 For *preferred* and *negotiatied* reading, see, Stuart Hall ([1973] 1980), "Encoding/decoding…", *op. cit.*

548 Simon Anholt (2007), distinguishes "brand image" as the perception in the mind of the audience/consumer.

549 Remarks by Malcolm Bell, *op. cit.*

550 Simon Anholt (2007), *op. cit.* p.5.

Interpellation: *An Galow*

The founders of the Cornish music organization, CUMPAS argue that, "you can try persuading people but it's better to attract them by what you do".[551] They are in effect issuing an open invitation to join in a dance that celebrates and expresses belonging, one that could be expressed by the final lines of the play, *The Creacon of the World*:

> Menstrels, gwrewgh dhyn ny peba,
> May hallen warbarth dauncya,
> Dell yw an vaner ha'n gis.[552]
> ('Minstrels pipe for us
> so that we may dance together
> as is the manner and the custom.')

This has been a theme in the previous chapters where the "usefulness" of Revivalist activity has been linked to its ability to appeal and attract, not just anybody but a socially inclusive cross-section of the population where the Cornish are sufficiently well-represented to shape the "structures of feeling" into which others are welcomed. Appealing, in the sense of calling out to people, may be related to the etymologically connected notion of interpellation (< Latin, *appellare*). Briefly, Althusser's concept, concerns how subjects' identities are constructed through the workings of institutions (from the scale of the family to that of the state) and discusses a process usually described in English as "hailing". Figuratively speaking, this involves a kind of naming whereby subjects are hailed during social interactions and may recognize the subject positioning that is proffered.[553] Althusser's theories have been discussed in relation to hegemony and the "Ideological State Apparatus" with the tentative suggestion that the Cornish Movement might be an "ideological state*less* apparatus", offering a counter hegemony and re-evaluation of cultural and symbolic capital. From this perspective, the Movement also hails people, influencing identity constructions. The annual Cornish Gorsedd includes this call or *galow* to Cornwall:

---

551 *Non verbatim.*

552 William Jordon, *The Creacion of the World*, 1611. Respelt.

553 Louis Althusser (1971), "Ideology and ideological State Apparatus".

177

Kernow a'n Howldrevel, clêw galow an Orseth!
Kernow a'n Barth Dyhow, clêw galow an Orseth!
Kernow a'n Howlsedhas, clêw galow an Orseth!
Kernow a'n Barth Cledh, clêw galow an Orseth![554]

Calling out to Cornwall, hailing and inviting people to further its cause, is essential to maximizing the usefulness of consciously Cornish cultures. Poor awareness of social, discursive and semiological issues—and the dangers of re-signification—have been identified in this regard. When it comes to interpellation, recruitment and creating something which working-class Cornish people—amongst others—might wish to take up, the issues are similar to those of social context and expectation that are considered in widening participation in higher education. The usefulness of Revivalism has therefore been linked to achieving accordance with popular identifications, aesthetic preferences and the dispositions and attitudes of habitus.

We may think of Cornishness as a set of discursive formations and hypothesise that language revitalization and other cultural activities may be conceived so as to mesh with existing discourses and achieve relevance to insiders. Revivalism is supposed to be all about articulating Cornishness and yet we have seen how some versions that are championed clash. Questions of connotation, social context, disposition and attitude (*habitus*) impact upon whether activities appeal to different sections of society and become embedded culturally. Interpellation and the effective communication of culture probably depend upon practitioners' ability to evoke the familiar while doing so in new, creative ways. Evoking the familiar means calling forth what is already there so as to draw out knowledge and feelings that people are not aware of having and this differentiates it from invoking or calling upon things from without. Its etymology suggests calling out or giving voice from within. It can bring buried knowledge and desires to the surface and be part of developing effective standpoints and articulating "myths" (in Barthes' sense of the term). Language revitalization, for example, already appeals to the familiar sounds of place-names and Cornu-English, evoking

554 A call to the four points of the compass. "East Cornwall, hear the call of the Gorsedd…"

memories, producing awareness and drawing out knowledge, but this might be enhanced by attention to tacit responses and feelings. This is a long way from appeals that present learning Cornish as a duty and even further from commercial justifications. It starts from the poetic and aesthetic imagination and engages the emotions with potentially beneficial outcomes.

Reconnecting

Cornwall's new circumstances are nothing if not destabilizing and they emerge from a series of traumas or "failed experiences"[555] which, in varying degrees, have left their mark. Industrial decline, chronic emigration, ongoing development trends, marginalization and deprivation—even a second language loss, that of Cornu-English—could be said to create a collective post-traumatic disorder that diminishes emotional prosperity. This may sound like "Celtic whinge"[556] of the kind that reproduces victimhood but these experiences lead into post-memory and community narratives. As David Lowenthal remarks of Ireland and the West Indies, "Many remember historical trauma as though past and present were contemporaneous."[557] Amongst these are the recent events that have produced fragmentation and displacement. Cornishness is now less distinct and bounded and although the resulting ambiguities and hybridities can give rise to creativity, there are anxieties and a rootlessness that undermines people's need for belongingness. Desires for re-attachment to place and group seem symptomatic of this. Deacon cites a "desire to patrol the ethnic boundaries" and connects it to "the surge of interest among the Cornish in family history since the 1970s".[558] It is commonplace, especially for younger people, to have indeterminate relationships with Cornish tradition and those who have grown up in Cornwall have experienced

555 Mieke Bal relates trauma to failed experience: Mieke Bal, Jonathan Crewe, Leo Spitzer (1999), *Acts of Memory, Cultural Recall in the Present*, Hanover New Hampshire: Dartmouth College.

556 Directed at the SNP by Jeremy Paxman, reported by Scotland on Sunday 18 September 2011.

557 David Lowenthal (1975), "Past Time, Present Place: Landscape and Memory", in *The Geographical Review*, Vol. 65 (1), (January, 1975), pp. 1-36.(p.28)

558 Bernard Deacon (2012), "The Unimportance of being Cornish in Cornwall", 24 November 2012, *op. cit.*

Cornishness as marginal and low-status. Many people who reasonably identify themselves as indigenously Cornish have one Cornish parent or just one grandparent and are very likely to have spent part of their lives elsewhere or to have been "born away" because of economic circumstances that have led their parents to move for work. Many amongst the Cornish Movement's activists and adherents have interesting personal accounts of how they feel strongly Cornish despite such displacements. A Ph.D. student from the Midlands whose mother is from St Austell was learning Cornish, a musician with one Cornish parent had spent his childhood in London and an academic from Devonport began to feel Cornish after becoming aware of influences from her North Cornwall family.

Thirty years ago, Perry found that a fifth of Cornish people were "return migrants" (and his category would not include the above examples) and the proportion is likely to be higher now because of the more recent collapse of traditional industries.[559] In addition, the range of possibilities for in-migrants to become integrated or assimilated as "New Cornish" has been discussed. A eucre (card game) evening in the Blue Anchor Inn at Fraddon illustrated how circumstances fuel desires for secure identities that are manifested in everyday life. A woman wearing a "Cornish by marriage" tee-shirt asked if I could play eucre and her obviously local husband chipped in to say it was, "our national card game [...] They play it in Canada but nobody up country have heard of it". Their son of about thirty-five with a trace of his mother's Watford accent, talked about playing online and added that "We should keep on being Cornish". At *Lowender Peran*, musicians in their twenties spoke of their attachments. One had been born elsewhere of Cornish parents and "come back to Cornwall" as a child. Another had left in her teens, a third had gone to a school which "wasn't very Cornish", and a fourth had left university in Leeds and found work there, saying that it was, "until I can find a job back home" and two more who said they felt Cornish were the locally-born children of in-migrants. Revivalist scenes unsurprisingly appeal to people on the fringes of "Proper Cornishness" who do not have some of its typical distinctions. The ranks are swelled by "return migrants" and others

559 Ronald Perry, *et al.* (eds) (1986), *Counterurbanisation...*, *op. cit.*, p. 84.

whose ambiguous coding might make them feel, consciously or not, that their tribal qualifications are unsure. This was voiced plainly by a Cornish learner in Camborne: "My mum is Cornish and my dad is English. I want to show I'm definitely Cornish."[560] Acknowledgements like this are rare but the phenomena of electing, achieving and negotiating personal Cornish identities are defining features that manifest themselves in small, common-place acts of disambiguation.

Whereas such unsettled personal circumstances might have been unusual a generation ago, they are now so common that a majority of the Cornish participants in Revivalist activities are sometimes concerned. Associated networks apparently provide some of the means by which individuals reaffirm their belonging to a Cornish community and reconnect and this process might be an indispensable part of maintaining the integrity of the group, constantly recreating it and increasing participants' resolve to make their lives in Cornwall. It means that instead of "patrol[ing] the ethnic boundaries"[561] and presiding over a shrinking, defensive identity, the most viable long-term strategy is the active interpellation of those who are in the position of choosing whether to be Cornish or not. The historical background of migration, transnationality and diaspora could provide themes that aid this process of physical and emotional (re)attachment. These include the ideas that it is Cornish to go overseas and mix with other people and that "Cousin Jennies" and "Cousin Jacks" can be born in far-away places but still belong.[562] By performing identity, the Cornish may both maintain their own attachments and interpellate others so that instead of inexorably declining, Cornishness may thrive and spread confidently.

A Cornish Project

Bringing about the changes proposed is a task that cannot be shirked or put off, but without genuinely Cornish institutions how may that be undertaken and by whom? Despite the risks of cultural prescriptivism and a "second wrong turn", the voluntary Cornish

560 A learner at a class in Camborne, October 2011.
561 Bernard Deacon, "The Unimportance of being Cornish in Cornwall", Address to the Institute of Cornish Studies, 24th November 2012.
562 Traditional nicknames for the Cornish overseas.

Movement has been identified as loosely bringing together agents for change from within the community and providing the only existing spaces and discursive formations from within which opposition to imposed policies and developments is organized. It has effects that permeate society and is taken, by affective association, to include everyone who to some extent embraces varying sets of identity discourses that have been (re)shaped by Cornish nationalism and Celtic Revivalism. It includes most of those whose feelings of belonging lead them to be concerned by the impact of economic and social trends on community and cultural continuity. A remarkable feature of the Movement is the maintenance of small, voluntary groups, such as the Cornish Social and Economic Research Group (CoSERG) and the periodic organization of ephemeral working parties. To be blunt, if the Cornish Movement does not take the initiative, nobody else will—but because it is fragmentary, plural and nebulous, there is no single body that is ideally placed to take on the role. Of course there are cultural organizations such as Bewnans Kernow and Gorseth Kernow that may intervene in specific ways but a comprehensive initiative is needed to take discussion beyond Revivalist centres of interest and convincingly connect to socio-economic matters and the interests of the disadvantaged. In casting around for ways to make things happen, Cornwall Council stands out as the only body that is both answerable to the public and has the means to bring about change. In fact, the outlook of some councillors and officers is already influenced to a marked degree by the Cornish Movement. Cornwall Council has also gained influence and responsibility through its role in the Objective One programme and has sought and started to acquire further powers, from time-to-time lending support to the campaign for a fully-fledged Assembly.[563] It is therefore proposed that a feasible approach would be for the Council and elements within the Cornish Movement to work in complementary ways to deliver a Cornish Project that links cultural identity to durable social and economic regeneration and fully explores the possibilities for appropriate decision-making and strategic planning within Cornwall.

563 E.g. Contributions of Alec Robertson, former Council leader, at the Cornish Constitutional Convention, 24 July 2010 and continuing internet links to the Cornish Assembly campaign.

Earlier it was proposed that the Council and its various agencies and companies develop joined-up policies on branding and image-making in order to combat versions that hinder beneficial economic activities and favour harmful developments. This was linked to strengthening useful and enabling narratives, some of which have been identified and related to promoting an image that connects Cornishness to the possibility of economic strategies that build upon the mythologies of a technological heritage and international connectedness. The principle of a cohesive approach should extend to the whole of the Council's policy so that a resilient, socially-inclusive, Cornish future is clearly envisaged as an ambition to strive for in all of its work. This would replace disjointed, contradictory practices with a coherent strategy that recognizes connections between culture, language, economics and emotional well-being and sets out a course of action to meet Cornish needs. Contradictory promotional efforts and unsustainable housing plans show that this is far from being the case now so there is a need to get beyond the understandable tendency for departments and agencies to take easy paths offered by received wisdoms, contradictory directives and funding criteria that exclude local knowledge.

Supporting culture's primary uses has implications for most areas of policy because factors such as access to housing, jobs, education and health-care support or undermine communities and their cultures—which exist in specific environments. In brief, cultures and languages may meet psychological needs but only exist because of particular communities of people who in turn have material requirements. If the Council wishes to support Cornish cultures, it therefore needs to take account of impacts in such diverse areas as education, economic development, environmental management, housing and social services, not just in branding, tourism and cultural events. For example, a local needs housing strategy that proactively and militantly opposes speculative residential development and second home ownership is a necessity without which it is hard to imagine an indigenous Cornish tradition in the long-term. Cornish people need access to homes in order to stay in Cornwall. This is understood by the Welsh Government and is explicit in its work on culture and language where providing "affordable homes" is identified as "a vital contribution to sustainable communities that can support the future of the Welsh language" and a legitimate concern for a committee responsible for "The Culture and Heritage of Wales".[564] Seeking further powers to intervene in the housing market would enable Cornwall Council to extend the principle that has recently led it to use planning law and taxation in trying to limit second homes. In debates about housing development targets, informed arguments about local needs could counter building lobbies and figures imposed by central government. Instead of meekly responding to ministerial instructions, the Council sometimes needs to bare its teeth and present sound counter arguments. The purpose here is not to venture into policy details but rather to highlight the need for an overall strategy. Once this is achieved, Cornwall Council should be forthright in demanding that other agencies take note of its wishes as an elected body. By challenging received wisdoms and imposed policies, a more articulate and purposeful Cornish Movement could help bring about an assertive Council with strong enough public backing to oppose decisions and government directives that undermine the Cornish community.

Since culture is related to most of the Council's responsibilities, its cultural strategy[565] should recognize this with a designated cabinet member and committee. Instead of having a single portfolio holder for "culture and tourism"—an association that privileges cultural tourism—a committee with specific responsibilities for culture could make a clear linkage between culture and society. This was apparent at an early stage in the work of the Welsh Government when a cabinet post was created with responsibilities for Culture, Sport and the Welsh Language. In the 2002 strategy it was recognized that "culture can add to the value of other existing cross-cutting themes for the Welsh Assembly Government—for example, as a bridge to social inclusion, equal opportunities and sustainable development."[566] Objectives included "support bilingualism, multiculturalism and the equality of opportunity" and "ensure that culture

---

564 "The Culture and Heritage of Wales", Welsh Government, 2011, wales.gov.uk/docs/strategies/110929chap12en.pdf (Accessed January 2013
565 "White Paper for Culture", Truro: Cornwall Council, (October 2012).
566 "A Culture Strategy for Wales", The Welsh Assembly Government, (January 2002), p.8.

helps tackle social disadvantage".[567] These themes have been developed with an emphasis on access and participation and the pivotal place of culture is reflected in the fact that the ministers for Housing, Regeneration and Heritage, for Education and Skills and for Business, Enterprise, Technology and Science share responsibilities for delivering the cultural strategy.[568] Producing appropriate policies and strategies is hampered by a democratic deficit in the relationships between the voting (and abstaining) public, councillors and civil servants so that community input is often minimal and indirect. In planning, for instance, "public consultations" on regeneration, planning and cultural policy reach few people. Several informed witnesses have celebrated the abolition of the Rural Development Agency and spoken about its consultation exercises on developments between Camborne and Redruth, which allegedly took no real account of public opinion. Others have mentioned the online consultation and public meetings organized to air Cornwall Council's "Core Strategy" and described a situation in which even elected committee members are sometimes taken aback by decisions. Matters are made worse when policies are shaped by "regional quangos" outside Cornwall without (with rare exceptions) the involvement of Cornish people as employees or consultants. Consequently, networking does not extend into the community and there is a feeling that "regeneration" projects are done *to* local people by others, irrespective of their interests, rather than *by* them in accordance with their wishes. Academics and informed campaigners sometimes network informally with Cornwall Council officers but there are no developed channels and structures of the kind found in Brittany or behind the Welsh Government's promotion of Wales, nor are there the intimate networks encountered in Galicia where I found that regional ministers and civil servants shared cultural affiliations with people from a range of social backgrounds and met them informally. To summarize, there are not enough democratic mechanisms to facilitate public engagement and this lack extends to the informed input that might come from organic intellectuals in the community. This results in an unclear public vision and direction

567 *Ibid.* p.57.
568 "The Culture and Heritage of Wales", Welsh Government, 2011, *op. cit.*

that does not connect with popular identities and aspirations. It is urgent to ensure genuine public discussion that goes beyond unheeded and relatively ineffective consultation exercises, such as those that accompanied the Core Strategy.

Councillors and officers may take a lead in improving decision-making and delivery but changing public discourse more widely is a prerequisite for longer term success. The desired outcome is to produce prevailing discourses in favour of Cornish resilience and social inclusiveness to inform policy and motivate voluntary activity across the board. We might consider how this works elsewhere in Europe. For example, "Catalanism" defines the tenure and general direction of public discourse in Catalonia, from the arts and football to politics. While that model might not fit Cornwall, it is possible to envisage conscious attention to an inclusive Cornishness informing policy and individual actions. The Cornish Movement has to make concerted intellectual, organizational and communicative efforts, striving for a climate in which policy changes can happen and be translated into firm actions. It has to be clearly and unambiguous involved in the politics of decision-making, avoiding the trap of turning cultural pursuits into displacement activities that distract participants from social and economic engagement. Even before it can do this, the Movement must develop greater sophistication in analysing the potential effects of particular courses of action so that its adherents avoid drifting into ill-considered actions that constitute a "second wrong turn". Having a clear, determined sense of purpose and ambition will not be enough without self-critical examination of practices and attention to social relevance.

In the absence of well-placed native elites and institutions, there is a need to find bottom-up strategies to build an epistemic community where knowledge is generated and applied. This is where the Cornish Movement has traditionally provided life-support, creating spaces where heretical valuations of culture and symbolic repertoires prevail in a vocational spirit that allows it to challenge imposed decisions and answer back. Reinforcing and expanding culturally facilitated networks with attention to ownership and purpose may be the only realistic way to create spaces from which to gain democratic control of governance and policy-making. It is a strategy that uses culture to strengthen the solidarity and knowledge needed for a credible, thought-out alternative to present trends and it means striving for a participative, democratic model and a shared project that makes tolerable development for local needs one of its principles. Instead of embracing the oxymoronic "sustainable development" or a preservationist presumption against any development at all, it could support work to meet the needs of Cornwall's population—including the poorest—without compromising the ability of future generations to meet theirs. This is necessary to overcome the situation in which decisions are largely removed from convincingly democratic processes and it could be facilitated by establishing a research group for Contemporary Cornish Studies. Academics, researchers and councillors have voiced the concern that there is no such body to inform policy and act as a consultancy, frustrations that now need to be translated into an initiative, preferably with the enabling support of Cornwall Council, higher and further education institutions and funding bodies. This is made more urgent by the precarious status of the University of Exeter's Institute of Cornish Studies, founded with the collaboration of Cornwall Council. Since 1970 it has provided the only dedicated academic site for studying Cornish society and has been a focal point for research but its academic staffing has been to reduced to part of the time of one historian. Cornwall Council needs to build upon the achievements of the Institute and encouraging attention to present-day issues. There is a need to extend involvement beyond academia, sharing knowledge and establishing purpose in the community at large. As part of its first programme, a research body could establish workshops, discussions and conferences similar to those organized by Cowethas Flamank, in the 1980s and 90s, which unified and motivated revivalists at a time when political differences and schismatic divisions were producing disengagement. A sufficiently motivated research body with a strong online and community presence could act as a hub around which to build lasting networks of common interest within which organizations and individuals could operate.

The Cornish Movement has the opportunity to challenge the systemic inertia of decision-making and bring about a shared

Cornish project, working through Cornwall Council to address disadvantage and bind diverse communities into a cohesive whole where social capital is enhanced by culture. Stuart Hall describes identity as, "an idea which cannot be thought in the old way, but without which certain key questions cannot be thought at all."[569] Taking a similar view that rejects an over-obsession with boundaries, this discussion has sought to recognize the plural, multi-dimensional realities of Cornishness and the mutability, not just of culture but of ethnicity itself. At the same time it recognizes that ethnicity is a deep construction that cannot just be invented and acted out as a lifestyle option. The lasting character of habitus has been underlined, as has the continuity of evolving tradition.

The playwright, Nick Darke (1948-2005), who was regarded as indisputably Cornish while being the child of in-migrants, insisted that, "A community that loses its past is in danger of losing its way."[570] In the same spirit, this discussion has attached importance to the ways in which we build our present and future through the stories we tell about ourselves. Cornwall has certainly been destabilized but we can consider new configurations for cultural practice that are compatible with circumstances in which many people are trying to both maintain and achieve geographically rooted identities. This neither pretends that the demographic transformations of the last fifty years have not happened, nor assumes that continuity is unimportant. Instead it starts from where Cornwall really is and looks to a future that is different, perhaps even unrecognizable to former generations, but nevertheless part of Nance's "cultural tradition that is definably Cornish".

50.1662°N, 5.1018°W

---

569 Stuart Hall, "Who needs 'identity'?" in, *Questions of Cultural Identity*, in S. Hall and Paul du Gay (1996), London: Sage, p.2.
570 Cited by Cornish National Cinema.

Bibliography

Aaron, Jane and Chris Williams (eds.), (2005), *Postcolonial Wales*, Cardiff: University of Wales Press.

Abercrombie, Patrick and J. Paton Watson (1943), *A Plan for Plymouth*, Underhill, (Plymouth). Ltd.

Accardo, Alain and Phillipe Corcuff (1989), *La Sociologie de Bourdieu*, Bordeaux: Le Mascaret.

Aldous, Philipa and Malcolm Wiliams, "A Question of Ethnicity" in P.J. Payton (ed.), *Cornish Studies, 2nd Series*, No. 9, (2001), pp.213-226.

Althusser, Louis, in Karl Marx (1969 [1867]), *Le Capital*, trans. J. Roy, Paris: Garnier-Flammerion, p. 585 (footnotes).

Althusser, Louis (1971), "On Ideology and Ideological State Apparatuses", in *Lenin and Philosophy and Other Essays*, New York: Monthly Review Press.

Anderson, Benedict (1996 [1983]), *L'imaginaire national : réflexions sur l'origine et l'essor du nationalisme*, La Découverte: Paris.

—— (1991), *Imagined Communities: Reflections on the Origin and Spread of Nationalism*, 2nd edition, London and New York: Verso.

Angarrack, John (1999), *Breaking the Chains: Propaganda, censorship, deception and the manipulation of public opinion in Cornwall*, Camborne: Cornish Stannary Publications.

—— (2008), *Scat t'Larrups. Resist and Survive*, Padstow: Independent Academic Press.

Anholt, Simon (2010-01-23), *Places: Identity, Image and Reputation*, Basingstoke: Palgrave Macmillan.

—— (2007-01-23), *Competitive Identity: the new brand management for nations, cities and regions*. Basingstoke: Palgrave Macmillan.

—— (2003), *Brand New Justice: the upside of global branding*, Oxford: Butterworth-Heinemann.

—— (January 2000), *Another One Bites the Grass: Making Sense of International Advertising*, New York: John Wiley and Sons.

Appadurai, Arjun (1986), *The Social Life of Things. Commodities in Cultural Perspective*, Chicago: University of Chicago Press.

Baumeister, Roy F. and Mark R. Leary, (1995), "The Need to Belong: Desire for Interpersonal Attachments as a Fundamental Human Motivation", *Psychological Bulletin, 117*, 497-529.

Bal, Mieke, Jonathan Crewe, Leo Spitzer (1999), *Acts of Memory, Cultural Recall in the Present*, Hanover New Hampshire: Dartmouth College.

Barthes, Roland (1982 [1957]), *Mythologies*, Paris: Le Seuil.

—— (1993), *Mythologies*, (English edition) translated by Lavaers, London: Vintage.

—— (1964), *Éléments de sémiologie*, Communications 4, Paris: Le Seuil.

Baudrillard, Jean (1983 [pub. in French, 1981]), *Simulacra and Simulations*, translated by Foss, New York: Semiotext(e), pp.1-13 and 23-49.

Becker, Gary (1994[1964]), *Human Capital: A Theoretical and Empirical Analysis with Special Reference to Education*, Chicago: University of Chicago Press.

Benjamin, Walter (1970 [1933]), "The Work of Art in the Age of Mechanical Reproduction", trans. Harry Zohn, in W. Benjamin, *Illuminations*, London: Jonathan Cape.

Billig, Michael (1995), *Banal Nationalism*, London, Thousand Oaks, New Delhi: Sage.

Biscoe, Bert, "The Hungry Beast. A View of the Media", in Simon Parker (ed.) (1998), *Cornwall Marches On!, Keskerdh Kernow 500*, Truro: Keskerdh Kernow Ltd., pp. 149-161.

Blakely, Tony and Kevin Dew, "Ethnicity, Acculturation and Health: Who's to judge?", *Journal of the New Zealand Medical Association*, (30th January 2004), vol.117 (1188).

Borlase, William (1769), *Antiquities Historical and Monumental of the County of Cornwall*, London: Bowyer and Nichols.

Bosenketh, Edward (1888), *Tin*, London.

Bottrell, William (1989 [1870,1873]), *Traditions and Hearthside Stories of West Cornwall*, Lampeter: Llanerch Publishers. (Originally published in three volumes Penzance.)

Bourdieu, Pierre (1972), *An Outline of a Theory of Practice*, trans. Richard Nice, Cambridge: Cambridge University Press.

—— (1979), *La Distinction, Critique sociale du jugement*, Le Sens Commun (coll.), Paris: Minuit.

—— (1979), "Les 3 états du capital culturel", in *Actes de la recherch en sciences sociales*, Vol. 30, November 1979, L'Institution Scolaire, pp. 3-6.

—— (1980), *Le sens pratique*, (coll.) *Le sens commun*, Editions de Minuit, Paris.

—— (1980), "L'identité et la représentation: Elements pour une réflexion critique sur l'idée de région", Actes de recherche en science sociale, no. 35, (novembre 1980), pp. 63-75.

—— (1982), *Ce que parler veut dire—L'économie des échanges linguistiques*, Paris: Editions Fayard.

—— (1982, 2001) *Langage et Pouvoir Symbolique*, Editions Fayard et Editions de Seuil.

—— (1984,1988), *Homo Academicus*, translated by Peter Collier, Cambridge: Polity Press.

—— (1985), "The Social Space and the Genesis of Groups", in *Theory and Society*, vol.14 (6), (November 1985), New York: Springer.

—— (1990), *Distinction: A Social Critique of the Judgement of Taste*, Cambridge: Cambridge University Press.

—— (1991), *Language and Symbolic Power*, Cambridge: Polity Press.

—— et Loïc J.D. Wacquant (1992), *Réponses pour une anthropologie reflexive*, Paris: Le Seuil.

BIBLIOGRAPHY

—— (1991)"Identity and Representation: Elements for a Critical Reflection of the Idea of Region" in Bourdieu (1991) *op. cit.* Part III, Ch. 10.

—— (1997), *Méditations pascaliennes*, coll. Liber, Paris: Le Seuil.

—— (2000), *Les structures sociales de l'économie*, coll. Liber, Paris: Le Seuil.

Bowman, Marion (1996), "Cardiac Celts: images of the Celts in paganism", pp. 242-251 in G. Harvey and C. Hardman (eds.), *Paganism Today*, Thorsons: London.

Bridge, Gary, "Bourdieu, Rational Action and the Time-Space Strategy of Gentrification", *Transactions of the Institute of British Geographers*, vol. 26, no. 2: (2001), pp. 205-216.

Brown, Terence (ed.) (1996), *Celticism*, Amsterdam and Atlanta GA: Rodopi.

Buck, Mary, Lyn Bryant and Malcolm Williams (1993), *Housing and Households in Cornwall: A pilot study of Cornish families*, Plymouth: University of Plymouth.

——, Malcolm Williams and Lyn Bryant, "Housing the Cornish: Containing the Crisis", in P.J.Payton (ed.), *Cornish Studies*, no. 1, pp.97-108.

Burley, Sally (2008), *A Report on the Cornish Language Survey Conducted by The Cornish Language Partnership*, Truro: Maga.

Burton, Rob (1997) "A Passion to Exist: Cultural Hegemony and the Roots of Cornish Identity", in P.J. Payton (ed.), *Cornish Studies*, 2nd Series, no.5, pp. 151-163.

Cameron, Deborah (1995), *Verbal Hygiene*, London: Routledge.

—— [n.d] "The one, the many and the Other: representing mono/multiculturalism in post-9/11 verbal hygiene", paper presented to "Multilingual 2,0?" Conference at the University of Arizona, (14th April 2012).

Camps, Cath. (n.d.) "Silencing the voice of the Cornish", unpublished Cert.Ed. assignment for Cornwall College.

Carrick District Council and PSEC Health and Housing Consultancy (1996), *Private Sector House Condition Survey*, Truro: Carrick District Council.

Chapman, Malcolm (1992), *The Celts: The Construction of a Myth*, London: Macmillan.

Charlesworth, Simon J. (2000), *A Phenomenology of Working Class Experience*, Cambridge University Press: Cambridge.

—— (2005), "Understanding Social Suffering: A Phenomenological Investigation of the Experience of Inequality", *Journal of Community and Applied Social Psychology*, no. 15 (2005) pp. 296-312.

Chevallier, Stéphane and Christine Chauvre (2010), *Dictionnaire Bourdieu*, Paris: Ellipses.

Clarke, Matthew (2012) "Cornish Culture in Business", A Guest blog for *Business Cornwall*, www.businesscornwall.co.uk/blogs/guest-blog-cornish-culture-in-business-123 (Accessed 13 April 2012.)

Coadic, Ronan le (1998), *L'Identité bretonne*, Deuxième édition, Rennes: Terre de Brume—Presse Universitaires de Rennes.

Coleman, Hilary and Sally Burley (2015), *Shout Kernow—Celebrating Cornwall's Pub Songs*, London: Francis Boutle.

Coleman, James (1988), "Social Capital in the Creation of Human Capital", in *The American Journal of Sociology*, Vol. 94, Supplement: Organizations and Institutions: Sociological and Economic Approaches to the Analysis of Social Structure, pp. S95-S120.

Commission for Racial Equality (1995), *Challenging Racism in the South-West: a one day seminar for Cornwall*, Truro.

Coleman, Will. Letter to the editor, *The Western Morning News*, 26th June 2007.

—— (2012), Unpublished documents concening the Kernocopia project.

Cornish Language Board—Kesva an Taves Kernewek [n.d.], *House-Names in Cornish*, Kesva an Taves Kernewek.

Cornish Language Partnership, "Cornish Language Survey", (July 2008).

Cornwall and Isles of Scilly Drug and Alcohol Action Team, "Alcohol Needs Assessment", (2010-11) and "Adult Drug Treatment Needs Assessment" (2010-11).

Cornwall Arts Partnership and Arts Council England, "Understanding the impact of cultural tourism", (June 2008).

Cornwall Council (2004), "Strategy for the Cornish Language", Truro.

Cornwall Council (2007), "West Cornwall Housing Requirements Study", Truro: Opinion Research Services (Swansea).

Cornwall Council, "Preventing suicide: a strategy for action in Cornwall and Isles of Scilly—2008-2013" [n.d.]

Cornwall Council (December 2007), "Cornwall's Creative Industries Strategy, 2007-2012", Truro.

Cornwall Council (2010), "Future Cornwall—2010-2030: A joint strategy, vision and objectives", (Sustainable Community Strategy), Truro.

Cornwall Council (2010), "The Cornwall Housing Market, Strategic Evidence Base 2010 Update: Executive Summary", Truro.

Cornwall Council (2011), "Draft Core Strategy", Truro.

Cornwall Council (2011), "Demographic Evidence Base", Truro.

Cornwall Council (2011), "Deprivation and Child Poverty", Truro.

Cornwall Council (2012), "White Paper for Culture", Truro.

Cornwall Council (2012), "Planning Future Cornwall", Truro.

Cornwall Enterprise (2000), "A Framework Strategy for Tourism in Cornwall: Delivering Distinctive Difference", Cornwall Enterprise: Truro.

Cornwall Enterprise (Projects Consultancy) (August 2008), "Commercial Use of Cornish", Truro.

Cornwall Rural Community Council (1990s), Parish Housing Surveys.

Council of Europe, *The European Charter for Regional or Minority Languages*, Council of Europe, (1992).

Courtney, Margaret A. "Cornish Feasts and 'Feasten' Customs", *The Folk-Lore Journal*, vol. 4 (3), (1886), pp.221-249.

Crang, Mike and Nigel Thrift (2000), *Thinking Space*, London: Routledge.

Curnow, Howard in *An Baner Kernewek*, no. 69, (August 1992).

Davey, Merv (1983), *Hengan: Traditional Folk Songs, Dances and Broadside Ballads Collected in Cornwall*, Redruth: Dyllansow Truran.

BIBLIOGRAPHY

Davey, Merv, Alison Davey and Jowdy Davey (2009), *Scoot Dances, Troyls, Furrys and Tea Treats: The Cornish Dance Tradition*, London: Francis Boutle Publishers.

Davey, Merv *"As is the manner and the custom"; folk tradition and identity in Cornwall*, unpublished Ph.D thesis, University of Exeter.

Deacon, Bernard (1993), "And shall Trelawney die? The Cornish identity", in P.J. Payton (ed.), *Cornwall Since the War* (below).

—— (1997), "'The Hollow Jarring of the Distant Steam Engine': Images of C between West Barbary and Delectable Duchy", in E. Westland (ed.) (1997) (below), Ch.1,

—— (2000), *The Cornish and the Council of Europe Framework Convention for the Protection of National Minorities*, Truro: Cornish National Minority Steering Group, supported by the Joseph Rowntree Reform Trust.

—— (2005), "From 'Cornish Studies' to 'Critical Cornish Studies': reflections on methodology"; *Cornish Studies*, no. 12, (2005). pp. 13–29.

—— (2007), *Cornwall: A Concise History*, Cardiff: University of Wales Press.

—— (2012) "The Unimportance of Being Cornish in Cornwall", Paper presented to the Institute of Cornish Studies, 24th November 2012.

Deacon, Bernard, Dick Cole and Garry Tregidga (2003), *Mebyon Kernow and Cornish Nationalim*, Cardiff: Welsh Academic Press.

Deacon, Bernard, Andrew George and Ron Perry (1987), *Cornwall at the Crossroads*, CoSERG: Redruth.

Deacon, Bernard and Philip Payton (19931), "Re-inventing Cornwall: Culture Change on the European Periphery", in P.J. Payton *Cornish Studies*, no. One (1993), pp. 62–79.

—— (1993b), "The Ideology of Language Revival", Ch.12 in P.J. Payton (ed.) (1993), *Cornwall Since The War*, (below).

Deacon, Bernard with Sharron Schwartz and David Holman (2004), *The Cornish Family: the roots of our future*, Fowey: Cornwall Editions.

Debord, Guy and Gil Wolman, "Mode d'emploi du détournement" first published in *Les Lèvres Nues*, no.8 (May, 1956), in translation by Ken Knabb, "A User's Guide to *Détournement*" in *The Situationalist International Anthology* (2006): www.bopsecrets.org/SI/detourn.htm (Accessed 8 November 2012).

DEMOS (2009), See Charlie Tims and Shelagh Wright.

Dorson, Richard "Is Folklore a] Discipline?", in *Folklore*, vol. 84, no. 3, (Autumn, 1973), pp 177-205, Taylor and Francis.
www.jstor.org/stable/1259723 (Accessed 15 December 2011).

Dorson, Richard (1976), *Folklore and Fakelore: Essays Toward a Discipline of Folk Studies*, Cambridge, Mass: Harvard University Press.

Drew, Samuel (1824), *The History of Cornwall*, Helston: William Penaluna.

Duranton, Gilles, Andrés Rodríguez-Pose and Richard Sandall, "Family Types and the Persistence of Regional Disparities in Europe", in *Economic Geography*, vol. 85, issue 1, (January 2009) pp. 23-14.

Eco, Umberto (1986), "Travels in Hyperreality" in *Faith in Fakes*, London: Seeker and Warburg.

—— (1987), *Travels in Hyperreality*, London: Picador.

Featherstone, Mike (1991), *Consummer Culture and Postmodernism*, London and Newbury Park, California: Sage.

—— (1995), *Undoing Culture: Globalization, Postmodernism and Identity*, London and Newbury Park, California: Sage.

Fiske, John (1987), "British Cultural Studies and Television Criticism", pp. 254-90 in R. Allen (ed.), *Channels of Discourse: Television and Contemporary Criticism*, London: Methuen.

Fiske, Susan T. (2009 [2004]), *Social beings: A Core Motives Approach to Social Psychology*, 2nd Edition, London: John Wiley and Sons.

Foot, Sarah, *Cornish Scene* (Magazine), 1987-1992.

Foucault, Michel (1970), *The Order of Discourse: An Archaeology of the Human Sciences*, London: Tavistock.

—— (1972), *The Archaeology of Knowledge*, London: Tavistock.

—— (1977), *Language, Counter-Memory, Practice*, Ithica: Cornell University Press.

—— (1978 [1972]), *The History of Sexuality: An Introduction, vol.1*, Harmondsworth: Penguin.

Fowler, Bridget (1997), *Pierre Bourdieu and Cultural Theory—Critical Investigations*, London: Sage.

Gendall, Richard (1988), Letter, in *Carn*, vol. 63, The Celtic League.

—— (1991), *A Students' Grammar of Modern Cornish*, Menheniot: The Cornish Language Council.

Gordon, Colin (ed.) (1980), *Michel Foucault: Power/Knowledge: Selected Interviews and Other Writings 1972-1977*, Brighton: Harvester.

Gramsci, Antonio (1998), *Selections from the Prison Notebooks and the Study of Philosophy*, in Q. Hoare and G. Nowell-Smith (eds.), London: Wishart.

—— (2006 [1994]), "Hegemony, Intellectuals and The State", in John Storey (ed.), pp. 215-221.

Hale, Amy (1996), "Foot in the Mouth, or Foot in the Door? Evaluating Chapman's *The Celts*" in P.J. Payton (ed.), *Cornish Studies*, no. 4, pp. 158-170.

—— (1997), "Genesis of the Celto-Cornish Revival? L.C. Duncombe-Jewell and the Cowethas Kelto-Kernuak", in P.J. Payton (ed.), *Cornish Studies*, no. 5, pp. 100-111.

—— (2001), "Representing the Cornish—Contesting heritage interpretation in Cornwall", in *Tourist Studies*, Vol. 1 (2), pp. 185-196, London: Sage.

—— (2002), "Whose Celtic Cornwall? The Ethnic Cornish Meet Celtic Spirituality", in David C. Harvey, Rhys Jones, Neil McInroy and Christine Milligan (eds.) *Celtic Geographies; Old Culture, New Times*, London.

—— (2006), "Selling Celtic Cornwall: Challenging Markets and Meanings?" in K. Meethan, A. Anderson and S. Miles (eds.) *Tourism, Consumption and Representation: Narratives of Place and Self*, Wallingford Oxon and Cambridge MA: C.A.B.I. International.

Hall, Stuart ([1973] 1980), "Encoding/decoding", in Centre for Contemporary Cultural Studies (ed.): *Culture, Media, Language: Working Papers in*

BIBLIOGRAPHY

Cultural Studies, 1972-79, London: Hutchinson, pp. 128-38.

—— (2000), "Culture, the Media and the 'Ideological Effect'", in James Curran, Michael Gurevitich and Janet Woollacott (eds.) *Mass Communications and Society*, London: Edward Arnold.

—— (ed.) (2003 [1997]), *Representation, Cultural Representation and Signifying Practices*, London: Sage.

—— (1996), "Cultural Studies: Two Paradigms", in John Storey (ed.) (2006 [1994]) (below), pp. 31-48.

Harding, Sandra (ed.) (2004), *The feminist standpoint theory reader: intellectual and political controversies*, London: Routledge.

Harvey, David, *et al.* (2001), *Celtic Geographies—Old Culture, New Times*, London: Routledge.

Hebdidge, Dick (1979), *Subculture: The Meaning of Style*, London: Routledge.

Hechter, Michael (1975), *Internal Colonialism—The Celtic fringe in British national development, 1536-1966*, London: Routledge & Kegan Paul.

Hechter, Michael and Margaret Levi, "The comparative analysis of ethno-regional movements", in *Ethnic and Racial Studies*, vol. 2, no 3, (July 1979).

Hewison, Robert (1987), *The Heritage Industry: Britain in a Climate of Decline*, London: Methuen.

Hill, Simon A., Colin Pritchard, Richard Laugharne and David Gunnel, (2005) "Changing Patterns of Suicide in a Poor, Rural County over the 20th Century: A comparison", in *Social Psychiatry and Psychiatric Epidemiology*, (September 2005).

Hitchins, Fortescue and Samuel Drew (1824), *The History of Cornwall*, Helston: William Penaluna.

Hobsbawm, Eric and Terence Ranger (eds.) (1983, 1989), *The Invention of Tradition*, Cambridge: Cambridge University Press.

Hofstede, Geert (1984), "The Cultural Relativity of the Quality of Life Concept", *Academy of Management Review*, vol. 9 (3), pp. 389–398, www.nyegaards.com/yansafiles/Geert%20Hofstede%20cultural%20attitudes.pdf (Accessed 4 May 2010.)

Hosken, Philip Marrack (1998), "The Cornish Overseas", in Simon Parker (ed.) (below).

Howells, Jane (2012), "Preliminary report on the Cornwall Council Core Strategy preferred approach equality impact assessment", Cornwall: Bewnans Kernow.

Home Office (H.M. Government) (1999), "The United Kingdom Report on the Council of Europe Framework Convention for the Protection of National Minorities", London: The Home Office.

Husk, Kerryn (2012) "Ethnic group affiliation and social exclusion in Cornwall: analysis, adjustment and extension of the 2001 England and Wales Census data", unpublished PhD thesis, University of Plymouth.

Ivey, Allan and Philip Payton (1994), "Towards a Cornish Identity Theory", in *Cornish Studies*, vol. 2, pp. 151-163.

Jackson, Peter (2003), "Mapping Culture", in Alisdair Rogers and Heather Viles (eds.) *The Student's Companion to Geography*, 2nd Edition, Oxford: Blackwell.

James, Simon (1999), *The Atlantic Celts—Ancient People or Modern Invention?*, London: British Museum Press.

Jameson, Frederic (1983), "Postmodernism or the Cultural Logic of Late Capitalism", *New Left Left Review*, No. 46, (1984).

—— (1988a), *The Cultural Turn : Selected Writings on thePostmodern 1983-1988*, London and New York: Version.

—— (1997), *Post-Modernism and Consumer Society*, in A. Gray and J.McGuigan (eds.) *Studies in Culture: An Introductory Reader*, London: Arnold, pp. 192-205.

Jay, Eric (1992), *Keep them in Birmingham, Racism in the South-West*, Commission for Racial Equality, Bristol.

Jenkin, Alfred K. Hamilton (1934), *Cornish Homes and Customs*, London: J.M. Dent.

Jenkins, Richard (1992), *Pierre Bourdieu*, London: Routledge.

Keating, Michael (2001). "Rethinking the Region. Culture, Institutions and Economic Development in Catalonia and Galicia", *European Urban and Regional Studies*, vol. 8, no. 3, pp. 217-234.

—— (2007), "A regional history of modern Europe. Territorial management and the state", in Bill Lancaster, Diana Newton and Natasha Vall (eds.) *An Agenda for Regional History*, Newcastle upon Tyne, Northumbria University Press pp. 149-164.

Kendall, Gavin and Gary Wickham (1999), *Using Foucault's Methods*, London: Sage.

Kennedy, Neil (1995), "Racial equality in Cornwall", in Commission for Racial Equality, *Challenging Racism in the South-West: report of a one day seminar for Cornwall*, Truro, pp. 18-21.

Kennedy, Neil and Nigel Kingcome (1998), "Disneyfication of Cornwall—Developing a Poldark Heritage Complex", in the *International Journal of Heritage Studies*, vol. 4, no. 1, Exeter.

Kent, Alan (2000), *The Literature of Cornwall, Continuity, Identity, Difference 1000-2000*, Bristol: Redcliffe Press.

—— (2002), *Pulp Methodism: The Lives and Literature of Silas, Josephe and Salome Hocking*, St Austell: Cornish Hillside Publications.

—— (2002), *Love and Seaweed*, StAustell: Lyonesse Press.

—— (2010), *The Theatre of Cornwall: space, place, performance*, Bristol: Redcliffe/Wescliffe Books.

—— "From Ingraine to Callin' 'ome Mouzel: Two Paradigms of Memory, Language and Literature in Cornwall", (Prepublication copy: 2012).

Kneafsley, Moya (2001), "Rural Cultural Economy: Tourism and Social Relations", *Annals of Tourism Research*, vol. 28, no. 3, pp.762-783.

Korey, Jane Smith (1992), *As we belong to be: The ethnic movement in Cornwall, England*, Thesis, Brandeis University.

BIBLIOGRAPHY

Kunc, Norman (2011 [1992]), *The Need to Belong: Rediscovering Maslow's Hierarchy of Needs*, Baltimore: Paul H. Brookes Publishers.

Lancaster, Bill, Diana Newton and Natasha Vall (eds.) (2007), *An Agenda for Regional History*, Newcastle upon Tyne: Northumbria University Press.

Lanyon, Andrew (1985), *The First and Last Straw*, [s.n]

Lechte, John (1994), *Fifty Key Cotemporary Thinkers—From Structuralism to Postmodernity*, London: Routledge.

Lowenthal, David (1998), *The Heritage Crusade and the Spoils of History*, Cambridge: Cambridge University Press.

Lowenna, Sharon (2004), "'Noscitur A Sociis': Jenner, Duncombe-Jewell and their Milieu", in P.J. Payton (ed.), *Cornish Studies*, no. 12, pp. 61-87.

—— (2011), "Charles Roger's 'Vocabulary of the Cornish Language', The Rylands Vocabulary, and gatherers of pre-'Revival' fragments", in P.J. Payton (ed.), *Cornish Studies*, no. 19, pp. 105-122.

Lowenthal, David (1975), "Past Time, Present Place: Landscape and Memory", in *The Geographical Review*, Vol. 65 (1), (January, 1975), pp. 1-36. www.jstor.org/stable/213831, (Accessed 25 January 2010.)

—— (1985), *The Past is a Foreign Country*, Cambridge: Cambridge University Press.

Lowerson, John (1994), "Celtic Toursim—Some Recent Magnets", in P.J. Payton (ed.), *Cornish Studies*, Vol. 2, pp. 128-137.

Malmesbury, William of (1125) *Gesta Regum Anglorum*, cited in Susan Pearce (1978) (below).

McArthur, Mary (1988), "The Cornish: A Case Study in Ethnicity", Unpublished M.Sc. Dissertation, University of Bristol.

MacKinnon, Kenneth (2000), *An Independent Academic Study on Cornish*, EKOS Ltd. & SGÙD for the Government Office of the South West, Plymouth.

Marx, Karl (1969 [1867, 1883, 1885]), *Le Capital*, translated by J. Roy, Garnier-Flammerion.

—— (1977 [1867, 1883, 1885]), *Capital*, vols. 1-3, translated by B. Fowkes, New York: Vintage Books.

—— (1990 [1867]), *Capital, Vol. 1: A Critique of Political Economy*, translated, Ben Fowkes, London: Penguin, p. 126.

—— *Capital*, vol. 3, in D. McLellan (ed.) (2000), *Karl Marx: Selected Writings*, Oxford: Oxford University Press.

Maslow, Abraham (1943), "A Theory of Human Motivation", first published in *Psychological Review*, no. 50, pp. 370-396. psychclassics.yorku.ca/Maslow/motivation.htm, (Accessed 16 September 2012.).

—— (1987 [1954]), *Motivation and Personality*, Cynthia McReynolds (ed.), New York: Harper and Row Publishers. ways-ahead.net/meditation/037-2-Maslow.pdf, (Accessed 3 May 2010.)

Maurier, Daphne du (1967), *Vanishing Cornwall: The spirit and history of Cornwall*, Harmondworth: Penguin.

Mauss, Marcel (1934), "Les Techniques du corps", *Journal de Psychologie*, 32 (3-4). Reprinted in Mauss, *Sociologie et anthropologie*, 1936, Paris: PUF.

Morgan, Prys (1983, 1989), "From a Death to a View: The Hunt for the Welsh Past in the Romantic Period", in Hobsbawm and Ranger (eds.) *op. cit.*

Murdoch, Brian (1993), *Cornish Literature*, Cambridge: D.S. Brewer.

Nance, Robert Morton (1949), "Cornish Culture", in *The Cornish Review*, no.1, April, p.3.

—— (1958 [1929]), *Cornish for All: A Guide to Unified Cornish*, 3rd edition, Federation of Old Cornwall Societies

—— (1925), "What we stand for", in *Old Cornwall*, no. 1.

Objective One Programme for Cornwall and the Isles of Scilly, "Single Programming Document", (December 2005).

Olivro, Jean (2010), *Projet Bretagne*, Rennes: Editions Apogée.

Ó Luain, Cathal (ed.) (1983), *For a Celtic Future: A Tribute to Alan Heusaff*, Dublin: The Celtic League.

O'Sullivan, Tim, John Hartley, Danny Saunders, Martin Montomery, John Fiske (1994), *Key Concepts in Communication and Cultural Studies*, 2nd Edition, London: Routledge.

Parker, Simon (ed.) (1998), *Cornwall Marches On!*, Keskerdh Kernow 500. Truro: Keskerdh Kernow Ltd.

Payton, Philip (1989), *Modern Cornwall: The Changing Nature of Peripherality*, Unpublished Thesis.

—— (1992), *The Making of Modern Cornwall: Historical Experience and the Persistence of 'Difference'*, Redruth: Dyllansow Truran.

—— (ed.) (1993-2012), *Cornish Studies*, 2nd Series, nos. 1-20, Exeter: Exeter University Press (Institute of Cornish Studies).

—— (ed.) (1993), *Cornwall since the War: The Contemporary History of a European Region*, Redruth: Dyllansow Truran and Institute of Cornish Studies.

—— (1996), *Cornwall*, Fowey: Alexander Associates.

—— (1999), "The Ideology of Language Revival in Modern Cornwall", in R. Black, W. Gillies & R. Ó Maolalaigh (eds.), *Celtic Connections: Proceedings of the Tenth International Congress of Celtic Studies*, Vol.1, *Language, Literature, History, Culture*, Edinburgh, pp.395-424.

—— (2002), "Industrial Celts? Cornish Identity in the Age of Technological Prowess", in P.J. Payton (ed.), *Cornish Studies*, vol. 10, pp. 116-135.

—— (2004), *Cornwall—A History*, Fowey: Cornwall Editions Ltd.

—— (2007), "'A Duchy in every respect un-English': discourses of identity in late-modern Cornwall", in Bill Lancaster, Diana Newton and Natasha Vall (eds.) *An Agenda for Regional History*, Newcastle upon Tyne, Northumbria University Press, pp. 321-332.

Payton, Philip and Bernard Deacon (1993), "The Ideology of Language Revival", in P.J. Payton (ed.), *Cornwall Since the War*.

Pearce, Susan (1978), The Kingdom of Dumnonia, Padstow: Lodenek Press.

Pelmear, Kenneth (1960), *Rugby in the Duchy*, An Official History of the Game in Cornwall, Falmouth: Cornwall Rugby Football Union.

Pengilly, John (1987), correspondence in *Cornish Scene*, vol. 2, no. 4, p.24.

BIBLIOGRAPHY

Perry, Ron (1997), "Celtic Revival and Economic Development in Edwardian Cornwall", in in P.J. Payton (ed.), *Cornish Studies*, no. 5, p.112-124.

—— (1999), "The Changing Face of Celtic Tourism in Cornwall, 1875-1975", in P.J. Payton (ed.), *Cornish Studies*, no. 7, (1999), pp.94-106.)

—— (1993), "Economic Change and Opposition Economics", in P.J. Payton (ed.) *Cornwall since the War*.

—— (2002), "The Making of Modern Cornwall 1800-2000: A Geo-Economic Perspective", in P.J. Payton (ed.) *Cornish Studies, no. 10*.

Perry, Ronald, Ken Dean and Bryan Brown (eds) (1986), *Counterurbanisation: case studies of urban to rural movement*, Norwich: Geo Books.

Philips, N. Roy (1987), *The Saffron Eaters*, Exeter: Devon Books.

Putnam, Robert D. (1993), *Making Democracy Work: Civic Traditions in Modern Italy*, Princetown, N.J.: Princetown University Press.

—— (1995), "Tuning in, tuning out: the strange disappearance of social capital in America", *Political Science and Politics*, no. 28, pp. 664-83.

—— (2000), *Bowling Alone: The Collapse and Revival of American Community*, New York: Simon and Shuster.

Quiller-Couch, Arthur T. (1898), *The Cornish Magazine*, vol. 1. p.237.

Reay, Diana (1996), "Insider Perspectives or Stealing the Words out of Women's Mouths: Interpretation in the Research Process", *Feminist Review*, no. 53, "Speaking Out: Researching and Representing Women", (Summer), pp. 57-73. www.jstor.org/stable/1395661 (Accessed 8 February 2011.)

—— (2004), "Gendering Bourdieu's concept of capitals?: Emotional capital, women and social class", in L Adkins and B Skeggs (ed.) *Feminism after Bourdieu*, Oxford: Blackwell.

—— (2004), "'It's all becoming a habitus': Beyond the habitual use of Pierre Bourdieu's concept of habitus in educational research", *Special Issue of British Journal of Sociology of Education on Pierre Bourdieu*, vol. 25, no 4, pp 431-444.

Rogers, Alisdair and Heather A. Viles (eds.) (2003), *The Student's Companion to Geography*, 2nd Edition, Oxford: Blackwell.

Said, Edward (2003 [1978]), *Orientalism*, London: Penguin Books.

Salmon, Tom (1983), *The First Hundred Years—The Story of Rugby Football in Cornwall*, Illogan: Cornwall Rugby Football Union.

Saltern, Ian (March 2011), "The Cornish National Minority Report 2", Redruth: Azook Community Interest Company.

Saunders, Tim (1983), "Cornish Symbol and Substance", in Cathal Ó Luain (ed.) *op. cit.*, pp. 253-258.

Saussure, Ferdinand de (1967 [1915]), *Cours de Linguistique Générale*, Paris: Payot.

Shaw, Gareth and Allan Williams (1988), "Tourism and employment: reflections on a pilot study of Looe, Cornwall", (Department of Geography, University of Exeter) in *Area*, vol. 20 (1), pp. 23-24.

Shaw, Gareth and Allan M. Williams (2004), *Tourism and Tourism Spaces*, London: Sage.

Skeggs, Beverley (1997), *Formations of Class and Gender*, London: Sage.

Storey, John (ed.) (2006 [1994]), *Cultural Theory and Popular Culture: A Reader* (3rd Edition), Harlow Essex: Pearson Education Ltd.

Symons, Joan (2012), in, "White Paper for Culture", Truro: Cornwall Council, (October), *Foreword.*

Tanner, Marcus (2006 [2004]), *The Last of the Celts*, New Haven: Yale University Press.

Tay, Louis and Ed Diener (2011), "Needs and Subjective Well-Being around the World," *Journal of Personality and Social Psychology*, vol. 101 (2), pp. 354–365. www.apa.org/pubs/journals/releases/psp-101-2-354.pdf. (Accessed 16 September, 2012.)

Thomas, Charles (1973), *The Importance of Being Cornish in Cornwall*, Redruth, Inaugural Lecture of the Institute of Cornish Studies.

—— (1997), "See Your Own Country First: The Geography of a Railway Landscape", in E. Westland (ed.) (below), pp. 107-128.

Thomas, Peter and Derek Williams (eds.) (2007), *Setting Cornwall on its Feet: Robert Morton Nance, 1873-1959*, London: Francis Boutle Publishers.

Thomassen, Bjørn (2010), "The Uses and Meanings of Liminality" in *International Political Anthropology*, no.3. www.politicalanthropology.org/ component/search/?searchword=liminality&ordering=&searchphrase=all (Accessed 5 May 2011.)

Thompson, John B. (1982, 2001), "Preface" in Pierre Bourdieu, *op. cit.*

Tims, Charlie and Shelagh Wright (2006), "Bidding for a competition that doesn't exist!—How Cornwall imagined a Region of Culture and found a future", DEMOS Report for Cornwall Council.

Tregidga, Garry (2012), "Celtic comparisons: Brittany and the Cornish Revivalist Movement", conference paper at, "Les rencontres, Bretagne/Monde Anglophone", Université de Bretagne Occidentale, Quimper, 29 June 2012.

Urry, John (2002 [1990]), *The Tourist Gaze*, 2nd Edition, London: Sage.

Vink, Caroline (1993), "'Be Forever Cornish!' Some Observations on the Ethnoregional Movement in Contemporary Cornwall", in P.J. Payton (ed.), *Cornish Studies*, no. 1, pp. 109-119.

Weatherhill, Craig and Paul Devereux (1994), *Myths and Legends of Cornwall*, Wilmslow: Sigma Leisure.

Welsh Assembly Government (2002), "A Culture Strategy for Wales", Cardiff (January).

Welsh Government (2001), "The Culture and Heritage of Wales", Welsh Government, Cardiff: 2011, wales.gov.uk/docs/strategies/110929chap12en.pdf (Accessed January 2013).

Westland, Ella (ed.) (1997), *Cornwall, the Cultural Construction of Place*, Penzance: Patten Press with the Institute of Cornish Studies.

BIBLIOGRAPHY

Willett, Joanie (2008), "Cornish Identity, Vague Notion or Social Fact", in P.J Payton (ed.), *Cornish Studies*, no. 16 pp. 183-205.

—— (2009), "Sustainable Communities, Innovation, Social Capital and the Inland China Clay Villages", in P.J Payton and S. Trower (eds.), *Cornish Studies*, no. 17, pp. 136-156.

—— (2009), "Why is Cornwall so Poor? Narrative, Perception and Identity," unpublished Ph.D. thesis, University of Exeter.

Williams, Carol (1995), "Housing in Cornwall: A two-tier system?", P.J Payton (ed.), *Cornish Studies*, no. 3, (1995), pp. 194-205.

Williams, Malcolm (1993), "Housing the Cornish", in P.J. Payton (ed.) (1993), *Cornwall Since the War, op. cit.*

—— (2002), "The New Cornish Social Science", in P.J. Payton (ed.), *Cornish Studies*, no. 10, pp. 44-66.

Williams, Malcolm (2003), "Why is Cornwall So Poor?, Poverty and In-Migration Since the 1960s", *Contemporary British History*, no. 17, pp. 55-70.

Williams, Malcolm and Eric Harrison (1995), "Movers and Stayers: A comparison of migratory and non-migratory groups in Cornwall, 1981-91", P.J. Payton (ed.), *Cornish Studies*, no.3, (1995), pp 176-193.

Williams, Malcolm, Peter Mitchell and Lyn Bryant (1995), "Movers and Stayers: Population and Social Change in Cornwall, 1971-1991", University of Plymouth.

Williams, Malcolm and Tony Champion (1998), "Cornwall, Poverty and In-Migration", P.J. Payton (ed.), *Cornish Studies*, no. in P, Payton (ed.), *Cornish Studies*, no. 6, pp. 118-126.

Williams, Nicholas (2006), *Cornish Today: An Examination of the Revived Language*, Third Edition, Westport, Co. Mayo: Evertype.

Williams, Raymond (1988), *Keywords—A Vocabulary of Culture and Society*, London: Fontana.

—— (2006), "The Analysis of Culture" in J. Storey (ed.) *op. cit.* pp.48-56.

Wills, Peter (1992), *Water, Water Everywhere*, Camborne: CoSERG.

—— (n.d.), Unpublished analysis of Cornwall Rural Community Council's Parish Housing Surveys, CoSERG. (Late 1990s).

Wright, Mary (1979, 2008), *Cornish Guernseys and Knit-frocks*, Polperro: Polperro Heritage Press.

Wynne, Derek (1998), *Leisure, Lifestyle and the New Middle Class*, London: Routledge.

Yack, Bernard (1999), "The myth of the civic nation", in Ronald Beiner (ed.) *Theorizing Nationalism*, New York: State University of New York, pp. 103-118.

Yu Wujin (2006), "Thing, Value, Time, and Freedom: A Consideration of Some key Concepts in Marx's Philosophical System", translated by Jie Tang in *Frontiers of Philosophy in China*, Vol.1 (1), (January), pp. 114-123, Springer. www.jstor.org/stable/30209956 (Accessed 22 July 2010.)

Frequently accessed websites:
Awen Productions: www.awen.org.uk
Bewnans Kernow: www.bewnanskernow.org
Business Cornwall: www.businesscornwall.co.uk
Cornish Constitutional Convention: www.cornishassembly.org
Cornish Dance Society www.cornishdance.com
Cornish Folk Arts Project: www.an-daras.com
Cornish Gorsedd—Gorseth Kernow: www.gorsethkernow.org.uk
Cornish Language Partnership, MAGA: www.magakernow.org.uk
Cornish Oafs: www.facebook.com/CornishOafs?ref=stream
Cornish Social and Economic Research Group, CoSERG:
 www.cornwallcoserg.org.uk
Cornwall Council: www.cornwall.gov.uk
Invest in Cornwall: www.investincornwall.com
It's Our Cornwall: www.facebook.com/itsourcornwall
Office of National Statistics: www.ons.gov.uk/ons/index.html and
 www.statistics.gov.uk/hub/index.html
Produit en Bretagne: www.produitenbretagne.com
This is Cornwall: www.westbriton.co.uk
Visit Cornwall: www.visitcornwall.com
Welsh Government: wales.gov.uk